Multi-Media

'As much an art book as a scholarly work, *Multi-Media* combines sophisticated, well-informed scholarship with artists' pages that transcend mere illustration to become a catalogue for a virtual exhibition. In terms of both subject and format, it's a worthy companion to Kaye's *Site-Specific Art*.'

Phil Auslander, *Georgia Institute of Technology, USA*

Multi-Media charts the development of multi-media video, installation and performance in a unique dialogue between theoretical analysis and specially commissioned documentations by some of the world's foremost artists. Nick Kaye explores the interdisciplinary history and character of experimental practices shaped in exchanges between music, installation, theatre, performance art, conceptual art, sculpture and video.

The book sets out key themes and concerns in multi-media practice, addressing Time, Space, the resurgence of ephemerality, liveness and 'aura'. These chapters are interspersed with documentary artwork and essays by artists whose work continues to shape the field, including new articles from:

- Vito Acconci
- The Builders Association
- John Jesurun
- Pipilotti Rist
- Fiona Templeton

Multi-Media also reintroduces a major documentary essay by Paolo Rosa of Studio Azzurro in a new, fully illustrated form.

This book combines sophisticated scholarly analysis and fascinating original work to present a refreshing and creative investigation of current multi-media arts practice.

Nick Kaye is Professor of Performance Studies at Exeter University and author of *Site-Specific Art* (2000).

Multi-Media

Video – Installation – Performance

Nick Kaye

Multi-Media: Video – Installation – Performance
is supported by

Routledge
Taylor & Francis Group

LONDON AND NEW YORK

Arts & Humanities
Research Council

First published 2007 by Routledge
2 Park Square, Milton Park, Abingdon, Oxon OX14 4RN

Simultaneously published in the USA and Canada
by Routledge
270 Madison Avenue, New York, NY 10016

Routledge is an imprint of the Taylor & Francis Group, an informa business

Typeset in Janson and Scala Sans
by Laserwords Private Limited, Chennai, India
Printed and bound in Great Britain
by MPG Books, Bodmin, Cornwall

British Library Cataloguing in Publication Data
A catalogue record for this book is available from the British Library

Library of Congress Cataloging-in-Publication Data

Kaye, Nick.
    Multi-media : video, installation, performance / Nick Kaye.
        p. cm.
    Includes bibliographical references and index.
1. Multimedia (Art) I. Title.
    N7433.92K39 2007
    700.9′05 – dc22

                                                    2006023843

ISBN: 978-0-415-28380-9 (hbk)
ISBN: 978-0-415-28381-6 (pbk)
ISBN: 978-0-203-96489-7 (ebk)

For Ben and Francesca

Contents

Notes on Contributors

Vito Acconci: one of the most influential artists of his generation. Developing from his work as a poet, after receiving a BA from Holy Cross College, Worcester, Massachusetts, in 1962 and an MFA from University of Iowa in 1964, Acconci's entry into visual art in the late 1960s established him as one of the most celebrated protagonists of body art, performance and video art. Focusing on art 'as an instrument in the world', Acconci's work extends across writing, installation, film, conceptual art, theatre, multi-media, site-specific and public art. From 1983 he became increasingly engaged with architectural projects. In 1988, Acconci formally established the Acconci Studio, based in Brooklyn, an architectural practice that has created proposals and projects for an eclectic range of sites across the USA, Europe and beyond. Acconci's emergence as one of the most important figures in the development of radical art-making practices across a wide range of fields has been marked by solo exhibitions throughout North America and Europe from the early 1970s as well as his participation in key group shows defining the development of time-based, media and site-related practices in the visual arts. These include *Street Works I–IV* (New York, 1969), *Software* (Jewish Museum, New York, 1970), *Information* (MOMA, New York, 1970), *Body Works* (MOCA, San Francisco, 1970) and *Video Art* (MOMA, New York, 1975), among many others. In 1987, *Vito Acconci: Domestic Trappings* provided a major retrospective of Acconci's work at the La Jolla Museum of Contemporary Art, California, and then across major galleries in the United States. Acconci's publications are prolific, as is the critical literature surrounding his work. His practice has been recognized through numerous awards and grants from institutions, including the American Academy in Rome, the Berlin Deutscher Akadamischer Austauschdienst, the Guggenheim Foundation and the National Endowment for the Arts. With Acconci Studio, his recent projects have included the creation of an artificial island on the river Mur in Graz, Austria, in collaboration with Robert Punkenhofer, ART & IDEA, and as part of the Graz European City of Culture project, 2003. The most recent major retrospective of Acconci's work, *Vito Acconci*, was shown in Mexico, New York, Barcelona and Amsterdam, among other locations, in 2005 and 2006.

John Jesurun: a playwright, director and designer based in New York. From the 1982 premiere of his celebrated play *Chang in a Void Moon*, Jesurun has been recognized as one of North America's leading avant-garde artists. After receiving a BFA from the Philadelphia College of Art in 1972 and an MFA in sculpture from Yale University in 1974, Jesurun developed his interests through filmmaking and in television production. Following a three-year role as associate producer for *The Dick Cavett Show*, where he produced shows featuring folk singer Odetta, Tito Puente, Papa John Williams and music producer John Hammond, Jesurun began writing and directing theatre performances using concepts derived from film. His theatre has subsequently engaged with increasingly complex relationships between live, mediated and recorded performance, in theatrical works incorporating television and film mediation and production. The first 36 weekly episodes of *Chang in a Void Moon*, with text, direction, design, video and film by Jesurun, were followed in 1983 by *Bird's Eye View*, and, among a wide range of projects, *Red House* (1984), *Shatterhand Massacree/Riderless Horse* (1985), *Deep Sleep* (1986), *White Water* (1986), *Black Maria* (1987), *Everything That Rises Must Converge* (1990) and *Ojo Caliente* (1994). His film projects include *Last Days of Pompeii* (1980) and *Fairground 88, The History of Theatre, Part II* (1988-9), while his work has also extended to video installations, including *Highway to Hell* (1988). Jesurun has collaborated with The Builders Association, who produced his text *Imperial Motel (Faust)* (1996), and his work is presented widely throughout the Americas, Europe and Japan. He has been the recipient of many honours and awards, among them the New York Foundation for the Arts Fellowship (1988); a Rockefeller Foundation Playwrights Fellowship (1987); an OBIE Award, best play (*Deep Sleep*); BESSIE Award for *Chang in a Void Moon*; MacArthur Foundation Fellowship (1996); and

US–Mexico Creative Artists Residency Grant, National Endowment for the Arts (1994). His work is published widely. In 2002–3, Jesurun was guest professor at the Kyoto University of Art and Design.

Pipilotti Rist: one of the world's most widely recognized video artists. Rist's work came to prominence in the mid-1980s in a transformation of the structures and vocabularies of television, advertising and music video toward a vivid language for contemporary media art and a political engagement with popular culture, feminism and the body. Her early work was influenced by her training in graphic design, illustration and photography at the Institute of Applied Arts at Vienna, and subsequent studies in audio communications and video in Basel, as well as her membership of the post-punk pop group *Les Reines Prochaines*, for which she created some of her first video works. Establishing herself internationally through single-channel tapes including *I'm Not the Girl Who Misses Much* (1986), *(Entlastungen) Pipilotti's Fehlerst* (1988) and *Pickelporno* (1992), Rist engaged with video installation from the early 1990s, including large-scale, site-specific and multi-screen installations. Following the first international showings of her work in 1988, Rist's video and video installation has been exhibited world-wide, including solo exhibitions at the San Francisco Museum of Modern Art; Contemporary Arts Museum, Houston; Luhring Augustine, New York; Museo Nacional de Arte Reina Sofia, Madrid; the Museum of Contemporary Art, Chicago; Museum Ludwig, Cologne; Shiseido Foundation, Tokyo; and the Stedelijk Museum, Amsterdam. She has participated in group exhibitions shown at MOMA, New York; Museum of Contemporary Arts, Taipei; Virginia Museum of Fine Arts; Kunsthalle, Vienna; Metropolitan Museum of Modern Art, Tokyo; ZKM, Karlsruhe; and many others. In 1997, she was awarded the Premio '2000' of the Venice Biennale for her video work *Ever Is All Over*. Her awards include the Zürcher Kunstpreis, Stadt Zurich; Wolfgang Hahn Preis, Museum Ludwig; and the Kwangju Biennale Award. Her publications include the book *Apricots Along the Street*, released by Scalo in 2001. Pipilotti Rist lives and works in Los Angeles, California, and Zurich, Switzerland.

Paolo Rosa: created the Studio Azzurro in collaboration with Fabio Cirifino and Leonardo Sangiorgi in Milan in 1982. In 1995, Stefano Roveda joined the group, bringing his expertise in interactive systems to bear on Studio Azzurro's work. Since its inception, Studio Azzurro has innovated across a wide range of artistic and commercial spheres, combining photography, visual art, cinema, graphics and animation to create video, interactive environments, installations and a wide range of influential theatre works and site-specific performances. Their 'videoenvironments' gained wide international recognition with *Il Nuotatore* (*The Swimmer*), first conceived in 1983 and shown at the Palazzo Fortuny, Venice, in 1984. In the mid-1980s, Studio Azzurro engaged in a major collaboration with the celebrated post-avant-garde theatre director Giorgio Barberio Corsetti to create a series of multi-media installations and performances including *Prologo a diario segreto contraffatto* (*Prologue to a Secret Counterfeit Diary*) (1985) and *La camera asttrata* (*The Abstract Room*) (1987), commissioned for the opening of Documenta 8, Kassel. From 1994, the group focused its artistic work on the development of complex interactive videoenvironments and theatre performances, including *Tavoli, perché queste mani in toccano?* (*Tables – Why Are These Hands Touching Me?*) (1995), *Il Giardino delle anime* (*The Garden of Souls*) (1997), *Giacomo mio, salviamoci!* (*Oh Giacomo, Let's Save Ourselves!*) (1998) and *Wer möchte wohl Kaspar Hauser sein* (2000). Studio Azzurro's videoenvironments and performances have been created for sites and theatres in Milan, Rome, Turin, Beirut, Amsterdam, London, Nuremberg, Paris and Tokyo, among many others. Their major exhibitions include *Videoenvironments 1982–1992* shown across galleries in Italy and Japan; as well as exhibitions at the ACE gallery, New York, 2000; ICC, Tokyo, 2001; Castel Sant-Elmo, Naples, 2002; Mori Art Museum, Tokyo, 2003; and Opernhaus, Stuttgart, 2004. The Studio Azzurro's most recent work includes *Meditazzioni Mediterraneo* (2003), a series of site-related interactive videoenvironments, and *Infinita Commedia* (2005), a multi-media work. Studio Azzurro has also created feature-length films, including *L'Osservatorio nucleare del sig. Nanof* (*The Nuclear Observatory of Mr Nanof*) (1985) and *Il Mnemonista* (2000), as

well as video and television programmes in Italy and abroad. Studio Azzurro's most recent publication is *Studio Azzurro: Immagini Vive*, released
by Electa in 2005.

Fiona Templeton: her work embraces performance, installation, video,
opera, plays and poetry, multi-media and site-specific practices. In the
1970s she co-founded the seminal UK-based performance art company
the Theatre of Mistakes. Fiona Templeton's performance and installation
work includes *Delirium of Dreams* (1991), 'an anti-biographical play
about the phenomenon and predicament of Camille Claudell', *Recognition*
(1996), a multi-media performance created in collaboration with Michael
Ratomski, and *Cells of Release* (1995), an installation created in the
abandoned Eastern State Penitentiary in Philadelphia, in collaboration
with Amnesty International. Templeton's award-winning *YOU – The
City*, created as 'an intimate citywide play for an audience of one'
in Manhattan in 1998, has since been recreated in six countries and
languages, including at the London International Festival of Theatre in
1989, and most recently as a key project of Rotterdam Cultural Capital
of Europe 2001. For the opening of the Lille European Cultural Capital
2004, she was commissioned to create *L'Ile* (*The Island*), a theatre game by
appointment. Templeton has received play commissions from Theater
Cocteau-Basel, Switzerland; Art Awareness, Lexington, NY; New York
State Council on the Arts; the Mickery, Amsterdam; among others. Her
awards include fellowships from the National Endowment for the Arts
in both Poetry and Visual Arts (new genres); an Abendzeitung München
Sterne des Jahres for theatre; and two fellowships from the New York
Foundation for the Arts for performance, as well as one for playwriting. In
1996–7, Templeton was senior writer-in-residence at the English Faculty
of Cambridge University, England, and 2000–2003 Arts and Humanities
Research Board Creative Fellow with the Department of Theatre Studies,
University of Lancaster, England. In December 2002 she received the
annual Foundation for Contemporary Performance Arts grant for theatre
in New York. Fiona Templeton's poetry has been published in a series of
volumes, including *London, Hi Cowboy* and *Airdrie*. Her other publications

include *YOU – The City*, released by Roof Books in 1990, and *Elements of Performance Art*, with Anthony Howell. Fiona Templeton's current project, *The Medead*, 'a performance epic retelling of the journey of Medea', is in progress. To date, parts of the performance have been shown in London, Glasgow and New York.

Marianne Weems and The Builders Association: Marianne Weems is artistic director of The Builders Assocation and has directed all of their productions. In addition to her work with the company, she recently completed a multi-media workshop with Disney Creative Entertainment and Walt Disney Imagineering, and is currently at work on a new theatre/music event with David Byrne and Fatboy Slim entitled *Here Lies Love*. She serves on the board of the Association of Performing Arts Presenters, is on the advisory committee of the Center for Research in Engineering, Media and Performance at UCLA, and is the board president of Art Matters Inc. In the distant past, she also worked as a dramaturg with Susan Sontag, the Wooster Group and others. She is the co-author of *Art Matters: How the Culture Wars Changed America*, released by New York University Press in 2001.

The Builders Association is a New York-based performance and media company that exploits the richness of contemporary technologies to extend the boundaries of theatre. Based on unusual collaborations and extensive periods of development, the company's productions feature a seamless blend of text, sound, architecture, video and stage performances that explore the impact of technology on human presence. Since 1994, with a growing circle of artists, the company has collaborated on nine large-scale theatre projects, including *Master Builder* (1994), *The White Album* (1995), *Imperial Motel (Faust)* (1996), *Jump Cut (Faust)* (1997), *Jet Lag* (1998–2000) with Diller + Scofidio, *Xtravaganza* (2000–1), *Alladeen* (2002–5) with **moti**roti, *Avanti* (2003–5) and *SUPER VISION* with dbox (2005). Their OBIE Award winning work has has been presented at venues including the Singapore Arts Festival, the Barbican Centre, Romaeuropa Festival, the Brooklyn Academy of Music, the

Festival Iberoamericano de Teatro de Bogota and the Melbourne International Arts Festival, among many others. For more information, visit www.thebuildersassociation.org.

Keith Kahn, Ali Zaidi and motiroti: With Marianne Weems, Keith Khan and Ali Zaidi are co-creators of *Alladeen*. Founded in 1990 by Keith Khan and Ali Zaidi, **moti**roti is twice winner of the *Time Out* London Dance and Performance Award and a recipient of the BBC Asia Award for Achievement in the Arts. **Moti**roti's substantial theatre and arts work has been developed with a range of collaborators drawn from visual arts, multi-media, live art and experimental theatre. The company purposefully creates its work through cross-disciplinary and cross-cultural dialogues. Since 2004, and following Keith Khan's departure from the company to become Chief Executive of Rich Mix, a new cultural and creative space for London, Ali Zaidi has been Artistic Director of the company.

Keith Khan is a multi award-winning artist whose work is recognized internationally. His commissions have included Director of Design for the opening and closing ceremonies of the Commonwealth Games 2002 and Artistic Director of *Celebration Commonwealth*. His work has occupied places such as the Tate Modern, the Royal Albert Hall and the Millennium Dome, where he designed the opening ceremony and worked with Mark Fisher and Peter Gabriel.

Ali Zaidi's work emphasizes digital design and new technologies. He is Indian by birth, Pakistani by migration and now British by choice, and cultural paradox and hybridity contribute creatively to Ali Zaidi's speculation around issues of identity and representation. His work engages with diverse forms, including film, theatre, live art, installation, site-specific design and new media. In addition to his collaboration with **moti**roti, Zaidi's works include *Reality Bytes*, commissioned by the Now Festival, Nottingham, UK, and *The Seed The Root*, a series of site-specific installations around Brick Lane in London's East End.

Figures

Acknowledgements

A book such as this rests on the interest and support of many individuals and organisations. The first and most significant of these contributions lies with the artists who have created the documentations that form such a central part of this project. It has been a particular privilege for me to develop this book in relation to the generous contributions by Vito Acconci, John Jesurun, Pipilotti Rist, Paolo Rosa and Studio Azzurro, Fiona Templeton, Marianne Weems and The Builders Association, and, through The Builders Association, Keith Kahn, Ali Zaidi and **moti**roti. In my own development of this volume, much of its value for me has been drawn from these exchanges.

This project has also received extensive institutional support. I am particularly grateful to the UK Arts and Humanities Research Council (AHRC) for a Small Grant in the Creative and Performing Arts that provided for essential research in archives in Rotterdam, Karlsruhe and New York, as well as contributing to permissions costs for illustrations. In addition, the AHRC supported the completion of the book through a Research Leave Scheme award. The Drama Department of the University of Manchester also provided support for travel costs, scans and permissions. I am also grateful to the University of Exeter for financial support for the cost of design and the preparation of camera-ready copy and to the Department of Drama, University of Exeter, for support for permissions costs for illustrations. In addition I am grateful to Simon Josebury for his time and interest in the project, his invaluable design work detailed below, as well the development of the book cover. I would also like to thank Lieselotte Giannachi-Mangels for directing me toward the work of Pipilotti Rist.

I would like to acknowledge the invaluable support of the staff and resources of the following libraries and institutions. In New York: the New York Public Library for the Performing Arts at Lincoln Centre, the Jerome Robbins Archive of the Recorded Moving Image at Lincoln Centre, The Kitchen and Electronic Arts Intermix. In Rotterdam: V2. In Karlsruhe: the library and archive of Zentrum für Kunst und Medientechnologie (ZKM).

All artists providing documentations to *Multi-Media: Video – Installation – Performance* retain the copyright to their contributions to the volume, which are reproduced by permission. Detailed credits for the documentation are as follows.

For Vito Acconci, *ACCONCI STUDIO AND THE MEKONS: THEATER PROJECT FOR A ROCK BAND, 1995*: reproduced by permission of Vito Acconci. For The Builders Association and **moti**roti, *Alladeen*: page design in collaboration with David Cabrera; text edited by Marianne Weems; photos and interview excerpts by Ali Zaidi; excerpts from scene dialogue by Rizwan Mirza, Tanya Selveratnam, Heaven Phillips and Jeff Webster; this documentation reproduced by permission of The Builders Association. Major U.S. support for *Alladeen* was provided by The Daniel Langlois Foundation for Art, Science and Technology; The Greenwell Foundation; the Lila Acheson Wallace Theatre Fund, established in the New York Community Trust by the founders of the Reader's Digest Association; the Jerome Foundation; the Curtis W. McGraw Foundation; the National Endowment for the Arts; the New York State Council on the Arts, a state agency; the Rockefeller Foundation Multi-Arts Production Fund, and the Tin Man Fund. Major UK support was provided by London Arts, the British Council, the PRS (Performing Rights Society) Foundation for New Music, and the Asian Music Circuit. For John Jesurun, *Snow*: text and photographs by John Jesurun; diagram by Bill Ballou; this documentation reproduced by permission of John Jesurun. For Pipilotti Rist, *Open My Glade*: photos by Dennis Cowley and reproduced by permission of Luhring Augustine Gallery, New York and the Public Art Fund; descriptions of *Open My Glade* provided by Luhring Augustine Gallery and reproduced with permission; statements by Pipilotti Rist are extracted from Hans Ulrich Obrist (2001) 'Hans Ulrich Obrist in Conversation with Pipilotti Rist' in P. Phelan, H. U. Obrist and E. Bronfen (eds) *Pipilotti Rist*, London: Phaidon Press, 6–30, and reproduced by permission of Pipilotti Rist; design by Simon Josebury (Secondary Modern). *Open My Glade* was commissioned by the Public Art Fund, New York. For Paolo Rosa, *Confidential Report on an Interactive Experience*: text reproduced by permission of Paolo Rosa; all images are © Studio Azzurro and reproduced with permission; translation from the Italian by Gregory Conti; design for this version of *The Confidential Report* is by Simon Josebury (Secondary Modern). I am pleased to acknowledge that the text reproduced in this book is edited from the original publication of *Rapporto confidenziale su un'esperienza interattiva* in F. Cirifino, P. Rosa, R. Stefano and L. Sangiorgi (eds) (1999) *Studio Azzurro: ambienti sensibili, Esperienze tra interattività e narrazione*, Milan: Electa, 156-67. For Fiona Templeton, *medium, remedy, mortality, fiction, acting, absence, capture, loss, recognition*: text, images and design by Fiona Templeton and reproduced with permission. I am also grateful to Simon Josebury of Secondary Modern for the preparation of camera-ready copy for Vito Acconci, *ACCONCI STUDIO AND THE MEKONS: THEATER PROJECT FOR A ROCK BAND, 1995*, and Fiona Templeton, *medium, remedy, mortality, fiction, acting, absence, capture, loss, recognition*. For their generous help with these contributions I am also grateful to Garrett Ricciardi and Mike Bellon of Acconci Studio; Natalie Afnan of Luhring Augustine Gallery, New York; Delphine Tonglet of Studio Azzurro; Marianne Weems and Claire Hellerau of The Builders Association; Anne Wehr of the Public Art Fund, New York.

With regard to the figures reproduced in this book, I am pleased to acknowledge the following credits. Figure 1.1, courtesy the Cunningham Dance Foundation; Figures 1.2 and 1.3, courtesy of Peters Editions Limited, London; Figure 2.1, courtesy dpa (Deutsche Presse-Angentur GmbH)/Goettert; Figures 2.2, 2.3, 2.4, 3.1, 3.2 and 3.3, courtesy Electronic Arts Intermix (EAI), New York; Figure 2.5, courtesy Joan Jonas and Galerie der Stadt Stuttgart; Figures 3.4, 3.5, 3.6 and 3.7, courtesy Donald Young Gallery, Chicago; Figure 4.1, courtesy Paula Court and the Wooster Group; Figure 4.2, courtesy Mary Gearhart; Figure 4.3, courtesy John Jesurun; Figure 4.4, courtesy Massimo Agus; Figure 4.5, courtesy Paula Court. In addition to the generous help of the artists and copyright holders named here, I also wish to thank the following for their assistance with regard to these images: Tanja Ploghaus of dpa; Clay Hapaz, archivist, the Wooster Group; Rayne Roper Wilder of the Gary Hill Studio; Sabrine Gschwandter and Josh Kline of EAI, New York; Sabine Gruber of Galerie der Stadt Stuttgart; Fiona Flowers of Edition Peters; Stacy Sumpman of the Cunningham Dance Foundation. I would also like to extend my thanks to Studio Azzurro for their generous permission to reproduce the image of *Dove va tutta'sta gente? (Where Are All These People Going?)* (2000), interactive video installation Festival Vision Ruhr, Dortmund, on the cover of the book.

In relation to my own writing, I am happy to acknowledge that parts of this book were developed in an earlier form as part of my article 'Hardware in Real Time: Performance and the Place of Video', published in *Contemporary Theatre Review*, vol. 15, 2 (2005): 203–18. This paper was developed from a presentation to the Stanford Humanities Center Research Workshop, 'Critical Studies in New Media', in November 2003 at the invitation of Professor Michael Shanks. The Research Workshop programme is supported by a grant from the Mellon Foundation.

At Routledge, I would like to thank Talia Rodgers, as always, for her patience and belief in this volume. I would also like to thank Rosie Waters for her support and assistance during the project's initial development and Minh-Ha Duong for her support during the book's evolution and completion.

Finally, and most of all, I would like to thank Gabriella Giannachi for her support in so many ways: for her invaluable discussions, perceptive insights and unfailing encouragement, without which this book would not have come to conclusion.

medium, remedy, mortality, fiction, acting, absence, capture, loss, recognition

Fiona Templeton

medium, remedy, mortality, fiction, acting,
absence, capture, loss, recognition

Fiona Templeton

Recognition was a performance work I created with my late collaborator Michael Ratomski in 1992–96. What began as a live duet had to change as Michael became increasingly ill with AIDS; we did not want to limit his ability to act according to a set level of necessary health, so the work incorporated the stages of his illness. The work was performed in preview at the National Review of Live Art just over a week after his death, then premiered in New York at the Kitchen and the ICA in London. The text is published by PAJ and can be read online at
http://muse.jhu.edu/journals/paj/v023/23.3templeton.html

"Death is an utter change in meaning"

A stage is an absence populated by the live performer. As a fictional representation it is a space to be defined, rather than the place it is as a theatre. When reality is staged it enters into the distancing of the documentary, of one choice of edit of the real over another, it is put into quotes. Michael's quotes are represented by the tv monitor. Mine are the props, the costume. Am I acting myself, or Fiona?

Michael's image on videotape is both witness and evidence.

The fictional place is a courtroom. The absences of its role-players too are the quotes. I play, eventually, all of them, except the jury who are real but not a real jury. In order to play each role I merely have to stand in a particular place, because a courtroom spatialises roles precisely. You could wake up there and know how you are identified in the constellation of its powers. It is opposition, right and wrong, on an axis crossed by authority and obedience, flanked by the speaker/see-er (witness or defendant) and the jury. The jury are simultaneously authority and public (drawn from the real public, who face the entire proceedings, further witnesses to this entire representation); and also imaginers, upon whose imaginative bridging of the 2 roles of witness and authority the ultimate identification of truth depends. The central authority translates this truth into a sentence, a second speech-act bridging the now pinned-down past to the future of the defendant. Until then, in the space and time of a courtroom, there is not one single narrative, but competition for the stamp of truth. The truth is a measurement of pain.

On stage, when Michael must bear witness, the tv monitor must bear it. I have to carry the monitor, I lean, cradle and grapple with the metal, plastic and electricity as if bearing a heavy body. "You are borne." The video-tape carries the imprint of Michael the person. My arms quote his real body. How fictional? How mortal? Within what frame within what frame? How big a screen?

The image is distant on the monitor. I added the larger screen. *"You had to be there."* The sound is badly recorded, his voice hard to hear. I have subtitled it. Is this what he is saying? The listener strains beyond the crackle of the medium. I have written the script for him to play himself. And then we rewrote it. In one scene, where he plays the *"out-of-work blind prophet"* Tiresias, I take the seat beside his witnessing and explain what he is saying. At first I begin by saying that he is saying it, but my use of the first person gives me his role, because I am facing the same way as he is.

And I face him, see him. He faces me. I on stage face him at home but both in the script, *"Change places with me."* It meant then, it meant now.

I face (watch) his image as an elsewhere, him at home playing at being an actor. I face in the room where he on the tape would be, facing me. He faces on tape my invisible body, visible on stage. *"You cannot be in two places at once."*

Onstage live I play him onstage on video playing himself or another. Onstage live I play myself onstage on video playing myself with him.

Speaking for Michael, moving for him. For me. Pretending he's there, speaking to and with the image, discussing him, him alone, him on screen with me, him acting, him reading, him speaking, me alone, the jury

After I edited the videotape of the shoot, the computer lost the file

reading my letter to him. Michael onstage, at home, in hospital, on videotape. *"Let me in, prisoner... And on the outside, a picture. A picture of what was inside now it's not?"*

 Michael is prostheticised: by the catheter implanted in his body; by plugging in that catheter several times daily to a drip solution containing the medications that allow him to survive. The catheter in his chest is attached, via a lead, to a wheeled stand for the drip bag enabling him to move around. His image on the monitor prostheticises his being, attached via a lead to the electricity that allows it to appear. Lead in hand, I wheel the plugged-in monitor around the space to simulate his moving presence there.

Lead in hand, Michael swings the drip stand into the toilet. Private. No image. In mask and wig, Michael emerges, lead in hand and drip stand as dance partner. *"What are you looking at?"* At a grotesque Madonna, as real as any

After I logged the moments to capture from the videotape, the technician could not find the images that I had seen

role in the time of the song. You no longer see the wires and you are unable not to. All the frames at once. *"The actor affirms, not the transience of life, but the permanence of the moment."* The medium of the work is the person, and being (a)live. The rest of the media are dead.

What is not fiction, what is not the naming power of the legal, is this movement. In law and in fiction, the corpse is found, is the marker. *"The stories go back to the moment of change, again, again, to lead us back forwards to a present changed by the uncovered past."* But all evidence is inadequate. Where is the visceral, the sticky, the body in the body of evidence? *"Would the witness please stick to the question?"* Even the inorganic medium decays. And *is* decay.

Michael's aria of witness is wordless sounds only. I could not have written it, and I can't quote it.

"The bird is in the hand
But the beat will not be held
Its breath is on the glass
and I have swallowed the world"

At the end of the piece, I unplug the video, with its image at that point of Michael's head, lying on the bed, the monitor laid at the head of the bed created from the courtroom tables. *"Our death is our own as dreams are."* It is not the life of Michael that I unplug but its artifice, the attempt to prolong what is real by what is not. It is my attempt to control his narrative that I give up on. The script too has been prosthetic, quoting him and returning his words to his mouth like a bird. *"So see your edge and end as privilege, poor thing. So write your terminal case."* In any case his image returns after I leave, unscripted, untragic, laughing at my behind-the-scene face, pulling the plug on my real or acted seriousness, the Michael I recognise.

The pictures are too dark. The image is too far away.
The pictures are too small. You can't see him.

Introduction:
Live Video

the more technology seeks to put things in their proper places, the
less proper those places turn out to be.

(Weber 1996: 124)

In performance, video amplifies division, difference and multiplication. Presented before a jury of the 'real public', Fiona Templeton's *Recognition* (1996) offers evidence for 'an utter change in meaning' signified in the passage between the live and the mediated. However, as Templeton attempts to set her collaborator Michael Ratomski's video performance onto the stage, the spaces and times of representation multiply. Here, Templeton proposes, where a stage is an 'absence populated by the live performer', *Recognition*'s allusion to the court ensures that '[i]n order to play each role I merely have to stand in a particular place, because a courtroom spatializes roles precisely'. Within this scheme, Templeton presents herself presenting Ratomski, as if to amplify the absence of the 'Michael' she represents: physically manipulating the monitor as if it were Michael's body, repeating and re-emphasizing his words, re-enacting and so doubling his recorded performance. Yet, even as *Recognition* asserts this difference, the 'real Fiona' and the 'recorded Michael' become enmeshed in exchanges between mediations. Templeton notes:

> When reality is staged it enters into the distancing of the
> documentary, of one choice of edit of the real over another, it is put
> into quotes. Michael's quotes are represented by the tv monitor.
> Mine are the props, the costume. Am I acting myself, or Fiona?

Indeed, in its staging of the recorded in the live, *Recognition* does not simply rest in an 'utter change of meaning' but plays on and echoes the ambiguities of *transmission*, of *the passage between* places and times.

In this meditation on forgetting, loss and erasure, then, 'Fiona' becomes the theatrical medium of Michael's performance: where the video brings Michael 'closer', 'Fiona' attempts to bring his performance closer still. In doing so, *Recognition* emphasizes a 'live' mediation: Templeton plays 'Fiona'; the theatre and its projections re-mediate the video; 'Fiona' enacts Michael's testimony. It is in this multiplication that *Recognition* explores 'Fiona's' desire to exchange places with 'Michael' and *make him present*, as if, in the passage of signs from 'the mediated' to 'the live', and in the manner of media's *transmission*, as the philosopher Samuel Weber argues, '[f]ar and near' may become 'no longer mutually exclusive but rather converge and overlap' (Weber 1996: 125).

This book is concerned with practices defined in movements between video, installation and performance: practices defined in video art's emergence and development from the mid-1960s in close and frequently paradoxical links to 'live' performance; in video installation's articulation of the interplay of the 'real' and 'virtual' times and spaces of its recordings, mediations and transmissions; and in multi-media theatre's subsequent elaboration and extension of the terms of 'the live' in the performance of mediation. Here, a history and development of explicitly multi-medial practices have been shaped not only in eclectic crossings of music, installation, theatre, performance art, sculpture and video, but in convergences and reversals between live and mediated times, spaces and performances.

Consistently with this, and counterpointing *Recognition*'s play on *transmission* in theatrical performance, the emergence of 'experimental television' in 1963 in the work of Nam June Paik, the single most influential figure in early North American video art, was linked, firstly, to the composer John Cage's experimental musical practices and emphasis on the 'unrepeatable' event. Following Cage, Paik's compositional strategies closely bound his 'experimental television' to an 'opening-out-to-the-world' (Kaprow 1993: 114) that embraced the unpredictability of audience interaction and participation. For Paik's contemporary, the German artist Wolf Vostell, whose highly influential 'dé-coll/age' Happenings had been initiated in 1958, television provided an analogous means of disrupting the stabilities of object-based work that separated art from its environment.

Indicating a tearing away, erasure or destruction of found or existing material, Vostell's 'dé-coll/age' defined actions and processes that threatened a dissolution of the artwork into its surroundings, whether through the dispersal of audience-performed activities across 'found' sites or the physical destruction of the instruments and objects of art. Recorded in Vostell's first film, *Sun in Your Head*, originally projected in one of a series of 'found' sites used for the happening *Nine – Non – dé-coll/ages* in September 1963, Vostell's work offered a record of his '"dé-coll/age" of a television programme' (Merkert 1974: 226). Following aspects of his unrealized score, 'TV dé-coll/age for millions' of 1959, a 'performance' to be conducted privately by television viewers in specific distortions of broadcast images and remade in six further versions from 1963 to 1967, Vostell identified these distortions 'with phenomena of decomposition, self-destruction or wearing out found in events [. . . that . . .] in my work implied the integration of the surrounding world in the form of events and real images' (Vostell in Merkert 1974: 226).

Such articulations *outward*, toward action and encounter, are evident, too, in the attention by visual artists to relationships between the 'recorded', the 'mediated' and the 'live', in their various senses, in single-channel video. For Peter Campus, whose highly influential single-channel tapes from 1971 tested the basic technical characteristics of early video in explorations of perceptual processes and psychological states, the projection of images onto the walls of the gallery revealed, for him, video's production of 'durational space' in the 'gallery-site' (Iles 2000: 255). Campus' remarks draw attention to the *threshold* of the video work, emphasizing exchange and liminality: an encounter with video defined in multiple measures, in dual times and spaces. For Bill Viola, whose highly poetic, allegorical and technically accomplished work developed from 1976 through single-channel tapes and multiple-screen installations, the fact that, he proposes, technically, video 'is in closer relationship to sound, or music, than it is to visual media of film and photography' (Viola 1995a: 62) drew him to the conclusion that '[a]ll video has its roots in the live' (Viola 1995a: 158). Here, Viola identifies the 'vibrational acoustic character of video as a virtual image' with 'the essence of its "liveness"'

(Viola 1995a: 158). Emphasizing the *occurrence* of this image as a 'dynamic energy field, a vibration appearing solid only because it exceeds our ability to discern such fine slices of time' (Viola 1995a: 158), Viola points to video's articulation of a 'real time' *in which* its virtual images unfold. Evidently, Campus and Viola's attention toward the 'real' time and space of video's reception presses toward the terms of installation and performance. Indeed, writing in *Virtualities: Television, Media Art and Cyberculture*, Margaret Morse identifies the broader emergence of video installation with the 'impulse toward "liveness" beginning in the 60 s, including happenings, performance, conceptual art, body art, earth art' (Morse 1998: 159). The video artist and critic Catherine Elwes similarly recounts early video art's material fragility and concomitant emphasis upon ephemerality and the event, in which 'the unreliability of video equipment gave the medium the reputation of being the only art form that was truly dematerialized' (Elwes 2005: 17). Consistently with this, Viola's understanding of the specific qualities of video echoes not only Paik's emphasis upon the ephemeral event or act, but also the values of 'liveness' in experimental music, values reflected in John Cage's seemingly paradoxical claim that in the performance of his electronic works 'live sounds really have a different quality [. . .]. They have a presence, and this presence is intact' (Cage in Cage and Charles 1981: 137).

Indeed, where video art, installation and multi-media theatre have presented a formal diversity that reflects their cross-disciplinary roots, these practices have been marked by a tendency toward a return or resurgence of specific notions of place, presence and media, while reflecting upon the experience of the body, the performing subject and subjectivity. In this context, *Multi-media: video – installation – performance* is concerned with that which persists across these practices: with the implications of the convergence of the live and the mediated; with the tensions between television and video's multiplication of the times and spaces of performance in their claim to simultaneity and *presentness*; with the diversity of forms and processes *in which* specific effects return.

In this context, too, Cage's remark concerning 'live sounds' directs attention to an erosion of oppositions between 'the live' and 'the mediated' reflected not only in these practices, but also in significant cultural commentary and performance theory. Thus, arguing against 'liveness as a pristine state' (Auslander 1999: 53), Phillip Auslander's influential study *Liveness* (Auslander 1999) observes the effect of 'mediatization' across a range of popular cultural forms. Proposing that 'mediatization' conventionally announces itself in *the absence* of the 'real' or 'live' event, Auslander deconstructs the binary opposition upon which this description rests. Here, Auslander's reading of 'mediatization' follows Jacques Derrida's attack on the privileging of speech over writing, and so of the 'presence' of the 'original' over its reproduction, supplement or trace (Derrida 1976, 1978). In doing so, it critiques influential ontologies of 'the live', in which, for example, the theorist Peggy Phelan locates an ontology of performance in its 'disappearance' and so in an eventhood and ephemerality that evade reproduction (Phelan 1993: 146–66). In this sense, Auslander's analysis attends, first, to the operation of language, leading him to argue thus:

> That the mediated is engrained in the live is apparent in the structure of the English word *immediate*. The root form is the word *mediate* of which *immediate* is, of course, the negation. Mediation is thus embedded in the *im-mediate*; the relation of mediation and the im-mediate is one of mutual dependence not precession [. . .]. Similarly, live performance cannot be said to have ontological or historical priority over mediatization, since liveness was made visible only by the possibility of technical reproduction.
>
> (Auslander 1999: 53–4)

Yet where Auslander's reading of the inscription of 'mediatization' *in* the live emphasizes the absences in which binary terms necessarily function – that is, that 'the live' is only known in its opposition to the mediated, and so in its *difference from and defferal to* 'the mediated' – Cage's remark and Viola's observations take a subtly different turn. Thus where Auslander reads 'the live' as the absent object of 'mediatization' and *vice versa*, Cage and Viola implicitly associate 'the live' with that which is produced *by* or *in* the system, and so with that which is *not exactly represented*, or, at least, whose 'object' is not specifically *elsewhere*. It is in this context that Cage articulates a fascination with *presence* in the media, implicitly proposing a return or resurgence of unrepeatability or ephemerality in the performance of electronic media. Viola similarly describes video's repetition *in* 'the live', such that '[v]ideo's roots in the live, not recorded, is the underlying characteristic of the medium' (Viola 1995a: 62).

Such readings may be set against theoretical positions that articulate the divisions and multiplications of television and video's operation. Writing in *Mass Mediaurus: Form, Technics, Media*, Samuel Weber proposes a highly influential analysis of 'the specificity of the televisual medium' (Weber 1996: 109). Consistent with Auslander's approach to 'liveness', Weber stands against 'ontologizing television' in order to avoid 'the risk of transforming, albeit unawares, a *differential determination* into a *positive* and *universal essence*' (Weber 1996: 109, original emphasis). Instead, and while noting the likely 'complicity' 'between the *medium of television* and the *world* composed by those forces' (Weber 1996: 112: original emphasis), Weber approaches television in its overcoming of distance. Here, he argues, television's operation confuses the relationship between representation and its object, for in bringing events 'closer' television sets before the viewer not simply the *reproduction* of the distant object but a mode of perception. In this operation, Weber proposes, television

> *transports vision as such* and sets it immediately *before* the viewer. It entails not merely a heightening of the naturally limited powers of sight with respect to certain distant objects: it involves a transmission or transposition of vision itself.
>
> (Weber 1996: 116, original emphasis)

In this sense, Weber concludes, television '*overcomes* distance and separation: but it can do so only because it also *becomes* separation' (Weber 1996: 116, original emphasis), as, in its operation, it comes to occupy a place which is *neither fully there nor entirely here.* What it sets before us, in and as the television *set*, is therefore split, or rather, it is a *split* or a *separation* that camouflages itself by taking the form of a visible *image*.

(Weber 1996: 120, original emphasis)

For Weber, it is television's transmission of vision *in these* divisions, its 'power to combine such separation with the presentness associated with sense-perception' (Weber 1996: 116–17), which lies at the root of television's specificity. Thus, where the 'simultaneity' of 'live' television, for example, at once emphasizes the distance, division and separation between viewing ('here') and its object ('there'), so it disguises this separation in the apparent continuity of view it *places before* the viewer, a 'camouflage' that asserts the *presentness* of vision. In its relationship to television, video extends this paradoxical *becoming separation*, providing for a further dispersal of relationships and terms through 'time-switching' (Webster 1995: 135) and its production of the 'timeshifted TV programme' (Cubitt 1993: xii). In its extension of the delays, divisions and dispersals of the time and space of production and reception, Weber thus argues, video amplifies television's fragmentation, its operational uncertainty, while reproducing the camouflage asserted by its continuity of view (Weber 1996: 122). Indeed, such tensions, in themselves, support 'the televisual medium's' *production* of the 'live' or 'liveness', and so a construction of an 'ideology of the live, the immediate, the direct, the spontaneous, the real' that earlier theorists such as Jane Feuer had observed was commonly 'taken as the very definition of television' (Feuer 1983: 14). Turning to the consequences of this transmission of vision, Weber notes that

one does not usually speak, in English, of 'seeing' television but rather of 'watching' it [. . .] we *watch* events whose outcome is in doubt, like sporting events. [. . .] To watch is very close to *watching out for* or *looking out for*, that is being sensorially alert for something that *may* happen.

(Weber 1996: 118, original emphasis)

In this condition, in which 'the simultaneity of television transmission remains a *quasi*-simultaneity' (Weber 1996: 123–4, original emphasis), the 'watching' Weber describes *acts out* the divisions and uncertainties television's 'visual image' attempts to suppress. 'To "watch"', Weber argues, 'is to look for something that is not immediately apparent. It implies effort, a tension and a separation' (Weber 1996: 119). It is a response provoked not only by the tensions in which television's visual image is produced, but in this image's concomitant resistance to being *placed*. Weber emphasizes that:

> Transmitted vision and audition 'contain', as it were, distance and separation while at the same time confounding the points of reference that allow us to determine what is near and what is far.
>
> (Weber 1996: 122)

'Watching', here, is a response to television's operational uncertainty through a *mode of attention* that implies the 'ephemeral' and 'the live': a 'looking out for', an active projection toward that 'whose outcome is in doubt', an anticipation of that which 'may happen'. Nor, in the absence of an 'ontology' of 'the live', can such an operation be defined simply in a *representation* or *simulation* of 'liveness', where liveness is the 'referent' or 'absent object' of television's functioning or the viewer's response. Indeed, for Weber the 'specificity of the televisual medium' is to be found precisely in its capacity to effect the uncanny return of that which it divides. Thus, where the 'television image' 'contains' the divisions it claims to overcome, so, in the very *uncertainty* of the 'where' and 'when' of its image's occurrence, it *presents a return* of that which 'mediation' and 'recording' would seem to defeat: the *presence* of vision to events elsewhere; the performance of 'the live' in 'the mediated'. Returning to Derrida, Weber concludes:

> The television screen is the site of such uncanny confusion and confounding. In the uncanniness of such confusion, what Derrida has called the irreducible 'iterability' of the mark – that

repeatability that both allows a trait to constitute its identity while splitting it at the same time – manifests itself in the only way open to it [...] namely, as the *undecideable being of the television images we see*'.

(Weber 1996: 121, original emphasis)

This 'undecideable being' and the concomitant uncertainties of watching are reflected in other analyses of television's 'visuality'. For Richard Dienst, then, proposing, in *Still Life in Real Time: Theory After Television*, to follow 'Nam June Paik's intuition [...] that the fundamental concept of television is *time*' (Dienst 1994: 159), television's image itself is subject to dual *times*. Arguing that '[t]ime moves in two directions on television, toward the still and toward the automatic' (Dienst 1994: 159), Dienst contrasts 'still time', which '[a]t the extreme [...] could be achieved only as a series of pure instants, without any relation whatsoever' (Dienst 1994: 161–2), with a 'mechanic visuality', an automatic time that extends the continuity of the camera's view. Television's image, Dienst concludes, is presented in the interdependence of these two movements, which operate 'in an alternating current: the instant disrupts the continuous and vice versa' (Dienst 1994: 161). In this rhythm he argues:

> Televisual stills are created by switching away from a picture, pushing past one toward another, by halting a movement or adding a different one. And these stills do not add up or follow one another: each turns over and disappears from view [...] automatic time appears when an image is switched on and left running, so that it is no longer an image of *something*; it is the time of the camera's relentless stare, persisting beyond the movements of objects and scenery that pass before it.
>
> (Dienst 1994: 159, original emphasis)

Such constructions displace the transmitted image from television's *presentness of view*, for '[i]f still time slices images and designates them as past, then automatic time opens onto an anticipated future: it is an image waiting for its event to happen' (Dienst 1994: 159). Here, the more clearly these intersections of *times* and *tenses* are revealed, the more television presses *its vision* toward the language of 'the live': toward that which is 'just passed', that which is 'about to occur'.

This articulation and resurgence of 'the live' in mediated practices, even as its divisions and differences are emphasized, provides a key point of departure in multi-media practice. For John Cage, then, in *Variations V* (Figures 1.1, 1.2 and 1.3), a key collaborative event performed at the Lincoln Centre, New York City on 23 July 1965, the crossing of live, mediated and recorded channels of address permitted a further dissolution of the certainties and stabilities of the conventional musical or theatrical 'object'. A '[p]erformance without score or parts' (Cage 1965: 1) produced in 'two rehearsal periods eight hours each on two days at least one day apart' (Cage 1965: 4), *Variations V* emphasized 'flow',

1.1 John Cage, *Variations V.* (1965), courtesy the Cunningham Dance Foundation. Photo: Hervé Gloaguen. Dancers: Merce Cunningham and Barbara Dilley Lloyd. Musicians: (l–r) John Cage, David Tudor, Gordon Mumma.

PERFORM AT CONTROL PANELS IN THE ROLE OF RESEARCH WORKER.

CHANGE TUNING OF SHORT WAVE RECEIVERS SELECTIVELY, FAVORING NON-REFERENTIAL NOISE AREAS.

SEPARATE CHANNELS (6+) WITH LOUD-SPEAKERS PLACED A-ROUND AND ABOVE AUDIENCE.

INTERMITTENT.

ADDITIONAL INDEPENDENT SOUND-SYSTEM (A) AVAILABLE FOR USE BY DANCERS INVOLVING OBJECTS WITH CONTACT MICROPHONES AFFIXED.

MIXER (G): VOLUME, TONE, AND DISTRIBUTION TO ANY OF 6 LOUD-SPEAKERS.

CHANGED FUNCTION OF COMPOSER: TO TELEPHONE, TO RAISE MONEY.

FROM NO OPERATION OF CONTROLS TO TWO OR MORE OPERATORS AT EACH CONTROL PANEL.

ALL TAPE RECORDINGS (H) THE SAME AND DIFFERENT, ORIG-INAL SUGGESTING BUT NOT HAVING INTENTION.

SOME OBJECTS USED BY DANCERS (OBJECTS WITH CONTACT MICROPHONES AFFIXED) ENTERING INTO MULTI-CHANNEL SYS-TEM, NOT INTO ADDITIONAL SYSTEM.

(G) DESIGNED BY MAX MATHEWS.

(H) MADE BY JOHN CAGE.

2.

"BREAKTHROUGH", BY MEANS OF COLLABORATION, INTO THE UNOR-
GANIZED AREAS IN THE REAR" OF THE UNKNOWN.

A POSTERIORI SCORE.

VARIATIONS III.

E.G. KITCHEN SINK ("BAD PLUMBING").

VARIETY OF TAPE MACHINES AND SHORT WAVE RECEIVERS
(ASSEMBLED, NOT OBTAINED FROM A SINGLE COMPANY).

LIGHTING (I) AS THE SOLUTION OF A PROBLEM: DANCE,
FILM, PHOTO-ELECTRIC CELLS (LIGHT, DARKNESS, BEAM
INTENSITY).

ACCEPT LEAKAGE, FEEDBACK, ETC.

QUESTION TO BE ANSWERED AFFIRMATIVELY (DURING RE-
HEARSALS AND PERFORMANCE): DO SOUNDS FLOW THROUGH
THE SYSTEM? (IF NOT, MAKE CHANGES SO THAT THEY DO.)

IRRELEVANCE.

CONVERSATION, CONSULTATIONS (NOT AS SOUND-SOURCES).

AS DANCE ENDS, TURN OFF AMPLIFIERS (IF, DUE TO LEAKAGE,
NECESSARY).

(I) BY BEVERLY EMMONS.

3.

'leakage', 'feedback', between apparently discrete activities and works, including Cage's earlier *Variations III*, while interrupting these exchanges with digressions, 'irrelevance' 'procrastination, mistakes' (Cage 1965: 4). In these respects, and in Cage's integration of chance method and indeterminacy into aspects of its composition and performance, *Variations V* followed Merce Cunningham and Cage's accord, that

> it is essential now to see all the elements of theatre as both separate
> and interdependent [. . .] I think it is livelier to have more than one
> activity going on at once, so that the eye and the ear of the
> spectator are not fixed, but are free to make for each observer his
> own experience.
>
>   (Cunningham in Cunningham and Lesschaeve 1985: 140–1)

Thus, where Cage, in collaboration with David Tudor and three other musicians, operated a sound system designed by Tudor, including 'continuously operating (tape machines (6+), short wave receivers (6+)', as well as 'oscillator(s)' devised by Robert Moog (Cage 1965: 1), other artists worked independently yet in coincidence with this emerging soundscape. As Cunningham and company performed his choreography, Cage's 'a posteriori score' 'Thirty Seven Remarks Re An Audio-Visual Performance' (Cage 1965) records that 'the audibility of sound system' was 'dependent on movement of dancers' through their 'interruption of light beams' (Cage 1965: 1), while ten capacitive antennas and contact mics served to generate further sound from the dancers' activity and the objects they manipulated. Simultaneously, 'television (preferably closed with image distortions)' designed by Nam June Paik and 'film (preferably multiple)' by Stan Vanderbeek provided a visual overlaying and interruption of events. In emphasizing the unpredictable and the 'unknown', whereby Cage and his collaborators might approach the performance of controls 'in the role of research worker' (Cage 1965: 1), *Variations V* extended a fundamental aspect of early electronic music. Here, technology itself was conceived as introducing uncertainties, distortions and spontaneity. Cage remarks:

> One of the very early principles of live electronic music was that
> through the use of amplification changes take place in the quality
> of sound – going through a sound system, coming through the
> loud speakers [. . .]. So we like to use amplification even when it
> isn't necessary.
>
> (Cage in Kaye 1996: 16)

In extending this principle toward a field of ostensibly distinct activities, *Variations V* fosters relationships in which 'sounds flow through the system', a *transmission* from the live to the mediated to the live that continually effects the interruption and contamination of separate 'works' to produce 'spontaneous' and unintended outcomes. It is a flow of elements foregrounded, too, in the intrusion of activities that evade the conventions of theatrical, musical and choreographic performance: Cage's 'theatrical' performance is ruled by the demands of the 'system', the media, placed on view before the audience; Cunningham's choreography is 'interrupted' by everyday activities as he rides a bicycle or moves an object; the function of the composer changes, '[t]o telephone. To raise money' (Cage 1965: 2). Here, task, everyday actions and the presence of technology itself breach the conventional boundaries of 'the work', while asserting their place *in* interruption and 'irrelevance' within this field. *Variations V*, in this sense, is comprised in the operation of elements *there* and *here*, simultaneously present to distinct works, even inside and outside the 'field' itself. In these ways, *Variations V* deploys technology and mediation to interrupt, divert and so amplify the spontaneity and ephemerality of 'live' activity.

The ambivalent 'return' *in mediation* of that which it ostensibly disrupts is reflected, too, in key critical narratives around video art's impact on the 'individual' work in art. For Rosalind Krauss, writing of *A Voyage on the North Sea: Art in the Age of the Post-Medium Condition* (Krauss 1999), video art's emergence marked a disruption of the modernist programme articulated in the writings of Clement Greenberg (1961) and Michael Fried (1968) and reflected in abstract painting and sculpture after abstract expressionism. In this projection toward 'the irreducible working essence

of art and the separate arts' (Greenberg 1962: 30), the artwork's legitimacy
was to be linked to its expression of the 'recursive structure' (Krauss 1999:
7) of the medium it sought to uncover. Thus, Michael Fried concluded
in his celebrated essay 'Art and Objecthood', 'the task of the modernist
painter is to discover those conventions that, at a given moment, *alone* are
capable of establishing his identity as painting' (M. Fried 1968: 123–4,
original emphasis). Here, then, painting as 'a medium' provides for a
statement by the 'individual work' of the formal ground or place in which
it stands, reflecting the fact that,

> in order to sustain artistic practice, a medium must be a supportive
> structure, generative of a set of conventions, some of which, in
> assuming the medium itself as their subject, will be wholly
> 'specific' to it, thus producing an experience of their own necessity.
>
> (Krauss 1999: 26)

Reflecting this trajectory, and that 'the nature of a recursive structure
is that it must be able, at least in part, to specify itself' (Krauss 1999: 7),
structuralist film of the late 1960s and early 1970s, in the work of Michael
Snow, Ernie Gehr, Hollis Frampton and Paul Sharits, among others,
sought to articulate a correspondence between the various formal aspects
of film's 'technical support' and operation and an experience of viewing.
Exemplified in Snow's celebrated *Wavelength* (1967), incorporating 'a
45-minute single, almost uninterrupted zoom' (Krauss 1999: 25), such
work, Krauss suggests:

> strove to construct the synecdoche for film 'itself' – motion
> reduced to and summarized in the ultimate camera movement
> (Snow's zoom), or filmic illusion typified in the flicker film's
> dissection of the persistence of vision (Paul Sharit's work) – one
> which, like any totalizing work, would be unitary.
>
> (Krauss 1999: 44–5)

In contrast, Jonathan Knight Crary remarks, after (Frederic Jameson
1991: 78), (Weber 1996: 118–19) and (Krauss 1999: 31), that 'the idea

of asking (as did the formalist art critic Clement Greenberg and others) "what are the essential properties of television and video" was a quixotic project from the beginning' (Knight Crary 2002: 25). Indeed, if, as Weber proposes, 'what is ostensibly "set in place" as the television set is also and above all *a movement of displacement*, of *transmission*' (Weber 1996: 125), then television *contests* the 'proper place' the modernist work would *state*, to define a movement between places: a *movement in place*. It would follow from this that television's operation *works against* the 'televisual work's' 'uncovering' of its own internal structural necessity, for television is an operation occurring at once *inside* and *outside, there* and *here*. Indeed, to look 'inside' the medium of television is, it follows, to become subject to this operational displacement, to the *undecidability* in which its transportation of vision functions, a displacement that video, in its relationship to television, only serves to amplify. Correspondingly, Krauss notes, and specifically with respect to 'video art', that 'television and video seem Hydra-headed, existing in endlessly diverse forms, spaces, and temporalities' (Krauss 1999: 30–1). Here, Krauss concludes that video art's proliferation in the late 1960s demonstrated that

> even if video had a distinct technical support – its own apparatus,
> so to speak – it occupied a kind of discursive chaos, a heterogeneity
> of activities that could not be theorized as coherent or conceived of
> as having something like an essence or unifying core [...] it
> proclaimed the end of medium-specificity. In the age of television,
> so it broadcast, we inhabit a post-medium condition.
>
> (Krauss 1999: 31)

Indeed, descriptions of video in relation to the subsequent emergence of new media and digital art practices have frequently invested this 'movement of displacement' into its 'identity' and 'history'. Thus, Sean Cubitt, in his influential *Videography: Video Media as Art and Culture*, positions 'video media' (Cubitt 1993: xi) as a state of passage or transition 'from film and towards another family of media whose core is the computer' (Cubitt 1993: xi), while, in *New Philosophy for New Media*, Mark

Hansen emphasizes the critical attention focused on the video image 'as a privileged mediator of the transition from the cinema to the digital' (Hansen 2004: 236). Such accounts of the evasive character of video as an historical and theoretical 'object of study' have served, too, as the basis of descriptions of video as peculiarly resistant to theorization (Jameson 1991: 71), leading Cubitt, for example, to state unequivocally:

> There is no video theory in the way that there is a body of knowledge called film theory or, rather differently, television studies. There never will be. Not being a really simple or discrete entity, video prevents the pre-requisite for a theoretical approach: that is, deciding upon an object about which you wish to know.
>
> (Cubitt 1993: xvi)

Yet these positions remain paradoxical, for, even in this fracturing of 'the medium', the 'video art work' evidently *comes back* in the activity and exchanges of numerous video artists, exhibitions and editions, reflecting television's *camouflage*. Indeed, the demise of 'the individual work' in video assumes a specific form of 'artwork', one that has acquired a solidity, permanence and uniqueness. It is a narrative unprepared, too, for video's capacity to reinstate, transform and recuperate 'the work' *in transmission*. Here, even as television and video disturb or evade the 'individual work's' assertion of its 'unique' *place*, so that work *returns* in its very availability, its proximity: an availability that is a function of its absence from *this place*.

In this respect, too, 'experimental television' and video art find a close relationship to performance, conceptual art and 'live art', even where mediation and recording may seem antithetical to the 'live event's' 'ephemerality'. Like performance, video art has provided a means of challenging the ground and location of conventional forms of work, while operating in relation to multiple fields and points of reference. Reflecting this, the critical narrative of this book focuses on three entries into video, installation and performance, and their implications and consequences. Thus, the book begins with Nam June Paik's inception of experimental television and video art through his transposition and critique of the experimental musical practices of John Cage and the aesthetically radical Fluxus movement. In this context, Paik's focus on the performance of a plurality of musical and visual times formed the basis of explorations of presence and presentness in post-minimal video installation by artists such as Bruce Nauman and Dan Graham and performance by Joan Jonas, among others. Subsequently, *Multi-Media* focuses on a second wave of video art and installation arising in the late 1960s and early 1970s linked explicitly to body art and an articulation of the presence of the performer in disjunctive relationships between 'real' and 'virtual' spaces, exemplified in the work of Vito Acconci and further elaborated by Studio Azzurro, Pipilotti Rist and Gary Hill. Finally, the book returns to the trajectory of multi-media theatre and the performance of mediation from the Wooster Group's early incorporation of film and video into their theatre pieces, to more recent work created by the writer and director John Jesurun and the New York-based theatre company The Builders Association. In the course of these narratives, too, *Multi-Media* emphasizes a series of divisions and multiplications in which key figures and themes return: the division between video time and performance time; between video space and performance space; and the multiplication of media in the theatrical re-framing and performance of mediation. Here, too, *Multi-Media* asserts another doubling, as these narratives are written in dialogue with a series of documentations by key artists working across and between these fields, documentations that variously challenge, echo and extend the relationship between critical speculation and the recuperation of practice in which this project operates.

In this dialogue between times, spaces and media, too, the work with which *Multi-media* is concerned implicitly engages with the complicity Weber observes 'between the *medium of television* and the *world* composed by those forces' (Weber 1996: 112, original emphasis), where the 'un-decidability' of the transmitted image serves the construction of place, identity and subjectivity. Such concerns are reflected across the spectrum of these practices. Thus, for The Builders Association in their collabo-ration with the London-based company **moti**roti for *Alladeen* (2002–5), the performance of place, identity and time, explored through the experiences of call-centre operators working from the Indian sub-continent to the United States, is crossed with myths and fantasies of transformation. Such division is reflected in the fabric of *Alladeen* itself: the project, devised across two continents, encompasses a theatre performance, a music video and a website; in performance, the stage is divided between cinematic and theatrical spaces; its subject matter is a making visible of the performance of a 'global' (American) identity. Characteristically of The Builders Association's work, *Alladeen* exposes its own processes of mediation: performers located live on stage are simultaneously re-presented in the cinematic space above, integrated into a series of transforming images and narratives. In its documentation, too, the company emphasizes *Alladeen*'s exposure of the *divisions* integral to transmission, yet the availability and *presentness* of the vision it transports. Here, in foregrounding the contradictions of 'performing American', these companies engage with the suppression and return of 'local' identity, geography and politics. In doing so, and as video gives way to performance and live performance gives way to mediation, The Builders Association responds to the demand articulated by Tim Etchells, the Artistic Director of the British theatre and media company Forced Entertainment, that 'the theatre must take account of how technology [...] has rewritten and is rewriting bodies, changing our understanding of narratives and places, changing our relationships to culture, changing our understandings of presence' (Etchells 1999: 97).

The New York-based company The Builders Association creates large-scale theater projects exploring the interface between live performance and media. Directed by Marianne Weems, our work uses current tools to interpret old forms. Since 1994, with a growing circle of artists, we have collaborated on nine large-scale theater projects, including MASTER BUILDER (1994), THE WHITE ALBUM (1995), IMPERIAL MOTEL (FAUST) (1996), JUMP CUT (FAUST) (1997), JET LAG (1998) with Diller + Scofidio, XTRAVAGANZA (2000), ALLADEEN (2002–5) with **moti**roti, and SUPER VISION with dbox (2005).

THE BUILDERS ASSOCIATION

THE BUILDERS ASSOCIATION/MOTIROTI'S
ALLADEEN

The *Alladeen* project encompasses three collaborative works: a crossmedia performance directed by Marianne Weems (The Builders Association); a music video directed by Ali Zaidi (**moti**roti) and a website directed by Ali Zaidi at ww.alladeen.com. All three were conceived collaboratively by Keith Khan,Marianne Weems,and Ali Zaidi. Although distinct, these three works were created in tandem, drawing on a common pool of information,with material from each project interwoven into the others.

Alladeen explores how we function as "global soul" caught up in circuits of technology, how our voices and images travel from one culture to another,and the ways in which we continually reinterpret each other's signs and stories.

The fantasies which lie at the heart of Aladdin's story are instantaneous wish fulfillment, endless wealth, and total personal transformation—fantasies which remain fiercely addictive today. In the call centers of Bangalore, India,we found a setting in which such transformations are being constantly and routinely enacted— culturally, socially,and economically—on both ends of the fiber-optic phone lines.

Alladeen is a lens through which we view the realm of contemporary technology and its dissonant mixing of the local with the global. The territory we survey is the social imagination in an age of corporate colonialism.

I've been making calls for the past 6 months now, probably 200 calls every day. So earlier my perspective about America was all too rosy since that's what you see on television and through the media—that it was the best country and the land of opportunity—and it is definitely. But I think the people there are very lonely and some of them are very depressed. Their family ties seem to be wavering off and I don't think it's all that nice. Every place has it's own problems.

Natasha Sabharwal
Electronic Relationship Officer

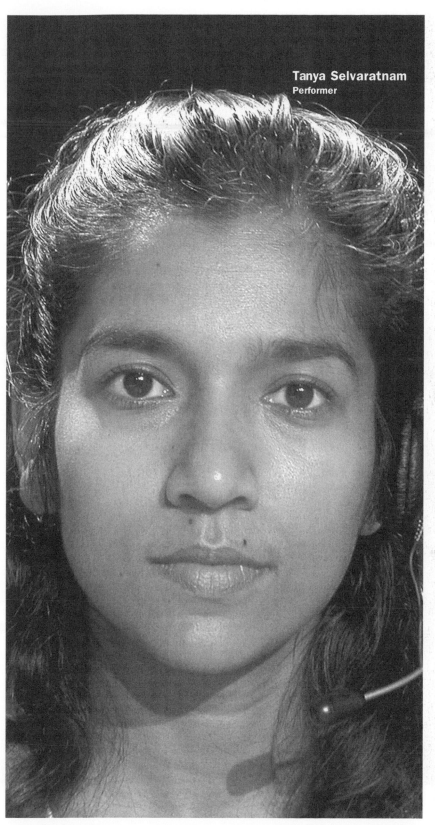

Tanya Selvaratnam
Performer

SCENE 5 EXCERPT

Phoebe
On the Road Customer Guidance. This is Phoebe, how may I help you?

Las Vegas Lady
Yeah. I just rented a car from you guys? And I'm trying to get from LA to LV and I was just wondering if you could give me some directions?

Phoebe
You're trying to get to Louisiana, m'am?

Las Vegas Lady
Oh, no. I'm in Los Angeles trying to get to Las Vegas and I lost the hoo-zee-what-sis thing, the thingamajiggy with the directions on it that you guys gave me. And I want to tell you that I am ready to gamble. I just won a gazillion smackaroonies in the PA lottery and I'm trying to triple my stash. I'm gonna blow the whole wad.

Phoebe
I think there is some-thing wrong with the connection. Can you hold on please?

Las Vegas Lady
Um? Sure?

Phoebe to Rizwan
(in an Indian accent) What is a "smack-rooni"?

Rizwan
Pasta. Spaghetti.

Phoebe
Not mac-a-roni, Smack-a-rooni...(she enters the word in Spellcheck, no response)...Hello m'am I'm back again...

SHARU JOSE
Trainer/Supervisor

SCENE 4 EXCERPT:
TELEPHONE TECHNIQUE

American Trainer
OK, Who am I speaking to this time?

Student
This is Bunny.

American Trainer
No, what's his American name? B,U double N–Y?

Student
Yeah Bunny.

American Trainer
Why don't we call him Brett—you know like a good American name. Bunny—I mean for Christ's sake—you're called Brett!

Student
Brett?

American Trainer
B-R-E-double T. Brett.

Student
Brett.

American Trainer
Alright? Or Brad. Or Joey. You're not called Bunny. Jesus Christ.

Student
(practicing) Jesus Christ...

American Trainer
Alright. Lets go....

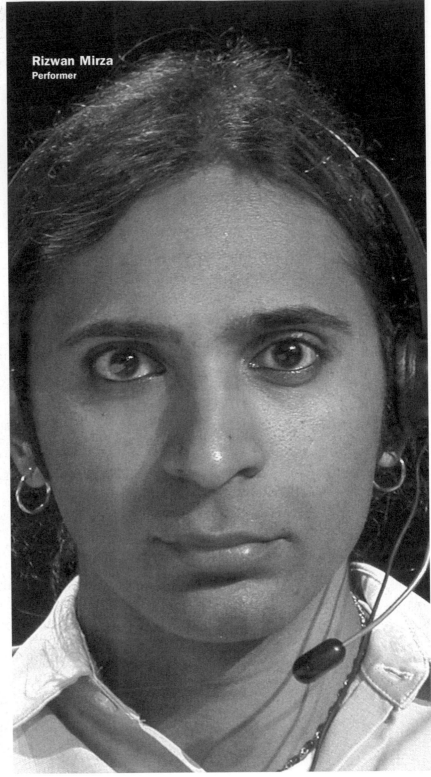

Rizwan Mirza
Performer

Is India getting exploited? Let me answer that by saying: we are not jerks. We're actually using the opportunity given by your company for our personal growth and the growth of our nation. And in turn what we're doing is cutting your costs and making it a valuable experience, to make you a lot more money. So if you think about it, the backup for word processors in your country is by the guys working over here, and that's for your own profit. So we're not the jerks, we're the dudes. Thank you.

Riaz Basha
Electronic Relationship Officer

Credits

The Builders Association/**moti**roti's
Alladeen
Conceived by Keith Khan, Marianne Weems, and Ali Zaidi

Page design in collaboration with David Cabrera
Text edited by Marianne Weems
Photos and interview excerpts by Ali Zaidi
Excerpts from scene dialogue by Rizwan Mirza, Tanya Selvaratnam, Heaven Phillips, and Jeff Webster

In Bangalore:
Ali Zaidi & Peter Norrman (Videography)
Jyoti Makhija (Research & Production)
Mike Isaac & Frame of Mind (Technical Production, hire & crew)

Invaluable assistance in India: Dr. Rathi Jafer (Manager,Arts,Culture & English Studies,British Council, India), Dr. B.K. Chandrashekar (Former Minister for I.T., Government of Karnataka, India), Nasreen Munni Kabir (Film Consultant), National Film Archive of India

www.alladeen.com

www.motiroti.com

www.thebuildersassociation.org

The Builders Association/**moti**roti
2003

Video Time/Performance Time

> Video art imitates nature, not in its appearance or mass, but in its intimate 'time-structure'.
>
> (Paik in Handhardt 2000: 15)

The emergence of 'experimental television' in North America in the early 1960s was closely bound to the new musical practices that emphasized an opposition to notions of the innate singularity of *the medium*. Here, in a reflection of the proposition that the 'technical support' upon which television and video rests is divided and multiple, the practices of Nam June Paik, the single most influential figure in early North American experimental television and video art, followed John Cage's emphasis on the *differences* at play in any medium or work. Such tendencies are evident in Paik's earliest practices and are bound to the close link between his experimental television and 'live' events or activities, in whose combination he frequently articulated one measure or passage of time in the context of another. Indeed, it is in Paik's address to the complexities of 'time-structures' in video and video installation that he has come to articulate terms fundamental to a multi-media and, specifically, a *multiplied* performance, where time, in *its* performance, is subject to variability, difference and multiplication.

Experimental Television: Nam June Paik

Originally trained in aesthetics, music and art history at the University of Tokyo (Decker-Phillips 1998: 24), following his family's evacuation during the Korean War, Paik's studies in Japan had culminated in a thesis on the work of Arnold Schönberg. In 1956, Paik moved to Germany to extend this work through doctoral research, registering for studies first at Munich and then Freiburg. In the summer of 1958, during the first of three years of work with the composer Karlheinz Stockhausen at Radio Cologne's Studio for Electronic Music, Paik attended Cage's series of key lectures on 'Composition as Process' (Cage 1968a) and accompanying concerts in Darmstadt. In these contexts, and while he approached Cage's concerts, Paik reported, 'with a very cynical mind, to see what Americans would do with Oriental heritage' (Decker-Phillips 1998: 25), Paik's encounter provoked a transformation in his own thinking; first, Edith Decker-Phillips suggests, in 'the insight that the boredom which he felt listening to Cage's music had its parallel in the philosophy of Zen Buddhism' and so 'in the idea of absolute emptiness' (Decker-Phillips 1998: 25). Subsequently, although his permanent relocation to New York in 1964 had ostensibly been on the occasion of the revival of Stockhausen's *Originale*, in which he had performed, he later emphasized that 'I came to the U.S. *only* because of John Cage' (Paik in Ross 1993: 59). Yet, while Paik's radical practices with regard to time in video directly responded to Cage's use of chance method and indeterminacy, which were derived from the aesthetic and ethical imperatives of Zen Buddhism, his work was also shaped in a critique of Cage's transformation of these aspects of his own cultural legacy.

For Cage, who had followed the teachings of D. T. Suzuki since attending his classes at Columbia University in 1951, Zen Buddhism provided the rationale for his radical revision of the content, form and purpose of musical activity. Proposing that 'art should introduce us to life' (Cage in Cage and Charles 1981: 52), Cage observed that, in the context of Zen, 'Nature', and so 'the real', occurs as a state of continual 'becoming', which the work of art is subject to, but which, *as an object in time*, it can neither embody nor represent. He remarks:

> You say: the real, the world as it is. But it is not, it becomes! It doesn't wait for us to change [. . .]. It is more mobile than you can imagine. You are getting closer to reality when you say that it 'presents itself'; that means it is not there, existing as an object. The world, the real, is not an object. It is a process.
>
> (Cage and Charles 1981: 80)

In this context, Cage's first lecture at Darmstadt, 'Changes', whose title refers to the *I Ching: Book of Changes*, reflected his earlier acceptance of

Ananda K. Coomaraswamy's proposition that 'the function of Art is to imitate Nature in her manner of operation' (Cage 1976: 31). It was this position that had brought Cage to the introduction of chance method into his work in 1952 and, subsequently, to compositions 'indeterminate' with respect to their performance, in which each realization may produce an unpredicted and continuously unpredictable outcome.

In his first solo exhibition, the *Exposition of Music – Experimental Television* of March 1963, in which Paik inaugurated his 'electronic art', he explicitly transposed these new musical practices and ideas toward the arenas of action, audience participation and the 'abstract time' (Paik 1993: flyleaf) of his television manipulations. Occupying every room of the suburban house that formed the Galerie Parnass in Wuppertal, Germany, and following his earlier, unrealized conception of a *Symphony for Twenty Rooms* of 1961 (Paik in Handhardt 2000: 41), the *Exposition* sought to realize Paik's declared imperative in his 'Postmusic' manifesto of the same year 'to renew the ontological form of music' (Paik 1979a). Seeking to extend Cage's notion that '[t]heatre takes place all the time wherever one is and art simply facilitates persuading one this is the case' (Cage 1968e: 174), Paik's manifesto proposed a '"Moving Theatre" in the street' (Paik 1979a) that would embed art within the time and circumstances of the everyday, suggesting that

> the sounds move in the street, the audience meets or encounters them 'unexpectedly' in the street. The beauty of moving theatre lies in this 'surprise *a priori*', because almost all of the audience is uninvited, not knowing what it is, why it is, who is the composer, the player, the organizer – or better speaking – organizer, composer, player.

> (Paik 1979a, original emphasis)

For the *Exposition* Paik sought to realize 'the next step toward indeterminacy', in which, he stated, 'I wanted to let the audience act and play itself' (Paik 2000: 53), so subjecting 'musical performance' to the vagaries of visitor choice, time and interest. In doing so, and while, in Cage's view, taking 'liberties [. . .] in favour of action rather than sound events in time' (Paik in Cage 1993: 22–3), the *Exposition* extended the iconoclastic dissolution of musical performance defining the 'violent "antisomething" aesthetic' (Paik in Ross 1993: 58) of Paik's early solo actions. Thus, where Paik's *One for Violin* (1962) had consisted of a five-minute action in which he carefully raised the instrument above his head only to destroy it in a single downward movement, the *Exposition* 'showed (violently) prepared pianos' (Blom 1998: 77) in a reflection of Paik's proposition that 'the piano is taboo: it must be destroyed'. *Klavier Integral* (1963), a piano already subject to seemingly violent interventions, thus invited visitors to the *Exposition* to 'play' keys that activated objects suspended from the piano case, electric switches, a transistor radio, a fan heater, film projectors and the lights of the exhibition room (Dreschler 1993: 46). Extending Cage's practice of inserting wood, metal screws, cardboard, rubber and other objects between a piano's strings to disrupt the relationship of notation to sound, such works also drew the uncertainties of audience action into Paik's dispersal of the instrument's performance into its environment. Along with a variety of *Objets Sonore* (sound objects) that traversed music, sculpture and action, the *Exposition* also presented various arrangements of dissembled record players and audiotape recorders, each under the title *Random Access*, that provided for the spectator's 'accidentally determined access to music pieces and other events' (Decker-Philips 1998: 34) through their active participation. Here, too, Ina Blom argues, in giving way to the particularities of audience participation, such works deferred to the concrete location, or specific site, of their performance. Referring, in particular, to the dual forms of *Random Access*, and implicitly acknowledging an indeterminacy effected through participation, Blom notes that here Paik's various

> apparatuses do not simply transmit or create sound, but constantly rewrite it [. . .]. Record players were taken apart and reconstructed as towering 'record-schaschlik's' where the pick-up could be moved at will across the vertical and horizontal axes of the construction. Magnetic tape (with sound recordings) were glued on the wall in criss-crossing patterns.
>
> (Blom 1998: 78)

As a consequence, Blom concludes, in '[l]istening by means of the loose soundhead of a tape recorder, one would trace the sound map of a wall terrain', so realizing 'a cartography of sound [...] in which sound is submitted to the dimensionality of concrete space and distance' (Blom 1998: 78).

Significantly, in focusing upon such 'encounters', Paik's work also participated in a subversion of musical performance linked to 'the concept of Concretism' to which George Maciunas had understood 'neo-Dada', or Fluxus, activity to be almost exclusively bound (Maciunas 1988: 25). Writing of 'Neo Dada in Music, Theatre, Poetry, Art', an essay performed, with Paik's and others' collaboration, by the artist Arthus C. Caspari in June 1962 as part of '*Après* John Cage', an evening of performances by Fluxus artists (Smith 1998: 59–60), Maciunas emphasized that rather than evoke an 'ideal' realm of musical form, '[a] material or concrete sound is' one that 'clearly indicates the nature of material or concrete reality producing it' (Maciunas 1988: 26). In these events, and through his destructive actions in particular, Paik violently extended Maciunas' concretism, drawing attention to the iconoclastic act and the spectacle of the object in use. Here, too, Paik set the *ephemerality of action* at the heart of his 'Postmusic', while expressing an engagement with indeterminacy and unrepeatability very different from Cage's. Paik remarks that

> [t]he most important things happen only once [...]. The reason I became so well known through destructive art was also because of nonrepeatability. Once you break an expensive piano, it cannot be put back together. Once you throw water on the ground, you cannot scoop it back up.
>
> (Paik in Isozaka 1993: 125)

It is a sensibility, too, that forms a common thread in Paik's construction of many of his early works, as, consistent with the emphasis in Fluxus on temporality and *the temporary*, he admitted uncertainties into the functioning of his technology that frequently required his intervention during its exhibition. In his major catalogue of Paik's work, *The Worlds of Nam June Paik*, John Handhardt notes that 'the ideas of process and change over time were integral to Paik's work. His work embodied a sense of hand fabrication, of things that would break down and require repair in the process of the concert/performance' (Handhardt 2000: 68). Thus, in preparing for the *Exposition*, Paik's collaborator, the Fluxus artist Tomas Schmit, later recalled, Paik purposefully subjected the completion of the piano works, such as *Klavier Integral*, to potentially unreliable schedules and elements. Here, he notes:

> the equipment used to enhance the piano was by no means put in place ahead of time. We were still fiddling around with things during the exhibition. Some of the improvised fittings were deliberately rather delicate and had to be replaced – or simply eliminated – so the spirit behind creating the pianos was driven by spontaneity and free randomness.
>
> (Schmit in Dreschler 1993: 44)

The result, Schmit concludes, was that the *Exposition* became 'more like a performance, a potential performance' (Schmit in Dreschler 1993: 44).

In this context, Paik's exhibition of 'TV-sets in which the transmission was being destroyed or transformed in various ways' (Blom 1998: 77) participated directly in his subversion and transformation of musical practice. Indeed, Paik's ongoing research into physics and electronics, to which he had dedicated himself following his first participation in *Originale* in October and November 1961 (Handhardt 2000: 34), had by the time of the *Exposition* brought him to the creation of televisual analogues to Cage's prepared pianos and Maciunas' concretism. Here, in a single installation in which '13 sets suffered 13 sorts of variation in their VIDEO-HORIZONTAL-VERTICAL units' (Paik 1964, original emphasis), and following his conclusion that television images could be "indeterministically determined"' (Paik in Kellein 1993: 31), Paik's interventions engaged with an *electronic state* identified with the operation of the television set that exemplified Cage's conception of the indeterminate work as one that 'returns to *make itself*. It becomes a current, a flux'

(Cage in Cage and Charles 1981: 177, original emphasis). Having tuned each set to the same programme, Paik intervened into the hardware of the monitors in order to produce varying and frequently unpredictable distortions of the scanned image through procedures analogous to his reconfiguration of audiotape recorders and record players. Paik thus recalled that, among other alterations:

B   A relay is intercepted at the A/C 110 volt input and fed by a 25 watt amplifier without rectifier [...]
C   10 meg ohm resistor is intercepted at the grid of the vertical output tube and then the waves from the generator are fed here, so that both waves interfere and modulate each other [...]
D   The waves from the taperecorder are fed into the horizontal output tube's grid, so that horizontal lines are warped according to the taperecorder's frequency and amplitude.

(Paik 2000a: 90)

While one of Paik's thirteen sets remained face down on the floor following its accidental destruction, Schmit recalled that of eight TVs raised from the floor and subjected to these alterations,

[o]ne of the televisions shows a negative running picture; in one case the picture is rolled into a cylinder around the vertical axis of the screen. In another case it is modulated around the horizontal [...] three independent sinusoidal curves chivy at the parameters of the picture.

(Schmit in Dreschler 1993: 46)

Here, too, Paik's interventions implied another realization of Maciunas' concretism. For Maciunas, Cage's notion of art as an indeterminate flux was also suggested by 'concretism' itself, in relation to which, he proposed 'a truer concretist rejects pre-determination of final form in order to perceive the reality of nature', concluding:

This requires the composition to provide a kind of framework, an
'automatic machine' within which or by which, nature (either in
the form of an independent performer or indeterminate-chance
compositional methods) can complete the art-form, effectively and
independently of the artist-composer.

(Maciunas 1988: 27)

Evidently, for Paik, the capacity of television to subvert or surpass
intention in this way was underpinned by the specific material conditions
in which it operated. As early as 1964, Paik emphasized that his work with
television and video necessarily operated 'within the given condition of
RCA-NSTC TV encoding system' (Ross 1993: 58), the effect of which
was to reverse conventional compositional practice:

In usual compositions, we have first the approximate vision of the
completed work (the pre-imaged ideal, or 'IDEA' in the sense of
Plato). Then, the working process means the torturing endeavor to
approach this ideal 'IDEA'. But in the experimental TV, the thing
is completely revised. Usually I don't, or *cannot* have any
pre-imaged VISION before working. First I seek the 'WAY', . . .
that means, to study the circuit, to try various 'FEED BACKS', to
cut some places and feed the different waves there, to change the
phase of waves, etc.

(Paik 1964, original emphasis)

It is an unpredictability further extended through the audience participation characteristic of the *Exposition* as a whole. So, Schmit notes, the four
remaining monitors invited visitors to intervene into their operation, as,
for these sets

the manipulations are such that each picture is determined or
influenced by material fed in from the outside. One is connected to
a foot switch in front of it; when pressed, short circuits from the
contact procedure make a firework display of points of light that

shower across the screen, then disappear immediately. One is
connected to a microphone; if someone speaks into it, he sees a
similar, but this time continuous, firework display of dots. *Cuba TV*
goes the furthest; it is connected to a tape recorder that feeds
music into it (and us). The parameters of the music determine the
parameters of the picture.

(Schmit in Dreschler 1993: 46)

In these various respects, Paik's radical innovations realized aspects
of Cage's and Maciunas' account of the relationship of art to 'the
real'. Indeed, Cage himself implicitly linked the operation of the new
technology and 'Nature', both through his innovations in electronic
music to produce 'composition which is indeterminate with respect to its
performance (Cage 1968a: 35) and in his call, in response to Paik, to the
listener to consider the mind as a 'receiver' (Cage 1976: 89). In Paik's
'experimental television', however, the 'imitation' of 'Nature' extended
to his engagement with performance and action, and specifically with the
object *in use*. Here, too, Paik's work persistently returns to paradoxical
plays between multiple times: between the time marked by the television's
operation, by the repetition and transformation of its images, by the
interventions of artist or visitor. Indeed, it is in these *interventions*, in
particular, that the time of television's operation is realized as *dual*, as,
simultaneously, an 'automatic machine' marking its *own time* and a time
articulated outward, in a 'real time' of incident beyond the confines of the
screen. In these respects, the *Exposition* marked out fundamental aspects
of video installation's operation and vocabulary, which, the influential
critic Achille Bonito Oliva proposes,

[documents] a twofold time. Twofold because of a double
possibility of measurement, one dictated by the internal cadence of
the technology and the other by the encounter between the
technology and materials that are steady in themselves and the
public, either still or in movement.

(Oliva in Paik 1993: 16)

For Allan Kaprow, who had initiated the first of the New York 'happening' performances in 1959, the 'destructive' impulse in Paik's work was inextricably bound to this entry into the 'real time' of events, as, he proposes, 'Paik's early performances terrified chiefly because we sensed the opening-out-to-the-world he was embarking on' (Kaprow 1993: 114). It is in Paik's response to Cage's innovation in this context, in particular, that his most influential development of video art takes place.

Unmeasuring Time: John Cage, Paik and Fluxus Video

Cage's concern to invest a corollary to the disciplines of Zen – in which, he noted, 'one sits cross-legged in order to come to *no-mind*' (Cage in Kaye 1996: 22, original emphasis) – in 'musical' composition, performance and listening, and so approach the operation of 'Nature' through art, is crystallized in his concept of 'silence'. First realized in 1952, the year in which Cage also inaugurated his use of aleatory techniques, Cage's first 'silent' piece, *4′33″*, served to exemplify the rigour and purpose of his giving up of 'intention'. Indicating a performance in three parts, where each part is designated 'TACET', *4′33″* prompts a specifically 'musical' event in which no musical instrument is to be played. Thus, in its first presentation at Woodstock, New York, from whose chance-determined duration the piece takes its title, the pianist David Tudor marked a turning away from notated sound through his closing of the piano's keyboard lid for the duration of each of its three timed 'movements'. Here, in directing the audience's attention to the 'chance' sounds occurring in the auditorium, Tudor's performance exemplified a fundamental tenet of Cage's work, that in the time of music

> nothing takes place but sounds: those that are notated and those
> that are not. Those that are not notated appear in the written
> music as silences, opening the doors of the music to the sounds
> that happen to be in the environment [. . .]. There is no such thing

as an empty space or an empty time. There is always something to see, always something to hear.

(Cage 1968c: 8)

Significantly, in opening the musical work to this 'silence' Cage proposes a collapse of the opposition within which 'musical time' conventionally takes its effect. Where, Jonathon Kramer argues in *The Time of Music*, music should be understood as 'a series of events, events that not only contain time but also shape it' (Kramer 1988: 5), so, he proposes, the experience of music arises in a phenomenological distinction 'between the time a piece *takes* and the time which a piece *presents* or *evokes*' (Kramer 1988: 7, original emphasis). In this regard, Kramer concludes, the time-structure characteristic of all music is defined by

at least two temporal continua, determined by order of succession and by conventionalized meanings of gestures. This duality makes musical time quite special: The past-present-future qualities of events are determined by their gestural shapes as well as their placement within the absolute-time succession of a performance.

(Kramer 1988: 161)

In sharp distinction to this 'parallel existence' of 'musical' and 'clock' time, in which, Kramer suggests, '*music creates time*' and '*time itself can (be made to) move, or refuse to move, in more than one "direction"*' (Kramer 1988: 6, original emphasis), *4' 33"* defines a structure seemingly indifferent to this duality. Indeed, as Cage made clear as early as 1954, in his lecture '45' for Speaker', the only structure in which 'silence' may be approached is one of 'no importance', one that 'simply allows anything to happen in it' (Cage 1968e: 159). Thus, Cage concludes, with respect to 'musical methods [. . .] [a]ll that is necessary is an empty space of time and letting it act in its magnetic way' (Cage 1968e: 177-8). Indeed, in this regard, *4' 33"* follows, in its form, the logic set out in this lecture, wherein, Cage notes, '[t]ime, which is the title of this piece (so many minutes so many seconds), is what we and sounds happen in' (Cage 1968e: 151). The paradoxical result, as the composer Christian Wolff suggests, writing 'On Form', is a 'time-structure', that, while marking a performance's structural distinctiveness, works toward the dissolution of its aural and spatial boundaries, so drawing its 'musical' identity into confusion. Thus, with regard to form, Wolff identifies a paradox in Cage's work, whereby

> [n]o distinction is made between the sounds of a work and sounds in general, prior to, simultaneous with, or following the work. Art – music – and nature are not thought of as separated. Music is allowed no privileges over sound. Yet the work is quite distinct. It can be timed [. . .]. But its distinctiveness implies no exclusiveness.
>
> (Wolff 1996: 58)

In *4'33"*, then, listeners find themselves at the centre of a 'musical' work by dint of their listening alone, and Cage provides no clear basis on which to map a hierarchy of sounds, follow a sense of development or come to any completion or resolution save that marked by the clock itself. It follows, Cage concludes in his 'Lecture On Nothing' of 1959, that in following this structure:

> Value judgments are not in the nature of this work as regards either composition, performance, or listening. The idea of relation (the idea: 2) being absent, anything (the idea: 1) may happen. A 'mistake' is beside the point, for once anything happens it authentically is.
>
> (Cage 1968d: 59)

Such authenticity, once accepted, precludes the 'error', the 'mistake' being merely a matter of judgement in listening itself, and so 'simply a failure to adjust immediately from a preconception to an actuality' (Cage 1968e: 170–1). In turn, Cage supposes, such a time-structure may act as a prompt and, after Zen, a mirror, to a specific mode of attention on behalf of the listener. Here, *4'33"* exemplifies the dual aspect of Cage's time-structures as both measure and discipline, leading Cage to note:

That music is simple to make comes from one's willingness to
accept the limitations of structure. Structure is simple because it
can be thought out, figured out, measured. It is a discipline which,
accepted, in return accepts whatever.

(Cage 1968d: 111)

It is in this time-structure, too, that Cage's approach to 'silence' returns
to Zen. Where such 'errorless music' is discovered *in listening*, the listener
may discover that, after Zen's approach to 'Nature', '[a] technique to be
useful (skillful, that is) must be such that it fails to control the elements
subjected to it [...]. And listening is best in a state of mental emptiness'
(Cage 1968e: 154). Here, each act of listening is located not only at the
centre of a musical performance, but in an ethical framework. In the
practice of such technique, and so within this music, Cage concludes,
'Art' fulfils its purpose, as '[t]he highest purpose is to have no purpose at
all. This puts one in accord with nature in the manner of her operation'
(Cage 1968e: 155).

Paik's response to this insight was articulated in works that ostensibly
countered Cage's claims to the transparency, purity and discipline of
the 'empty structure', reflecting his equivocal response to the Western
assimilation of Zen, in which he remarks: 'Zen is responsible for Asian
poverty. How can I justify ZEN without justifying Asian poverty?' (Paik
in Blom 1998: 79). Here, then, in works that frequently re-framed scores,
events and objects in a manner reflecting his subsequent re-use of single-
channel tapes in the various configurations of his video installations, Paik
referred to Zen in presentations that qualified his relationship to Cage's
practice and ethos. Thus, *Zen for Head* (1961) (see Figure 2.1), Paik's
interpretation of the composer La Monte Young's *Composition No. 10,
1960 (for Bob Morris)*, which invited the reader to 'draw a straight line and
follow it' in a reflection of Young's characteristic use of an extended single
note or repetition, was transformed through Paik's volatile performance
in which he marked an extended line with red paint. *Zen for Walking* (1962)
adopted a similar tone, offering a variation of Paik's score, *Dragging Suite*
(1962), whose instruction reads: 'Drag by a string along the streets, stairs,

2.1 Nam June Paik, *Zen for Head* (1962). Photo: dpa/Goettert.

floors: large or small dolls, naked or clothed dolls, broken, bloody or new dolls, real man or woman, musical instruments, etc.' (Paik 2000: 52).

Subsequently, in the *Exposition*, *Zen for TV* offered the re-presentation, as an individual work, of one of Paik's thirteen 'manipulated' TVs, whose picture, destroyed in its transportation to the Galerie Parnass, had been 'reduced to a horizontal line' (Decker-Phillips 1998: 36). In the context of *4'33"*, however, it is *Zen for Film* (1964), which precedes by one year his acquisition of the video Portapack, that marks Paik's engagement with the 'absolute emptiness' in which Cage reflected on the disciplines of Zen. Published as a characteristic box edition by Fluxus, designed by Maciunas and containing only a short loop of blank 16 mm leader tape (*ill.* Herzogenrath 1999: 86), in its projection *Zen for Film* offers no more than the illumination of 'particles of dirt and dust' (Handhardt 2000: 95), so, Decker-Phillips suggests, 'providing the audience with the empty white wall which is usually used in Zen meditation' (Decker-Phillips 1998: 151). In this way, *Zen for Film* offered, Cage later recalled, 'an hour-long film without images' in a demonstration of the fact that '[t]here is never nothing to see' (Cage 1993: 117).

Reflecting Maciunas' concretism, however, *Zen for Film* is a transcription in 'real time', and, by implication, a *continuous recording* of the physical degradation of the blank leader tape by the 'real' conditions of its projection. '[A]s it is projected', Blom notes, this 'loop of blank film leader [. . .] gets gradually scratched-up and dusty. It's a perfect repetition in which the image always changes' (Blom 1998: 83). It follows that where Cage relates its projection to the Zen axiom that '[t]he mind is like a mirror; it collects dust; the problem is to remove the dust' (Cage 1993: 117), over time *Zen for Film* effects an erosion of the mirror's transparency that cannot be recovered. As a result, *Zen for Film* points to a *plurality* of times, playing across the *present-tense* contemplation invited by the white wall, the accumulating traces inscribed by its past and present projection, as well as its future *erasure* in the mechanics of the film medium itself. In this regard, and as a response to *4'33"*, *Zen for Film* poses the question of what it means to be at the threshold of the medium; a threshold defined not simply around the spatial limits of the screen. Indeed, *Zen for Film* specifically attends to the *time-structures* that mark the limit of the work and its medium, effecting its own gradual destruction in *exchanges between* the film and its environment, a corruption acknowledged by Cage in his understanding of its affinity to the 'numerous acts of destruction and gestures of refusal in Paik's work' (Cage 1993: 24). Thus, in its projection, *Zen for Film* is, properly speaking, not *the film*, but the degradation of the 'mirror' in this *intersection of times*, in a structuring of what Paik describes as 'abstract time: time without contents' (Paik 1993: flyleaf). In its early projection, such concerns were further articulated through Paik's performed interventions in its screening, where, at the New Cinema Festival 1, New York, of November 1964, for example, he placed himself in the light of the projection, throwing his shadow on the screen in an amplification of the film's operation across several spaces and events (*ill.* Handhardt 2000: 95).

As this engagement with silence suggests, Paik's reflection upon the times of film and video is not a simple departure from Cage's position and aesthetic, but a response to the implications of Cage's transformation of music within another field. Indeed, Paik's attention, in *Zen for Film*, to the *threshold* of the work responds directly to the implications of Cage's thinking. Thus, where, after Wolff, one might read the time-structure of *4'33"* as proposing to *encompass* 'silence' within the frame of an ostensibly 'musical' event, *Zen for Film* directs attention to the threshold of the 'frame' itself. Within the context of Fluxus, a number of whose key participants had attended Cage's classes in New Musical Composition at the New School for Social Research in New York in 1958 and 1959 (Sohm 1970), this direction toward the value of the 'everyday', of events beyond the scope of conventional 'form', however radical, was fundamental both to the emergence and influence of Fluxus and to its impulse toward performance. Here, the 'silence' toward which Cage directs attention, and with which many Fluxus artists explicitly engaged, does not simply concern those sounds 'that are not notated' and yet that *have become* the 'musical work', or, in Paik's case, are caught in the illumination of the screen, but, more precisely, that 'sound' which evades any *proper place* within the 'musical object'. Thus, reflecting on the importance of this point of *undecidability*, Cage remarked that 'music itself is an ideal situation, not a real one' (Cage 1968b: 31–2), noting, later, that, as a consequence, his 'music' comes to the paradoxical position of 'bringing into existence what music is when there is *not yet* any music'

(Cage in Cage and Charles 1981: 222). 'Silence', in this context, is that which *interrupts the order* in which the 'musical object' is constructed, occurring as that which is at once 'inside' and 'outside' the work. In relation to time, and consistent with Paik, such 'silence' is not available simply *in* the time of the work, but at the *threshold* of the work and its *times*. In this regard, Cage proposed, his 'musical work' strove to offer a paradoxical 'introduction' to 'silence', in which its elements and, finally, its *time* must remain open to question or uncertainty, for '[w]hat counts is that the sound be transformed and restored simultaneously [...]. It is life. Time is with the sounds, in each one of them' (Cage in Cage and Charles 1981: 138).

Indeed, if, as Cage implies, the 'sounds of the environment' are to be encountered, in some sense, in their 'own times', then Cage's notion of 'silence' poses further questions concerning how the 'real' time 'in' each sound might be approached and described. Here, too, the work of Cage, Paik and Fluxus converges toward a description of a *performance of times*. In his revision to *4'33", 0'00" (4'33" No. 2)* (1962), whose composition and first performance coincided with early Fluxus activity, Cage proposed a measure of 'musical' and 'performance' time based on separate and discrete events, in a time-structure whose implications are taken up in Paik's video art. Importantly, in this score Cage stripped away the three-part structure and concert-hall circumstances of *4'33"* to describe simply an action 'to be performed by any one in any way' (Cage 1962), a 'composition' whose duration was to be determined in its realization by the disciplined act (of performance or listening) of which it consists. In turn, Cage requires, there is 'no attention to be given the situation (electronic, musical, theatrical)' (Cage 1962) in an implicit evasion of the formal definition of *4'33"* as a 'musical' work. 'Zero time', here, refers to an action or event that determines this work's duration, meaning, he notes, with regard to 'experimental' performance, 'what happens *before* one has *had the time* to measure it' (Cage in Cage and Charles 1981: 129, original emphasis). More simply, Cage remarks, '"zero time" exists when we don't notice the passage of time' (Cage in Cage and Charles 1981: 209). Significantly, time, here, is expressed as an *event*, as *something done*, while *0'00''* concerns itself with a performance of time *in action*, rather than a performance of actions within a given time.

This notion of time is directly reflected in the practices and concepts that underpinned Fluxus activity. Thus, writing in her essay 'Boredom and Oblivion', Ina Blom recalls the Fluxus artist and poet Jackson Mac Low's comment on his early chance poems from 1955, in which, he suggests 'the metric unit is *the event* rather than the foot, the syllable, the caesura or the cadence' (Mac Low in Blom 1998: 67, original emphasis). Fundamental to Fluxus sensibility, the 'event' pervades Fluxus work, shaping the characteristic Fluxus 'event scores' of George Brecht, Paik, Dick Higgins, Mac Low and other artists, but also extending to objects in the sense of an attention to the 'event' of relationship, of encounter, of uncertainty, of 'observer-observed' (Brecht 1991: 65). For Brecht, this understanding extended to all aspects of his work, in which, whatever form it takes, he notes, 'an event is always intended or implied' (Brecht 1983). Significantly, Blom concludes with regard to Mac Low's poetry, yet in a remark of importance to Fluxus events more widely:

> When the metric unit becomes the event, it crosses the threshold of [its] structure, opening the work to temporality *in general* [. . .] : Or one could simply say that it collapses the notion of art-time into real time.
>
> (Blom 1998: 67)

However, as Cage's 'silent' pieces suggest, the opening of 'art' to temporality *'in general'* works, paradoxically, against any *general* measure of time. Indeed, 'event time', in the sense of Cage's *0'00''* and the attention in Fluxus work to the 'event' of the viewer's encounter with the object or 'event score', is the *specific* time of action, the *something happens* of 'time in general', marked only by the particularities of lived experience. It is this *particularity* with which Cage is concerned that underpins Fluxus activity and shapes Paik's approach to 'Nature' in the time-structure of video.

In Paik's single-channel video and video installation, then, his engagement with these *particularities* is quite evident. Thus, where Maciunas notes that '[i]n music a Concretist perceives and expresses the material sound with all its inherent polychromy and pitchlessness and "incidentalness"' (Maciunas 1988: 26), Paik's video has, from its inception, sought an analogous 'polychromy' and 'incidentalness' in its approach to time. Where *Zen for Film* plays across past, present and future tenses, or the malfunctioning of Paik's equipment prompts interventions in a 'spontaneous' or 'free' time, Paik's single-channel video, developed in relation to his performance and film work from 1965, following his acquisition of a Sony Portapack, has foregrounded its own multiple times of production and reception. Thus, *9/23/69 Experiment with David Atwood* (1969) (see Figures 2.2 and 2.3), a densely collagic eighty-minute video work, which marked Paik's first use of the Paik/Abe-Synthesizer later developed for Sony, repeatedly recalls, replays and implies 'performances' in different and discontinuous times. Realized over the course of a single day, *9/23/69* combines abstract sequences, produced in a manipulation of the monitor's hardware, with synthesized and electronically distorted and overlaid

2.2 Nam June Paik. In collaboration with David Atwood, Fred Barzyk, and Oliva Tappan. **"9/23/69: Experiment with David Atwood," 1969**. *Courtesy Electronic Arts Intermix (EAI), New York.*

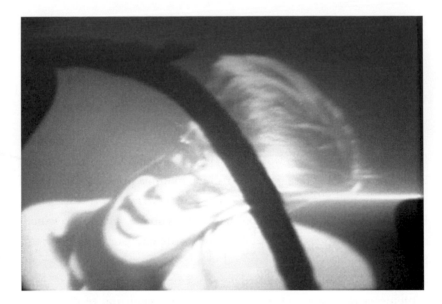

2.3 Nam June Paik. In collaboration with David Atwood, Fred Barzyk, and Oliva Tappan. **"9/23/69: Experiment with David Atwood," 1969**. *Courtesy Electronic Arts Intermix (EAI), New York.*

broadcast images evidently recorded and recomposed at various times. Amid its collages, the tape periodically reveals and documents occasions of Paik's manipulation of an already manipulated image through his performed interventions with his *Demagnetizer (Life Ring)* (1965) (see Figure 2.3), a 46 cm diameter handheld magnet that Paik also exhibited in its own right. Here, Paik intervenes into the disjunctive but continuous play of the electronic collage by placing himself and the *Demagnetizer* between what is, as a consequence of his intervention, revealed to be a camera positioned in front of a TV screen. In opening such a space for performance before what becomes, evidently, a re-mediated TV image, Paik exposes and overlays *various times* of *9/23/69*, which include the times of broadcast, recording, distortion and 'live' performance.

In contrast, *Video Commune* (1970), whose sequence incorporates parts of *9/23/69*, poses questions over the times of reception. Reflecting Paik's remark that '[g]enerally I either make it very fast or very slow' (Paik in Zurbrugg 1991: 138), *Video Commune* offers, like *9/23/69*, a rapidly transforming collage of overlaid images, yet warns the viewer at the outset that '[t]his programme runs for four hours without interruption. Treat it like electronic wallpaper. This programme has no beginning, no end' (Davis 1993: 118). Here, in its rapidly changing imagery, Paik's collage invites close scrutiny, yet, in its extended duration and the even rhythm in which the camera's *looking at change* is foregrounded, such attention becomes impossible. Sustaining, in this sense, the rapid 'cutting away' of Dienst's 'still time' only *to reveal* the extended exposure of the camera's 'automatic time' (Dienst 1994: 159), *Video Commune* poses the question of *how* to watch, of *which time* should structure the viewer's attention. Here, too, and in a reflection of his initial response to Cage, Paik welcomes 'boredom' into the experience of the work, remarking:

> In the beginning it is (probably) interesting, then later on it is
> boring – don't give up! Then it is (probably) interesting again,
> then once more boring – don't give up! Then it is (probably)
> interesting again, then once more boring – don't give up!
>
> (Paik in Blom 1998: 77)

Such 'electronic wallpaper' looks toward an *inconstant* time-structure, a time recomposed, or re-performed, in a coming and going of viewer attention over its extended duration, even at the risk of the 'destruction' of the work's reception through discontinuities or erosion of attention. Significantly, too, this 'inconstancy' has its corollary in the practices of early electronic music and the functioning of the hardware that underpinned it. In the first of his lectures at Darmstadt, Cage pointed toward a contemporary inexactitude in the time of the machine itself, noting:

> Exact measurement and notation of durations is in reality mental:
> imaginary exactitude. In the case of tape, many circumstances
> enter which ever so slightly, but nonetheless profoundly, alter the
> intention [. . .] some of these circumstances are the effect of
> weather upon the material; others follow from human frailty [. . .]

still others are due to mechanical causes, eight machines not
running at precisely the same speed.

(Cage 1968b: 29–30)

In conclusion, Cage noted, while '[f]ormerly for me time-length was a
constant. Now it, too, like everything else, changes' (Cage 1968e: 162).
Later, in conversation with Daniel Charles, Cage elaborated this position
in terms that, while fundamental to his practice, also seem integral to *Video
Commune*'s operation, where the viewer is implicated in the 'performance'
of its times. Cage proposes that

time is inevitably beyond measure. It can't ever be clock time.
Another way of saying it is to affirm that writing is one thing,
performing another, and listening a third; and that there is no
reason for these three operations to be linked. If I write by
imposing a particular measurement of time, the listener will not be
confronted with time itself, but with the way the performer
understands what he has read. And the performer will not have
read time, but one measurement of time.

(Cage in Cage and Charles 1981: 129)

Importantly, too, and specifically in relation to Fluxus, this 'production'
of a *plurality* of times, of relational terms and durations that are both
particular and *unpredictable*, reflects post-Einsteinian models in science
and philosophy. In this context, these practices may be read in relation
to concepts of Relativity and Einstein's rejection of 'absolute time' (Kern
1983: 19). Such a rejection was grounded, the cultural historian Stephen
Kern notes, in Einstein's realization that 'time only existed when a
measurement was being made, and those measurements varied according
to the relative motion of the two objects involved' (Kern 1983: 19),
leading him to remark that 'every reference body has its own particular
time' (Kern 1983: 19). Indeed, these models, as well as ideological and
theological concerns with uncertainty, chance and contingency, were a key
influence on Fluxus activity. Thus, where Paik grounded his 'experimental

television' in his extended study of physics and electronics, George Brecht, one of the most influential figures in the inception and development of Fluxus, had trained and continued to work in the sciences while collaborating with Maciunas. In his notebooks from October 1958 to April 1959, in which he diaried his responses to Cage's classes in New Musical Composition at the New School, Brecht specifically identified Cage's practices with concepts of Relativity (Brecht 1991: 64), while speculating toward 'The Structure of a New Aesthetic' linked to 'space-time relativity' or that might be 'a consequence of Relativity', concerned with:

> Uncertainty Principle
> Probability
> Observer-observed
> Paradox as a reflection of inability to imagine a simple model of the universe.
>
> (Brecht 1991: 65)

More recently, an analogous 'aesthetics' in postmodern literature has given rise to further elaborations in literary theory and criticism of the experience of *reading times*: of relationships between the reading of 'fictional' times and the time of reading. Developed without reference to this performance history or its sources through Mac Low, for example, in literary experiment, such models nevertheless draw on concepts of Relativity and Einstein's rejection of 'absolute time' (Kern 1983: 19), providing a further context through which the multiplication of times in video and performance may be described.

For the critic and theorist Elizabeth Ermarth, then, writing in *Sequel to History: Postmodernism and the Crisis of Representational Time* (Ermarth 1992), the 'postmodern' texts of Jorge Luis Borges, Julio Cortázar, Alain Robbe-Grillet and Vladimir Nabokov, among others, serve to challenge literary practices that have assumed and rehearsed the values of 'single-point perspective and unified time/space' (Ermarth 1992: 26) associated with the conventions of 'historical time' in the novel. Identifying 'perspective' with implicitly *teleological* times, in which the meaning and experience of the 'present' are always subject to the direction, purpose and goal of a linear history, Ermarth proposes that the creation of a unified narrative in fictional time inevitably eclipses the present time of reading (Ermarth 1992: 34). In contrast to the stabilities of such fiction, in which readers are *set apart* from the time of which they read, Ermarth proposes that in Borges' *The Garden of Forking Paths*, for example, the demand that the reader entertain alternate narrative possibilities forces a shifting *between* points of view, so producing a 'rhythmic time' that encompasses *the time of reading* itself. Here, Ermarth argues:

> The story forces reader attention into play between alternate semantic systems, and that play is what constitutes rhythmic time. The echoes of those multiple systems shine through, pullulate in the transparent moment, and force a reader to be aware that at any point multiple turnings are possible. Reader attention alternates between contradictory possibilities, and the rhythm of this attention cannot be reduced to a statement.
>
> (Ermarth 1992: 68)

In this way, Ermarth proposes, *The Garden of Forking Paths* resists the 'absolute' position, continuity or value inscribed in the conventions of 'historical time', in favour of a play of narrative possibilities that are '[n]o longer *fixed* by an inflexible conception like point of view' (Ermarth 1992: 23). In contrast to the linearity, unity and so 'otherness' of 'historical time', the 'rhythmic time' that arises in this play, Ermath suggests, 'is not neutral and absolute but a function of position, literally reader position', arising as it does in a conflation of the act of reading and that which is read, where '[t]he sentence read *is* time and time is a sentence: a defined part of a defined sequence before another sequence, another *conjugation*, begins' (Ermarth 1992: 22). Indeed, 'rhythmic time', Ermarth concludes, in its articulation and provocation of an awareness of the *time of reading*, describes a specifically 'postmodern time', a time, which 'is coextensive with the event, not a medium for recollecting it in tranquillity' (Ermarth 1992: 21). Consistent with Jean-François Lyotard's description of the postmodern as an 'incredulity toward metanarratives' (Lyotard 1984: xxxiv), such a 'rhythmic time' resists the totalizing effect of a linear or teleological 'historical time', asserting itself, Ermarth notes, as 'an exploratory repetition, because it is over when it's over and exists for its duration only and then disappears into some other rhythm' (Ermarth 1992: 53).

While both Cage's and Paik's work has exemplified a pursuit of the 'unrepeatable phrase' and a concomitant multiplication and fracturing of the *times* of the work, Ermarth's characterization of 'rhythmic' time also captures key aspects of the time-structures of Paik's film and video. Thus in *Zen for Film, 9/23/69 Experiment with David Atwood* and *Video Commune* Paik reflects upon the 'real time' of viewing through structures in which distinct, conflicting and multiple or varying times of production and reception are exposed, so effecting, in this sense, a 'rhythm' of deferral between *different*, yet interdependent, tenses, rhythms or measures. This play across times has been further extended in Paik's video installations. Thus, in *TV Clock* (1963), the first of his series of 'clock' pieces, which includes *Swiss Clock* (1988), *Moon is Oldest TV* (1965) and *TV Clock* (1997), Paik presented the monitor's marking of *its own* times, revealing, in this process, distinct yet interdependent measures of the viewer's engagement. First shown following the *Exposition of Music*, *TV Clock* (1963) comprises twenty-four manipulated black and white televisions, in which, after *Zen for TV*, each screen has been reduced to a single, still line of light that, in the sequence of monitors, marks the passage of twelve hours. Explicitly measuring *its* times, *TV Clock* juxtaposes narratives of 'clock time' and 'day time' with the viewer's choice and negotiation of *their own time* in the installation room. Simultaneously, the placement of twenty-four TV screens operating in a single installation serves to amplify the 'vibrational acoustic' (Viola: 1995: 158) that, Bill Viola has suggested, marks the 'real-time' operation of the machine, an operation which is *other to*, yet may be mapped by, these allusions to the hours and days of its installation.

The implications of such a 'rhythmic time' are wide ranging. Thus, Ermarth points to its reflection of a 'crisis of the subject' (Ermarth 1992: 107), evident not only from the fractured narratives of this literature but from its production of a shifting, de-centred relationship between reader, text and narrative possibility. Such strategies reflect, again, the implications of Relativity itself, as a consequence of which, Ermarth notes, '[j]ust as the classical object has been redefined in physics, so the phenomenological subject is no longer discrete, apart from the event, but, like time and space themselves, functions of specific events and bound by their limitations' (Ermarth 1992: 7). Correspondingly, in this postmodern novel:

> Narrative no longer inscribes the time that makes possible the perception of invariant identities like 'subject' and 'object'; instead it concentrates phenomenologically on the reader-events that collapse the distances between object and subject, inside and outside.
>
> (Ermarth 1992: 22)

Reflecting this emphasis upon the *particularity* of the temporal moment, in which '[e]ach time is utterly finite' (Ermarth 1992: 53), Ermarth has gone on to associate the 'event time' of reading with a 'phrase time'. Maintaining that, under postmodernism, 'time is no longer a neutral medium' (Ermarth 1992: 140), and writing in her later essay 'Time and Neutrality' (Ermarth 1998), Ermarth takes forward the implications of the 'uniqueness' of the particular temporal moment under this 'rhythmic time', in which 'each moment contains its specific and unique definition' (Ermarth 1992: 53). 'Postmodern time', Ermarth concludes, 'is bonded to the phrase, to the unrepeatable phrase [. . .]. Another term for this finite, postmodern temporality is "Ph[r]ase time"' (Ermarth 1998: 363–4).

Indeed, latterly, significant elements of Paik's work have foregrounded the paradoxes of 'real-time' recording and playback and live mediation to construct 'phrase times' at once defined by and in opposition to each other. For *Real Fish/Live Fish* (1982), part of a series including *Real Plant/Live Plant* (1978), *Video Fish* (1975) and *Fish Flies on Sky* (1975), Paik's closed-circuit video installation juxtaposed 'real' fish in an aquarium set within a television casing against their 'live' mediation *via* a black and white closed-circuit television (CCTV) camera to an adjacent monitor. Playing across the media's seemingly paradoxical capacity to unify terms defined in their difference, including relationships between 'production' and 'reproduction', 'real' and 'live', 'mediated' and 'recorded', this work poses the question of a collision of opposing states. Here, then, Paik's mediation binds together ostensibly distinct 'times' in an undecidable way, producing a paradoxical 'conjunction' and exchange of opposites in which the 'real'/'live' fish are reproduced in 'live'/'real' time. In his analysis of *Video Fish* 1975 (1982 version), a large-scale three-channel installation with multiple monitors and aquariums, John Handhardt notes:

> In this piece, twenty monitors are lined up in a row and placed at eye level on an elevated pedestal. Each monitor displays an edited videotape that synthesizes different images, from flying planes and fish to Merce Cunningham dancing in a rapidly collaged movement of imagery. In front of each monitor is a tank filled with water and fish. To see a monitor, one looks through a fish tank – in the process, the fish tank becomes a television and the television becomes a fish tank. Paik achieved this remarkable conversion of images by playing on the depth of the video space, which he manipulated through the editing of the videotape.
>
> (Handhardt 2000: 148)

Just as he confounds the 'space' of this installation in this reversal of 'the real' and 'the recorded', so, Handhardt observes, Paik approaches time 'as a two-plane co-ordinate: through the stored and edited time of the videotape and the unfolding and changing action of the fish' (Handhardt 2000: 148). Here, in opposition to the re-presentation of a unified image, space or time, and in explicitly approaching the events and materials of 'Nature', Paik confronts spectators with their own conflicting and unstable negotiation of the times of performance, mediation and viewing. Indeed, in *Video Fish*, even the opposition and exchange between the 'real fish' and the edited tape is interrupted, as, Handhardt notes, '[a]t random points on the looped videotape, a fish that is collaged into the image appears to fly or swim in its own space, further abstracting the representational dynamic of the installation' (Handhardt 2000: 148).

Exemplifying Paik's articulation of a multiplication of 'real times' and 'real spaces' through video, *Video Fish* fractures the viewer's perception of a 'unified' time, challenging the tenses in which its elements might be perceived and their *presentness* to one another established. In turn, this disturbance of the work's unity reflects upon the times and time-structures in which the 'Nature' he explicitly holds up to view is constituted. In this regard, again, Paik's work anticipates the multiplications of times Ermarth identifies in the postmodern novel, a multiplication that reflects the fact that 'postmodern subjectivity is without a subject', for 'the subject is dispersed in the world it observes' (Ermarth 1992: 123). Indeed, after Paik and in the context of post-minimal process, site-specific and installation art, it is precisely this dispersal of the subject that video art came to further articulate in the performance of its times.

Dividing the Present Tense of Space: Bruce Nauman, Dan Graham

Where Paik's time-structures in video, video installation and performance drew on experimental music to explore a 'Nature' and subjectivity fractured in time, the subsequent wave of video installation and early multi-media performance emerging from the late 1960s and early 1970s brought these concerns into explicitly sculptural contexts and processes. Indeed, in the wake of minimalist art, sculpture itself had turned toward process-based and durational concerns. In this context, the sculptor Robert Morris traced the new engagement with time in sculptural practices emerging in response to the minimalist aesthetic which his own work, along with that of Carl Andre, Donald Judd, Richard Serra and others had defined. Observing, in his influential essay 'The Present Tense of Space' how, since the emergence of the 'specific object' integral to minimalist presentations, sculpture had come in a variety of ways to engage with 'a state of being I will call "presentness"' (Morris 1993: 175), Morris proposed this engagement with time as a distinct break from earlier twentieth-century sculptural practices. In this new work, Morris suggested, 'images, the past tense of reality, begin to give way to duration, the present tense of immediate spatial experience. Time is in this newer work in a way that it never was in past sculpture' (Morris 1993: 176).

Explicitly phenomenological in emphasis, the invariably site-related practices of artists such as Mary Miss, Vito Acconci, Robert Irwin, Richard Serra, Alice Aycock and Robert Smithson, to whom Morris refers, focused, he noted, 'on space, both internal and external, as much as on the materials and objects that delimit or articulate these spaces' (Morris 1993: 193). Such work, Morris argued, 'opens more than other recent art to a surprising directness of experience', one that is 'embedded in the very nature of spatial perception' (Morris 1993: 176). Approaching explicitly architectural concerns with 'surrounding space' (Morris 1993: 185), this work frequently implicated the viewer in physical and psychological negotiations with installations, architectonic constructions and found sites. For Morris, these sculptural concerns with 'real space' and so with 'behaviour facilitated by certain spaces that bind time more than images' (Morris 1993: 194) necessarily emphasized experience in the 'present tense', where '"presentness" is the intimate inseparability of the experience of physical space and that of an ongoing immediate present. Real space', Morris concluded, 'is not experienced except in real time' (Morris 1993: 177–8).

Yet the incorporation of video into such spaces served to challenge the unity of this 'direct' spatial experience. Here, in the work of Bruce Nauman, Dan Graham and Joan Jonas, in particular, video prompted a further elision of distinctions between sculpture, installation and performance through work that mirrored a fragmentation of the performing subject in space and time. Thus Nauman's first video installations elaborated concerns with the complexities of the 'real times' of action and encounter explored in pieces such as *Performance Corridor* (1969), which comprised the first of a series of pieces including *Corridor Installation, Nick Wilder Installation* (1970), *Live-Taped Video Corridor* (1970) and *Corridor Installation with Mirror – San Jose Installation* (1970–4). Originally created, Nauman recalled, as 'just a prop for a videotape I was making [...] of me walking up and down the corridor' (Nauman in Sharp 2003: 114), *Performance Corridor* presents a 20 inch wide, 20 foot long corridor formed by two facing wallboards that Nauman occupied for the film/performance *Walk with Contrapposto* (1968). Here, though – and while consistent with the post-minimal work of artists such as Doug Wheeler, Robert Irwin and Michael Asher, which sought, the architect and theorist Bernard Tschumi observes, to restrict 'visual and physical perception to the faintest of all stimulations', such that 'the subjects only "experience their own experience"' (Tschumi 1994: 42) – Nauman complicates and divides this occupation of space. Thus, Janet Kraynak argues, the very fact of the visitor's *re-occupation* of Nauman's performance space serves to complicate this apparently *present-tense* experience, for

> the *Corridor*'s meaning issues not from an individual act of bodily
> intervention, performed by the viewer in the presence of the
> artwork, but from a compression of many moments: the past traces
> of Nauman's 'original' performance; their repetition in video; and
> their present and future reiterations by the audience.
>
> (Kraynak 2003: 30)

It follows, Kraynak concludes, that *Performance Corridor* 'is a performance not in the singular (the event, the act, the performance) but in the plural (performative, repetitious and ritualistic) in which any one enactment contains and anticipates traces of others' (Kraynak 2003: 30). In this context, CCTV added a further complication to these layers, as Nauman articulated this complexity by capturing the viewer's *acting out* of the media's interruption and division of its spaces. Thus, in his first use of a closed-circuit system, *Corridor Installation, Nick Wilder Installation* (1970), a piece, Cose van Bruggen notes, emphasizing 'concealment, dislocation, enclosure' (van Bruggen 1988: 19), the visitor encounters a series of corridors occupying the whole gallery space that variously permit or prohibit entry, while incorporating relays, *via* video and CCTV, of their own and others' occupation of the installation. In anticipation of the installation, Nauman proposed:

The distance between the walls will vary from three feet to about
two or three inches [. . .]. Within the wider corridors, some
television cameras will be set up with monitors so you can see
yourself. Body parts of me or someone else going in and out of
those corridors will also be shown on videotape. Sometimes you'll
see yourself and sometimes you'll see a videotape of someone else.

(Nauman in Sharp 2003: 112)

The resulting encounter confuses the presence, mirroring and recording of the body, fragmenting the visitor's capacity to take up the
installation's apparent invitation to simultaneously 'watch' and 'perform'.
In the first of these interruptions or distractions, Nauman arranged cameras and monitors such that 'when you walk down the wall you can see
yourself just as you turn the corner [. . .] you can just see your back going
round the corner' (Nauman in Sharp 2003: 113). While this mediation
throws the visitor's attention back toward the immediate past of the *space
just left*, as 'you can see yourself just as you turn the corner, but only then'
(Nauman in Sharp 2003: 114), in another of its corridors the *Installation*
disrupted the spatial unity of the visitor's experience:

When you walked into the corridor, you had to go in about ten
feet before you appeared on the television screen that was still
twenty feet away from you. I used a wide-angled lens, which
disturbed the distance even more. The camera was ten feet up, so
that when you did see yourself on the screen, it was from the back,
from above and behind, which was quite different from the way
you normally saw yourself or the way you experienced the corridor
around yourself. When you realized you were on the screen, being
in the corridor was like stepping off a cliff or down a hole

(Nauman in Sharp 2003a: 151)

Here, rather than invite a 'directness of experience' in 'the present tense
of space', *Corridor Installation* provokes a perception and experience of
the body in a collocation of times and spaces: in a realization of events

just passed; in spaces reversed and superimposed *in action*; in a mediation of space and the body that disrupts and divides the 'space' and 'time' of action.

In Dan Graham's video installations, the visitor's performance of multiple times and tenses becomes even more explicit. Arising out of his engagement with performance and film from 1969 (Graham 1999: 142–3), these installations further elaborated his early performance's disruptions of ostensibly 'present-tense' experiences and contaminations of distinctions between past, present and future tenses. Thus, for the video-taped performance *Past Future Split Attention* (1972), Graham's 'premise' is that '[t]wo people who know each other are in the same space. While one person predicts continuously the other person's behaviour, the other person recounts (by memory) the other's past behaviour' (Graham 2001: 139). Countering the implication arising, Graham proposes, under 'a strict phenomenology of the present' that 'every present would be equal to the present that just passed', *Past Future Split Attention* values the 'just past present', in order to contest an 'amnesia' that, he proposed, Walter Benjamin identified with the valorization of the immediate moment in 'consumer culture' (Graham 1999a: 76). Here, then, each performer's attempt to see the other in 'the present' is defined in a 'doubled attention': for the first performer, a reading of 'the present' as a sign of behaviour about to occur; for the second, in a recollection of that which is 'just past'. In recounting the performance, Graham explicitly reads this definition of 'present (attention)' after a video-feedback system, noting:

> For one to see the other in terms of the present (attention) there is
> a mirror reflection or closed figure-eight feedback/feedahead loop
> of past/future. One person's behaviour reciprocally
> reflects/depends upon the other's, so that each one's information
> of his moves is seen in part as a reflection of the effect that their
> own just-past behaviour has had in reversed tense as perceived
> from the other's point of view.
>
> (Graham 2001: 139)

Where *Past Future Split Attention* alludes to the visual feedback of CCTV system as a 'mirror' of the performer's 'past/future' behaviour, Graham's subsequent video installations explicitly drew their visitors into performative plays *between* 'tenses' and 'times'. Exemplifying this, in 1974 Graham produced a series of time-delay installations, including *Present Continuous Past(s)*, *Two Rooms/Reverse Video Delay*, seven permutations of *Time Delay Room* and *Opposing Mirrors and Video Monitors on Time Delay* (see Figure 2.4). Each of the time-delay installations offered an integration of multiple monitors and video cameras in the gallery that would explicitly record visitor activity, only to play it back to the viewer, and other visitors, following a delay of up to eight seconds. In such combinations of present-time action and time-delayed feedback, Graham aimed at once to 'foreground an awareness of the presence of the viewer's own perceptual process', yet to 'critique it by showing the impossibility of locating a pure present tense' (Graham 1999: 144). In the later installations, including *Present Continuous Past(s)*, *Two Rooms/Reverse Video Delay* and *Opposing Mirrors and Video Monitors on Time Delay*, this process is lent further complexity through the strategic placement of wall-size mirrors within the space. Arguing that '[m]irrors in enclosures exteriorize all objects within the interior space', so simulating the 'flat visuality of Renaissance painting' (Graham 1979: 67), Graham explicitly compares the effect of the mirror within these installations with Renaissance architecture and perspective. In this context, the mirror's effect is analogous to the 'single-point perspective and unified space/time' (Ermarth 1992: 26) that Ermarth associates with a transcendence of the reader's (or viewer's) 'own' time. Consistently with this, Graham argues:

> The symmetry of mirrors tends to conceal or cancel the passage of time, so that the overall architectural form appears to transcend time [. . .]. As the image in the mirror is perceived as a static instant, place (time and space) becomes illusorily eternal.
>
> (Graham 1979: 67)

2.4 Dan Graham. *Opposing Mirrors and Video Monitors on Time Delay* (1974),
detail from **"Video/Architecture/Performance," 1995**. *Courtesy Electronic
Arts Intermix (EAI), New York.*

In contrast, in the video image, he notes, 'geometrical surfaces are lost
to ambiguously modeled contours and to a translucent depth' (Graham
1979: 67), while, even in its 'live' mediation of a viewer's activity, and so
in *functioning* as a mirror, the video image is never congruous with the
action it relays, for

> a video image on a monitor does not shift in perspective with a
> viewer's shift in position [. . .]. A video monitor's projected image
> of a spectator observing it, depends on that spectator's relation to
> the position of the camera, but not on his relation to the monitor.
>
> (Graham 1979: 67)

Offering one of Graham's most complex interleaving of these elements,
Opposing Mirrors and Video Monitors on Time Delay operates between two
large mirrors set on the end walls of a single gallery room. Facing each

mirror is a television monitor with a camera positioned immediately on top of its casing. Here, Graham notes, '[t]he length of the mirrors and their distance from the cameras are such that each of the opposing mirrors reflects the opposite side (half) of the enclosed room (and also the reflection of an observer within the area who is viewing the monitor/mirror image)' (Graham 2001: 159). Within this symmetrical arrangement, each 'camera sees and tapes this mirror's view' (Graham 2001: 159), relaying this 'live' feed, on a five-second time-delay, to the monitor at the *opposite* end of the room. The arrangement is such that, in considering the installation as divided into two opposite but identical areas (A and B):

> A spectator in area A (or area B), looking in the direction of the mirror, sees: 1. a continuous present-time reflection of his surrounding space; 2. himself as observer; 3. on the reflected monitor image, five seconds in the past, his area as seen by the mirror of the opposite area.
>
> (Graham 2001: 159)

While, with regard to the closed-circuit system and delay:

> A spectator in area A, turned to face monitor A, will see both the reflection of area A as it appeared in mirror B five seconds earlier and, on a reduced scale, area A reflected in mirror B now.
>
> (Graham 2001: 159)

Importantly, too, in this combination of the mirror and the video system, the juxtaposition of present and past *reflections* of behaviour is underpinned by the specific time of the delay. Noting that '5 to 8 seconds is the limit of "short term" memory or memory which is part of and influencing a person's (present) perception' (Graham 1979: 69), Graham ensures that, in this installation, not only is the time-delay between camera and monitor five seconds, but the distance between the monitors and mirrors takes five seconds to traverse, allowing the viewer-participant to 'walk' the time-delay. As a result, Graham notes, 'as you walk physically you're inside the time delay and also inside the actual time you take to walk from one side to the other side' (Graham 1995). Such an arrangement amplifies the *continuity* of exchange between the 'present', 'delayed' and 'anticipated' time of activity, inviting a play between what is done *now* (reflected in the mirror), the '*just-past*' action (relayed in the time delay) and an *anticipation* of its *future delay*. Indeed, in this dynamic, *Opposing Mirrors and Video Monitors on Time Delay* captures the individual viewer within the dynamic of *Past Future Split Attention*, where action in 'the present' is constituted in a 'feedback/feedahead loop of past/future'. Here, then, I see my 'just-past' in a *present* behaviour that performs to my *future viewing*. In this dynamic, too, the 'private' operates, in the installation, in *public* performance, so dispersing action, perception and reaction not only across past, present and future moments, but 'out' toward 'exterior' spaces. Thus, Graham notes:

> if a perceiver views his behaviour on a 5 to 8 second delay *via* video tape (so that his responses are part of, and influencing his perception), 'private' mental intention and external behaviour are experienced as one. The difference between intention and actual behaviour is fed back on the monitor and immediately influences the observer's future intentions and behaviour.
>
> (Graham 1979: 69)

It follows, Graham argues, that '[b]y linking perception of exterior behaviour and its interior, mental perception, an observer's "self", like a topological moebius strip, can be apparently without "inside" or "outside"' (Graham 1979: 69). Indeed, in its divisions of 'the present moment', *Opposing Mirrors and Video Monitors on Time Delay* explicitly articulates that 'postmodern subjectivity' in which, Ermarth proposes, 'the subject is dispersed in the world it observes' (Ermarth 1992: 123). Here, then, 'the subject' performs the 'real times' of action through a system in which the delays and divisions of mediation are deployed to mirror and articulate a structure of experience that the claim to *presentness* would suppress.

Delay and the Subject: Joan Jonas

In this context, too, Joan Jonas' contemporaneous multi-media performances served to transpose these divisions toward the performance and
reading of identity. Providing one of the earliest and most influential
departures, in video, toward an explicitly theatrical multi-medial practice,
Jonas' work is rooted in her training as a sculptor in the early 1960s and
her work with postmodern choreographers, including Trisha Brown and
Yvonne Rainer, from 1967 to 1969. In these regards, too, Jonas' earliest
use of video extended her address, in performance, to complex inter-
plays between 'real' and 'represented' space and 'delays' or, as Douglas
Crimp suggests in his record of Jonas' performance, 'de-synchronizations'
(Crimp 1983: 8) in time. Jonas' first performances in specific sites and
gallery spaces, between 1968 and 1971, had incorporated mirrors to
reconfigure the space of performance; her subsequent series of outdoor
pieces from 1970 engaged with distortions in viewers' perceptions in
time. Thus in *Mirror Piece I* (1969) and *Mirror Piece II* (1970) Jonas' performers manipulated large mirrors to divide and fragment each others'
bodies, while explicitly framing audience activity within mirrored, and
so multiple, spaces for performance. Such work drew explicitly on the
use of mirrors within site-specific sculpture and installation by Robert
Morris, Robert Smithson and Rebecca Horn, while participating in this
sculpture's characteristic disturbance of oppositions between between the
'inside' and 'outside' (Kaye 2000: 183–201). Extending this concern with
a complex layering of spaces, Jonas' later site-specific choreographies,
including *Jones Beach Piece* (1970) and *Delay Delay* (1972), articulated
dislocations in time by setting her audience at considerable distances
from her performers in large exterior locations. In these events, Douglas
Crimp notes in his documentation of Jonas' early work:

> performers made loud noises by clapping blocks of wood together
> in wide overhead arcs. Because of the vast distance between
> performers and spectators, the gestures were seen well in advance
> of the sound it produced [*sic*], making the gesture one of silence

and the sound seem to come from nowhere. Both because of the
number of performers clapping blocks and because the sounds
were repeated with their own echoes, it was impossible to link
gesture and sound.

(Crimp 1983: 8)

In her video performances, Jonas' further elaborated these displace-
ments. Rooted in her experiments with video following her encounter
with Noh theatre in Japan in 1970 (Jonas in Kaye 1996: 89) but also
drawing directly on Borges' novels (Iles 2000a: 156), Jonas recalls that
her first video performances, *Organic Honey's Visual Telepathy* (1972) (see
Figure 2.5) and *Organic Honey's Vertical Roll* (1972) arose in an exploration of the camera's multiplications. Jonas notes that: 'the way I started
working with the Portapack was to sit in front of the TV screen or the
camera in a closed-circuit situation and work with myself and try on
different disguises' (Jonas in Kaye 1996: 89–90). Through 'a complex
layering of elements' (Jonas in Kaye 1996: 93), this video practice, in
which she also incorporated the use of the mirror as a screen, explicitly
sought to create spaces whose boundaries were unclear. Thus, Chrissie
Iles notes, where in one sequence within *Organic Honey's Visual Telepathy*
the performers are able to see their actions projected live onto the wall,
correspondingly:

A large mirror on wheels is rolled in front of the audience, echoing
the video imagery's juxtaposition of real and mediated space, and
suggesting a parallel between video and the mirror. Just as the
performers witness their actions live on the video screen, the
audience can see themselves in their reflection.

(Iles 2000a: 157)

As a result, Jonas' performances developed within complex installation
spaces that, in the manner of her mirror pieces, served to ensure that 'the
audience was in the space of the piece' (Jonas in Kaye 1996: 97). Here,
too, the incorporation of video articulated Jonas' performance in hidden

2.5 Joan Jonas, *Organic Honey's Visual Telepathy/Organic Honey's Vertical Roll*
(*1972*). Installation Galerie der Stadt Stuttgart, 2000. Photo: © Uwe H. Seyl.

'live' spaces, delays in time, and a multiplication of 'live', mediated and recorded spaces and frames. For Jonas, such multiplications amplified her exploration of the division and fragmentation of her own persona through the use of mask, costume and role. In this work, Jonas later emphasized: 'Video performance offered the possibility of multiple simultaneous points of view. Performer and audience were both inside and outside. Perception was relative' (Jonas 2000a: 108). In this context, too, Jonas articulated her performance *in transmission*. Here, where '[t]he audience sees [. . .] the process of image-making in a performance simultaneously with a live detail', Jonas notes:

> I was interested in the discrepancies between the performed
> activity and the constant duplicating, changing and altering of
> information in the video. The whole is a sequence of missing links
> as each witness experiences a different series by glancing from
> monitor to projection to live action. Perception was relative.
> There was a range of choices. Time and space in these
> performances was like [*sic*] Borges' *Garden of the Forking Paths*.
> Here were parallel worlds. I could inhabit, simultaneously,
> different fields of view, different channels.
>
> (Jonas 2000a: 108)

In this process of deflection of attention, and transition, in which image-making or 'drawing passes through the medium' (Jonas 2000b: 140), Jonas' representations of her alter ego, Organic Honey, themselves become subject to transition and delay. Thus, in articulating a 'female identity [. . .] expressed through a rapid switching between distance and closeness, revealing and concealing, using the mirror, the camera lens and the mask' (Iles 2000a: 159), these performances foreground tensions between Jonas 'herself' and her constructed persona, whose relationship and *difference* can never be resolved. In this context, Jonas subjects her image, and the imagery in which *she herself* might be 'shown', to continual movement, reversal and remaking. It is a process directly reflected in Jonas' narrative of the making of *Organic Honey's Visual Telepathy*. Thus,

Jonas recalls, this exploration of her own multiple presences in the 'real' and 'mediated' spaces of the installation

> evolved as I found myself continually investigating my own image in the monitor of my video machine. I then bought a mask of a doll's face, which transformed me into an ironic seductress. I named this TV persona Organic Honey. I became increasingly obsessed with following the process of my own theatricality, as my images fluctuated between the narcissistic and a more abstract representation [. . .] I attempted to fashion a dialogue between my different disguises.
>
> (Jonas 2000: 106)

In this process, Jonas introduces plays on time and its reversal into this exchange between disguises. It is here, too, that the slip between Jonas' fragmentary identities is most clearly expressed. At one point in *Organic Honey's Visual Telepathy*, on video, Iles recalls:

> Jonas puts on all the masks worn by the other performers, as though attempting to integrate their various personae within a single mask, or self. Simultaneously, the video monitor shows live imagery of her removing each one, slowly revealing the masks' different identities, until her own face is revealed, bare of any adornment. The impossibility of wholeness, expressed in this double, contradictory action, is repeated throughout the performance.
>
> (Iles 2001: 159)

Jonas' video performances articulate a fractured subjectivity, a performance of the signs of self not only across multiple spaces but in reversals and slips of tenses and times. Operating in the transitions between the live, mediated and recorded, *Organic Honey's Visual Telepathy* thus poses the question of *where* and *when* the subject is constituted and encountered, to present a performance of identity in shifts between media and in a crossing of the threshold of the screen.

PIPILOTTI RIST
OPEN MY GLADE (2000)

VIDEO INSTALLATION
16 DIFFERENT IMAGES, 1 MIN.

VIDEO SEGMENTS SHOWN ON THE
NBC ASTROVISION BY PANASONIC
VIDEO SCREEN AT QUARTER PAST
THE HOUR FROM 9AM TO
MIDNIGHT.

TIMES SQUARE, NEW YORK,
APRIL 6 TO MAY 20, 2000.

COMMISSIONED BY THE PUBLIC
ART FUND.

ALL PHOTOGRAPHS BY DENNIS COWLEY/COURTESY PUBLIC ART FUND

Pipilotti Rist *Open My Glade* (2000).

Pipilotti Rist *Open My Glade* (2000).

FOR THE CENTER OF MEDIA-FRENZIED TIMES SQUARE, PIPILOTTI RIST HAS CREATED A SERIES OF VIDEOS FOR THE ASTROVISION MEGA-BOARD THAT OVERLOOKS THE TRAFFIC JAMS, FLASHING LIGHTS, HIGH-TECH SCREENS, AND BILLBOARDS OF THIS FAMOUS NEW YORK CROSSROADS. VISITORS TO TIMES SQUARE WILL SEE ONE-MINUTE SEGMENTS THAT COMPRISE RIST'S NEW ARTWORK *OPEN MY GLADE*, INTERSPERSED WITH ORDINARY NBC PROGRAMMING AT A QUARTER PAST EVERY HOUR FROM 9:15AM THROUGH TO 12:15AM. AMONG THEM WILL BE IMAGES IN WHICH A PERSON FLATTENS HER/HIS FACE

AS IF SHE WANTS TO BREAK OUT OF THE SCREEN AND COME DOWN INTO TIMES SQUARE OR A SEGMENT IN WHICH THE SUN SHINES THROUGH DIFFERENT BODY PARTS WHICH APPEAR RED AND ORANGE (FOR COFFEE TIME). IN ANOTHER SEQUENCE THE SCREEN ITSELF IS "EATEN" BY A GROUP OF PEOPLE. WHILE IN THE SEQUENCE (MAYBE AT NOON) EYES TURN SLOWLY, THE LITTLE VEINS AND STRIPES IN THE IRIS ARE VISIBLE. ANOTHER SEQUENCE SHOWS BURNING TVS, WHICH IS ALWAYS REFRESHING (FOR HAPPY HOUR). AND FINALLY TO CALM US NEW YORKERS DOWN PIPILOTTI RIST IS FEATURING PEOPLE, FIRST

FAR AWAY AND SMALL ON THE HORIZON JUST STANDING THERE WITH HER/HIS ARMS WIDE OPEN WAITING FOR YOU TO APPROACH. ALL THESE SEPARATE SEGMENTS AND OTHERS COME TOGETHER TO CREATE PIPILOTTI RIST'S <u>OPEN MY GLADE</u>, A COLLECTION OF FILTERED POETIC IMAGES THAT ARE EXPLODED DETAILS OF OUR SUBCONCIOUS AND OUR DAILY LIVES.

TIMES SQUARE'S RHYTHM OF UNCOORDINATED FLASHING, GRABBING ATTENTION FROM ONE ADVERTISEMENT TO THE NEXT, ONE NEWS BROADCAST TO ANOTHER, NEUTRALIZES ALL THIS VISUAL INPUT INTO A MEMORY OF

ELECTRONIC OVERLOAD. RIST'S SERIES OF VIDEOS, SET AGAINST THIS BACKDROP, ARE SUBJECTIVELY SLOWED DOWN, LITERALLY IN SLOW MOTION, RELAYING POETIC, PHILOSOPHICAL AND POLITICAL STATEMENTS THROUGH HER IDIOSYNCRATIC SUPER CLOSE-UPS, HAND-FLYING CAMERA SHOTS AND INTENSE COLORS.

Pipilotti Rist Open My Glade (2000).

I SEE TIMES SQUARE AS AN OVERWHELMING SPACE FULL OF ELECTRIC BLOSSOMS AND ELECTRONIC TWINKLE THAT HIT VISITORS LIKE A SLAP IN THE FACE. I USE THE ENERGY OF THIS 'SLAP' TO FUEL MY VIDEO SEGMENTS. THE VIDEO WAS BROADCAST FOR SIXTY SECONDS EVERY HOUR, SIXTEEN TIMES EACH DAY. VIEWERS SAW A WOMAN FLATTENING HER FACE AGAINST THE SCREEN AS IF SHE WANTED TO BREAK OUT AND COME DOWN INTO THE SQUARE. THE FLATTENED FACE LOOKS VERY DEFORMED AND NEEDY. YOU WANT TO SET HER FREE, AND WITH HER ALL THE GHOSTS ON THE SURROUNDING SCREEN.

Above: Pipilotti Rist *Open My Glade* (2000).

I THINK THAT "TRYING TO BE DIFFERENT" IS EXACTLY THE SYSTEM ALREADY AT WORK IN TIMES SQUARE, WHERE THOUSANDS OF ADVERTISERS ARE ALL TRYING TO ATTRACT YOUR ATTENTION AT ONCE. ADVERTISING EXISTS TO GRAB OUR ATTENTION, AND TEAMS OF ADVERTISING EXECUTIVES SIT AROUND TABLES ASKING, HOW CAN WE BE DIFFERENT? AND OF COURSE THEY END UP NEUTRALIZING EACH OTHER. SO, HOW CAN WE REALLY BREAK WITH THE RESULTING HOMOGENEITY?

THE SCREENS ON TIMES SQUARE BLINK AND FLASH AND HAVE THEIR OWN UNCOORDINATED RHYTHM.

Below: Pipilotti Rist *Open My Glade* (2000).

THE ONLY GENUINELY "DIFFERENT" IMAGE WOULD BE ONE IN WHICH THE VIEWER CAN SEE AND FEEL THAT THERE IS NO COMMERCIAL INTENTION BEHIND IT: THIS WOULD TRULY BE A SHOCK. I DON'T PRETEND YOU CAN REALLY KNOCK TV OUT OF ITS HABITUAL HECTIC RHYTHM OR PROVOKE MUCH REFLECTION AMONG VIEWERS, EVEN IF THIS, OF COURSE, IS WHAT MOST ARTISTS WOULD LIKE TO PROVOKE – A DISTANCED REFLECTION ON SOCIETY, TO SHIFT THE VIEWERS JUST OUTSIDE THEMSELVES AND EXPERIENCE A FLASH OF IDENTIFICATION.

PURE SUBVERSION IS NO LONGER

POSSIBLE BECAUSE OUR REALITY IS TOO COMPLEX AND DISPARATE: IT IS ALREADY SUBVERSIVE IN ITSELF. I THINK MASS MEDIA PRODUCTION, WITHOUT THE PRESSURE OF GAINING A LARGE AUDIENCE (ALTHOUGH I USUALLY AIM FOR THAT AS WELL) IS PROBABLY WHERE THE RUPTURE OCCURS. THE FACT THAT AN ARTIST – WHO HAS NOTHING TO SELL BUT IDEAS, WHO HAS NO DIRECT COMMERCIAL IMPETUS, AND NO POWERFUL COMPANY BEHIND HER – IS GIVEN PRECIOUS ADVERTISING TIME ON TIMES SQUARE IS QUITE GOOD. ART PROTECTS ME EVEN IN THIS DEEPLY COMMERCIALIZED SITE; IT IS MY BODYGUARD.

TIMES SQUARE, WITH ALL THE BIG CORPORATIONS, NETWORKS, AND ADVERTISING COMPANIES IN THE NEIGHBORHOOD, IS THE SYMBOL OF THE PSEUDO-DEMOCRATIC IDEA THAT YOUR MESSAGE CAN BE HEARD BY THE WHOLE WORLD, ALL AT ONCE. NEW MEDIA DOES HAVE SOME REAL, DEMOCRATIC POSSIBILITIES, BUT FOR THE MOMENT THIS IDEA STILL SEEMS AN ILLUSION TO ME. IN TIMES SQUARE PHYSICAL SPACE MELTS INTO VIRTUAL SPACE. REMEMBER THE NEW YEAR'S EVE 2000 CELEBRATIONS THERE, WHERE YOU COULD WATCH 100,000 PEOPLE WATCH THEMSELVES WATCHING THEMSELVES ON HUGE SCREENS?

Pipilotti Rist *Open My Glade* (2000).

I WANT PEOPLE TO PAY ATTENTION TO TECHNOLOGY, TO REGISTER ITS LIMITS AND ITS POTENTIAL FOR DECEIT. TECHNOLOGY IS SO IMPORTANT IN OUR LIVES! IN THE SPIRIT OF PAIK, PEOPLE SHOULD BE MORE AWARE OF THE DISTINCTION BETWEEN TECHNOLOGICAL DEVICES THEMSELVES AND THEIR VIRTUAL CONTENT. THEY SHOULD BE AWARE OF TECHNOLOGY AS A SIMPLE "OBJECT," AS THE FURNITURE OF EVERYDAY LIFE.

Pipilotti Rist *Open My Glade* (2000).

Video Space/Performance Space

> [P]resence now is always complicated and layered, a thing of degrees, and in these strange times one can feel closer to a person, sometimes, when they are further away than when they are fully and simply before us.
>
> (Etchells 1999: 97)

Video art's burgeoning in North America from 1968, following Sony's release of the video Portapack in 1965, emerged in the wake of post-minimal departures in body art, process and time-based work. In this context influential 'video artists' came to include Vito Acconci, Dan Graham, Bruce Nauman, Dennis Oppenheim, Howard Fried, Terry Fox and Joan Jonas, all of whose work explicitly linked video to their engagements with live performance. Indeed, as early as 1971, exhibitions such as *Ten Video Performances* at the Finch College Museum of Contemporary Art in New York (Viola 1995: 129) reflected a sense that, as Laura Cottingham subsequently proposed, '[m]uch of the most interesting work in video made between 1968 and 1978 can accurately be described as "a video of a performance"' (Cottingham 2002: 13). Here, too, relationships between performance, documentation and the video work became uncertain or multiple. Thus, Joan Jonas' *Vertical Roll* (1972), one of the most celebrated of early single-channel video works (Elwes 2005: 30), was, in fact, produced in the process of Jonas' multi-media performance *Organic Honey's Vertical Roll* (1972), which was itself the subject of a separate documentary video work (Electronic Arts Intermix 2006). Indeed, such interweaving of live, mediated and recorded performance had also frequently come to position video and photographic 'documentation' as the principal or only means of accessing ephemeral events. Many of Dennis Oppenheim's actions and earth works from 1968 were thus presented through videotape, film and photographic documentation, in gestures linked to the contemporary exhibition by artists of the photographic remainder as a trace and index of performance's ephemerality

(Kaye 2006). Bruce Nauman's early film and video similarly elided distinctions between performance, time-based art, video documentation and
the film or video work, through recordings of his studio-based actions,
including *Wall-Floor Positions* (1968), *Walk with Contrapposto* (1968) and
Stamping in the Studio (1970). For Vito Acconci, in turn, the multiple
relationships between the performed event, the production of mediated
and recorded 'video art', and an engagement with the time and place
of a tape's exhibition and installation intrinsically linked video to live
performance. Here, too, in a reflection of Paik's fracturing of the *present
tense*, Acconci's work, among others, frequently set the 'presence', 'sign'
and 'trace' of the performer at the centre of a practice that articulated
the 'screened' body's definition in and of multiple spaces. Indeed, it is in
the articulation of the performer across these transitions and exchanges,
in particular, that this second wave of video art pressed toward the
vocabulary and implications of an explicitly multi-media practice.

In and Out of Performance*: Vito Acconci

Extending those concerns and processes rooted in poetry and sculptural
practice that had brought him to his engagement with performance,
Vito Acconci's highly influential single-channel tapes, exhibited from
1970, and subsequent video installations from 1973 frequently disturbed
conventional distinctions between 'live' and 'mediated' spaces and times.
In this relationship, and in his explicit negotiations of spaces before
and behind the screen, 'performance' provided the ground for Acconci's
interrogation of video, even as this video worked to challenge and extend
the terms of his live work. In these ways, Acconci's video work is bound to
the terms of 'performance', while his work has developed through radical
steps into and out of these media.

   Acconci's entry into 'Performance' in 1969 had been prompted, in
part, by his encounter with the minimal art object's 'theatricality'

---

*This subheading is drawn from Acconci's essay of 1979, 'Steps into Performance (and
Out)', published in A. A. Bronson and P. Gale (eds), *Performance by Artists*, Toronto: Art
Metropole, 27–40.

(M. Fried 1968: 135). Constituting, the critic Michael Fried argued in his celebrated essay 'Art and Objecthood' of 1967, a corruption of the values of an autonomous modernist art, these forms, associated with the white, geometrical 'unitary forms' of Robert Morris and related work by Donald Judd, Carl Andre and others, were read by Fried as denying the viewer an internal, sculptural dynamic by which an artwork necessarily defined *its own* transcendence of quotidian space and time (M. Fried 1968: 125). Exhibited from 1964, and acting as site-specific interventions into the conventional 'White Cube' gallery space, Morris' unitary forms interrupted the gallery's assertion of the art object's formal and aesthetic isolation by provoking the viewer's self-reflexive awareness of their own presence. Strictly geometric in form, yet implicitly anthropomorphic in size, these 'specific objects' produced, Morris later suggested,

> a confrontation with the body. It was the notion that the object recedes in its self-importance. It participates in a complex experience that includes the object, your body, the space, and the time of your experience. It's locked together in these things.
>
> (Morris 1997)

Acconci, like many of his contemporaries, responded to this deflection of the viewer's attention toward the act and conditions of viewing by reconsidering the artwork in terms of the '"real space time" [...] "actual space time"' (Acconci 1978) of encounter. For Acconci, in particular, where minimalism 'was the art that made it necessary to recognize the space you were in' (Acconci 1982), 'performance' came to provide a means of *acting out* the terms of this 'theatricality'. After minimalism, Acconci recalled, 'art obviously had to be this relation between whatever it was that started off the art and the viewer' (Acconci 1982).

Yet, for Acconci, and consistent with the 'complex experience' Morris' describes, *this relation* introduces 'performance' into the terms of ostensibly diverse practices, where 'action' provides not so much a form for a work as a means of disturbing the ground on which the text, the photograph, film, video and even 'performance' itself is produced, received and recorded. Reflecting on 'Performance After the Fact' in 1989, Acconci recalled that at the time of its emergence '[w]e hated the word "performance"' because '"performance" had a place, and that place by tradition was a theatre'. A theatre, he argues, is a place which, in providing 'a point you went toward' and 'enclosure', could only be 'abstractions of the world and not the messy world itself' (Acconci 2001c: 353). In fact, in his earliest work, and in direct response to minimalism, Acconci's impulse towards action was explicitly linked to practices *embedded* in the world, where 'performance' indicated a 'real-time' incursion into a place already occupied and *acted in*. In seeking to embed his performance in such occupied places, he concluded, 'we wanted [. . .] a region that was a section of the accustomed world that everybody knows and that you simply as a matter of course passed by' (Acconci 2001c: 353). It is a tactic expressed, too, in the eclecticism of Acconci's work, as his prolific output from 1969 developed across film, audiotape, 'Performance', 'Activities' and, from 1970, single-channel video. At this time, Acconci recalled in 1979, he came to the conclusion that

> if I specialize in a medium, I would be fixing a ground for myself, a ground I would have to be digging myself out of, constantly, as one medium was substituted for another – so, then, instead of turning toward 'ground,' I would shift my attention and turn toward 'instrument,' I would focus on myself as the instrument that acted on whatever ground was, from time to time, available.
>
> (Acconci 1979: 28)

This *disturbance* of the medium or form *in action* is evident in Acconci's earliest work in 1967 and 1968 as a poet, in his address to a 'literal page-space', an approach concerned not so much with *the page itself* as with 'questions of movement' across it: '[w]ays to go from left to right of the page. Ways to go from one page to another' (Acconci 1978). Thus, early works such as *RE* (1968), which deployed language to prompt, interrupt and map the act of reading, explicitly provoked the reader's self-reflexive awareness of relationships between text, space and eye movement. Addressing the event and trace of action, this engagement with the page provokes the reader's awareness of text as a place of *performed activity* that nevertheless remains *embedded within* reading.

Where Acconci's work for the page invariably deferred attention to an oblique presence, a presence felt at the margin or in the provocation or recollection of action, his performances turned toward a direct encounter with the viewer. Yet, here, while developing an interest 'in setting myself up as a point that absorbs a certain amount of time or space that belongs to another person' (Nemser 1971: 21), Acconci invariably structured such 'meetings' through conditions that countered his apparent availability. In the untitled project for Pier 17 (1971) Acconci invited his audience to individual meetings, announcing through the gallery:

> From March 27 to April 24, 1971, 1am each night, I will be at Pier 17, an abandoned pier at West Street and Park Place, New York; I will be alone, and will wait at the far end of the pier for one hour.
>
> To anyone coming to meet me, I will attempt to reveal something I would normally keep concealed: censurable occurrences and habits, fears, jealousies – something that has not been exposed before and that would be disturbing for me to make public.
>
> (Acconci 1971)

In *Claim* (1971), he occupied the foot of a stairwell within a two-level space for three hours, while a closed-circuit mediation of his activity took the place of the text. Here:

> At street level, there's a video monitor next to the door leading downstairs to the basement; the monitor functions as an announcement, a warning [. . .]. In the basement I'm seated on a chair at the foot of the stairs; I'm blindfolded, I have with me two lead pipes and a crowbar; I'm talking continuously, talking aloud, talking to myself: '. . . I'm alone here in the basement . . . I want to stay alone here in the basement . . . I don't want anybody to be

here in the basement with me . . . I'll stop anybody from coming
down here to the basement . . . '

(Acconci in Kirshner 1980: 16)

In these performances, Acconci announces and acts out a defence of
'his space', amplifying the visitor's experience of 'the state of being before,
in front of' (Onions 1973: 1,659) and so a sense of presence defined in
'the place or space in front of a person, or which immediately surrounds
him' (Onions 1973: 1,659). On these occasions, Acconci recalled, '[it]
seemed like what I was getting at were [sic] almost ways to say hello
to a viewer, but make that "hello" as difficult as possible' (Acconci
in Kunz 1978). In the project for Pier 17, then, the 'viewer comes
into [. . .] this warehouse pier at – at the door near the street, but they
don't see what – they can't really see what's around, so they're groping
their way along this pier in order to get to me. It's like this kind of,
you know, perilous journey' (Acconci in White 1979: 22). In *Claim*,
Acconci reports, 'viewer is forced to come toward me [. . .] it had this
notion of "I'm-this-focal-point" that viewer [sic] is sort of forced to be
confronted with' (Acconci in White 1979: 22). Here, Acconci works to
amplify his presence and authority, asserting a direct yet paradoxical
claim to the privileged space of the unique art object, whose 'aura' is
constituted in its unavailability, 'a sense of distance, no matter how close
an object may be' (Pearson and Shanks 2001: 95). Here, too, Acconci
mimics the object's garnering of significance, where '[a]ura refers to
the sense of associations and evocations that cluster around an object,
correspondences and interrelations engendered by an object' (Pearson
and Shanks 2001: 95). In this development, Acconci recalled, 'the I and
you, the viewer – were never really on equal ground [. . .] it was always
announced, I was always the artist, it was very much – "I" – "I-as-art-
star" meet you, the viewer' (Acconci in White 1979: 19). As a result, and
as the art object's claim to space, authority and exclusivity is transposed
by Acconci into the performance of public and personal transactions,
so he asserts the exclusivity of the 'art space' through these found sites,
returning, paradoxically, to the gallery:

> Once I set up a point – once I set myself up as the point – at one
> end of a space, the space around fades away: the space, whatever its
> shape, narrows into a channel between 'you' and 'me' [. . .] the
> space is only there to advance the plot.
>
>   (Acconci 2001a: 359)

In developing this modulation of 'presence', Acconci's subsequent
gallery performance, *Seedbed* (1972), turned toward the viewer as the
scheme for action in a radical reoccupation of the gallery space. Here,
Acconci recalled, in approaching space 'as a meeting place, a place to start
a relationship' (Acconci 1979: 34),

> I wanted myself as a presence that would exist during the viewer's
> presence, that would be more than one point – I wanted myself to
> be a part of the space in which the viewer was.
>
>   (Acconci in Bear 1982: 234)

For *Seedbed*, then, Acconci constructed an installation in an otherwise
empty 'conventional gallery room twenty-five feet by forty feet'. Here,

> halfway across the room, the floor turns to a ramp that rises to a
> height of two feet at the far wall [. . .]. The piece [. . .] is activated
> three times a week; each day, the piece lasts from opening to
> closing time, from 10 am to 6 pm: I'm under the ramp, I'm moving
> around under the floor where the viewers walk, I'm maintaining a
> constant masturbation – in order to do this I use the viewers as an
> aid, I build up sexual fantasies on viewer's footsteps, my fantasies
> keep my masturbation going.
>
>   (Acconci in Kirshner 1980: 17)

Reflecting Acconci's later remark that '[i]n order to make myself
vulnerable I need strong attacks at the barriers' (Acconci in Nemser
1971: 21), *Seedbed* proposes that in *hiding the body* Acconci might *come
closer*. In this intense conflation of 'private' and 'public' spaces and realms,

Acconci recalled, '[i]t was no longer that "I" was such a definable point in space. Rather, the viewer became a part of the space, rather than facing "me"' (Acconci in Wijers 1979: 10). Here, where, Acconci imagines, 'you are performing for me as much as I'm performing for you':

> [t]he viewer, entering the gallery, walks across the floor and, almost without thinking about it, up the ramp. The viewer hears my voice come up from below: '. . . the person to my left . . . I'm doing this with you now . . . I'm touching your hair . . . I'm running my hand down your back . . . I'm touching your ass . . . ' Whenever I reach climax, the viewer might want to pick himself or herself out of the crowd; the viewer might want to think; he's done this for me, he's done this with me, he's done this because of me.
>
> (Acconci in Kaye 1996: 49)

In this 'disappearance' of the body, too, Acconci's tactics subvert a condition of art viewing, in which, he proposes, 'viewer enters exhibition area, viewer centers in on art-work, or art-object, viewer is aiming toward art-work as if towards a target' (Acconci in White 1979: 15). Now activating the room 'by my presence underground, underfoot – by my movement from point to point' (Acconci in Pincus-Witten 1977: 144), he repositions the visitors, targeting the viewers by including them within his circle of attention:

> My aids are the visitors to the gallery – in my seclusion, I can have private images of them, talk to myself about them: my fantasies about them can excite me, enthuse me to sustain – to resume – my private sexual activity. (The seed 'planted' on the floor, then, is a joint result of my performance and theirs.)
>
> (Acconci in Pincus-Witten 1977: 145)

Eliding the performer's 'being there', *before* the viewer, *Seedbed* explores the paradox that *in his absence* Acconci may encroach more effectively onto the viewer's ground. In doing so, *Seedbed* works to disturb the conventional ground of 'performance', hiding the 'performer', placing the performer neither 'here' nor 'there'. In this respect, too, this performance operates in activities *uncertain* of their place: where 'meeting' is made difficult in order to *come closer*; where the physical divisions between performer and viewer serve to conflate roles and purposes; where Acconci's 'presence' to the visitor is amplified in his 'retreat' behind the screen.

This articulation of the performer's 'presence' in a dispersal of the body's 'place' provides a key to Acconci's use of video. In contrast to his Super-8 films that, in their projection, Acconci suggested, produce the body as 'landscape', leading to 'something too large to be a person' and so 'silence' (Acconci 2001: 361), video implied '[t]hinking of person [*sic*], close-up' (Acconci 2001: 363). Here, where the dimensions of the television monitor mimic the body such that '[t]he close-up literalizes television [. . .] on a TV screen a close-up face is approximately the same size as an actual face' (Acconci 2001b: 372), the specific quality of early mono video evidently amplified, for Acconci, a simulated 'intimacy', a 'closeness' offered in the private time of viewing:

> Video-viewer sits close to the screen – the distance Edward Hall
> [Hall 1966] calls 'personal distance', where three-dimensionality is
> emphasized. But the image on video is flat, grainy – video, then,
> serves to decrease distance, to approach Hall's 'intimate distance'
> where vision is blurred and distorted (appropriately, the video
> image presents itself in dots).

> (Acconci 2001: 361)

In this encounter, Acconci suggests, '[s]ince the image is poorly defined, we're forced to depend on sound more than sight' (Acconci 2001: 363), prompting him toward a directness that 'live' performance militates against. If, as Acconci proposes, '[p]araphrasing Godard: video might be the fear of dots, of grayness, of neutrality, of flatness' (Acconci 2001: 362), then video's mediation might define a resistance to play and perform against, demanding an intensified attention *outward*.

It is in this context that, in single-channel tapes such as *Theme Song* (1973) (see Figure 3.1), Acconci explicitly *acts out* and so amplifies the close-up in an apparent attempt to become 'present to' the viewer's 'private' time and space. Here, in a continuous 33-three minute and 15-second take, lying down, drawing himself close to the camera, Acconci speculates toward a 'face-to-face' encounter, by turn serenading the viewer and inviting and imagining a closer exchange:

> Of course I can't see your face. I have no idea what your face looks like. You could be anybody out there, but there's got to be somebody watching me. Somebody who wants to come in close to me ... Come on, I'm all alone ... I'll be honest with you, O.K. I mean you'll have to believe me. I'm really honest.
>
> (Acconci in Electronic Arts Intermix 2004)

Playing on the monitor *as* the body, Acconci's pressing, here, from a past recording toward the present tense of the viewer's encounter forces him to 'cling to my position' (Acconci 2001: 362), as, if both 'image and sound are only "basic", only "outlines"', Acconci might 'be humanly "pushy": I can push up against the screen, as if to throw myself on the viewer, as if to fight the neutrality of the situation, push myself through' (Acconci 2001: 361).

Where *Theme Song* mimics the blurring of vision of this 'intimate distance', so it at once reflects earlier theoretical analyses of media's 'extension' of the body while articulating television and video's spatial multiplications. Thus, as Acconci's approach to the viewer implicitly presses toward Marshall McLuhan's celebrated accounts of media's 'extension of consciousness' (McLuhan 1964: 4), in its simulation of intimacy and intrusion this 'recovery' of a relationship with the viewer nevertheless emphasizes the divisions in which it appears. Here, Acconci's work is consistent with Samuel Weber's more recent observation of television and video's operation in a multiplication of space and place. Noting that in its three operations of production, transmission and reception,

3.1 Vito Acconci. **"Theme Song," 1973.** *Courtesy Electronic Arts Intermix (EAI), New York.*

'television [. . .] *above all differs from itself'* (Weber 1996: 110), Weber emphasizes that

> by definition, television takes place in *at least three places at once*: 1. In the place (or places) where the image and sound are 'recorded'; 2. In the place (or places) where those images and sounds are *received*; and 3. In the place (or places) *in between*, through which those images and sounds are transmitted [. . .]. It overcomes spatial distance only by splitting the unity of place and with it the unity of everything that defines its identity with respect to place: events, bodies, subjects.
>
> (Weber 1996: 117)

In underlining Acconci's *absence* in his very *pressing to* the viewer, then, this performance of the 'screened body' suggests an *acting out* of Weber's proposition that television's '"being there and here" goes on *at the same time*' (Weber 1996: 120), or, as Acconci proposes, that 'television represents an absence, a difference' (Acconci 2001b: 374). Indeed, it is *in* this 'difference', in the fact that, Acconci proposes, 'television is the absence of the body' (Acconci 2001b: 374), that these single-channel tapes make a paradoxical advance on *Seedbed*'s strategies. Where in *Seedbed* it is precisely in 'the absence of the body', and so under the condition of a 'certain distance', that Acconci encroaches on the 'time or space belonging to another person', so in *Theme Song* Acconci's 'screened body' is defined in its 'proximity' to bodies *elsewhere*: to Acconci's 'past' performance; to the viewer's 'present' watching. Here, Acconci notes, in a reversal of cinema, but in an implicit extension of *Seedbed*'s projection over the viewer *in language*: 'Television is a rehearsal for the time when human beings no longer need to have bodies [...] the television "shoots" images into the viewer: the viewer functions as a screen' (Acconci 2001b: 374).

In certain of Acconci's single-channel tapes this 'projection' becomes emphatic. In *Undertone* (1973), for example, the viewer is positioned as auditor and arbiter of Acconci's fantasy. In this single-channel tape:

> Acconci sits at the end of a long table, arms hidden underneath, facing the camera/viewer. Looking down, he begins a hypnotic monologue as he tries to convince himself that there is a woman under the table rubbing his thighs, or, alternately, that it is himself rubbing his thighs.
>
> (Zippay 1991: 14)

Constructing the onlooker's viewpoint as a mirror of his own, *Undertone* insists on the viewer's complicity with Acconci's act of fantasy, positioning the visitor as a partner, who may, by turn, excise or intensify his illusion:

> I want to believe there's no one here under the table ... I want to believe there's a girl here [...]. I need you to know your place at the head of the table. I need to know I can count on you [...]. I

3.2 Vito Acconci. **"Centers," 1971.** *Courtesy Electronic Arts Intermix (EAI), New York.*

need you to screen out my lies, filter out the lies from the real
point of view.

(Acconci in Zippay 1991: 14)

Earlier, in *Centers* (1971) (see Figure 3.2), Acconci had set the agenda
for this 'projection' in a response to the viewer's 'targeting' of the
artwork. Here, Rosalind Krauss notes, in her early, influential essay on
video art, 'The Aesthetics of Narcissism', '[w]hat he does is literalize the
critical notion of "pointing" by filming himself pointing to the centre
of a television monitor' (Krauss 1976: 51). As Krauss' essay implies, and
consistently with the later *Seedbed* and *Undertone*, *Centers* is defined in an
intensely self-regarding action, as, for twenty minutes

Acconci faces the camera, his head and arm in close-up, he points
straight ahead at his own image on the video monitor, attempting
to keep his finger focused on the exact center of the screen [. . .]. As

the tape proceeds in real time, the only changes in the
performance action are slight adjustments in the position of his
finger as his endurance falters.

(Zippay 1991: 12)

Yet this is a circle of attention designed to enmesh and implicate
the viewer through video's spatial complexity. First, and evidently, '[i]n
pointing at the image of himself, Acconci is also directly pointing at
the viewer' (Electronic Arts Intermix 2006). In this, Acconci's gesture
is transformed and fragmented as (for himself) Acconci looks *with* the
viewer, while (for them) Acconci replies to the viewer's 'targeting' by
pointing back. In this aspect, Acconci suggests:

(the TV image) turns the activity around: in pointing away from
myself, at an outside viewer – I end up widening my focus onto
passing viewers (I'm looking straight out by looking straight in).

(Acconci in Zippay 1991: 12)

Arising in his attention to self, and so in his participation *with* the
visitor's targeting of his performance, *Centers* articulates Acconci's occupation of the multiple centres of production, recording and reception,
and so his occupation of a series of conjoined 'spaces' defined in each
other. Here, Acconci's performance of the 'screened body' emphasizes its
absence from *this* space; the differences *between* spaces; its dispersal *across*
spaces subject to reversal and delay. In Acconci's projections to the viewer,
Undertone transposes this dispersal toward emotional and psychological
exchange. Acconci's looking 'inward', into fantasy, is reversed: 'the television "shoots" images onto the viewer', Acconci projects 'himself' over
a future partner in performance; the viewers 'screen out' the lies, participate or vacillate, re-performing Acconci's projection in their private time
of viewing. Here, in both *Centers* and *Undertone*, Acconci presses toward
a repositioning of 'self' and 'other' that questions distinctions between
before and behind the screen, between 'mediated' and 'real' spaces and
acts. Here, too, Acconci's performance of the 'screened' body approaches

a performance of presence that provides a key element in the description of multi-media practice.

Aura and Division: Acconci's *Command Performance*

For Chantal Pontbraid (1982), Josette Féral (1982), Eleanor Fuchs (1985) and, in response to these articles, Phillip Auslander (1992), a critique of 'presence' in performance has been linked to technologies of 'mediation' in relation to which the 'aura' and so 'authority' of the performer might be exposed and denuded. Grounded in Walter Benjamin's celebrated essay 'The Work of Art in the Age of Mechanical Reproduction' (Benjamin 1992), such strategies have been proposed as effecting an interruption, or, Auslander suggests, 'a deconstruction of presence and of the structures of authority in performance' which, under the tactics of postmodernism, may be 'coupled with a refusal to offer "alternative" representations' (Auslander 1992: 47). In advancing this influential thesis, Auslander cites Pontbraid, who proposes that

> [t]he more performance is expressed by technical means, the more chance it has of being removed from the theatre or theatricality; the more it withdraws from representation into simple presentation; the more it draws away from aura into simple actuality; the more it withdraws away from classical presence to assert a new and different presence, a radical presence.

> (Pontbraid 1982: 156)

In his celebrated essay of 1936, on which this analysis rests, and which remains a point of reference in media as well as performance theory (Manovich 2001: 170–5), Benjamin proposed a key definition of 'aura' as 'the unique phenomenon of distance, however close it may be' (Benjamin 1992: 216). In this context, and implicitly conflating object and performer, Benjamin proposed that the performer's 'aura is tied to his presence' (Benjamin 1992: 223), where 'presence' refers to the performer's, or the object's, proper and so unique *occupation of its place*. Thus, he concludes, '[e]ven the most perfect reproduction of a work of art is lacking in one element: its presence in time and space, its unique existence at the place it happens to be' (Benjamin 1992: 214). In this context, the effect of the repetition and proliferation of the substitute through mechanical reproduction is to replace, and so *displace*, the 'original', eliding the 'unique phenomenon of distance' by succumbing to 'the desire of the contemporary masses to bring things "closer" spatially and humanly' (Benjamin 1992: 216–17). In absenting the 'original', it follows, the very availability of such reproductions heralds 'the disappearance of this aura' (Pontbraid 1982: 155). In the case of the performer, Benjamin similarly concludes, where 'the camera is substituted for the public [. . .] the aura that envelops the actor vanishes' (Benjamin 1992: 223). Under the performer's 'mediation', it follows, the 'authority' claimed by 'classical' (live) 'presence' is elided and may be 'deconstructed', in the manner of Jacques Derrida's profoundly influential exposure of the contradictions and limits of philosophical and literary texts. Yet, in relation to Acconci's work, as well as Benjamin's and Derrida's writings, this opposition between 'aura' and 'technology' may come under question. Indeed, it is through the relationship between Benjamin's and Derrida's work that Samuel Weber considers 'aura's' *transformation* within electronic mediation while raising the possibility of its production *in* this very mediation.

In Derrida's project, aimed at a deconstruction of concepts of 'presence' and its concomitant oppositions and hierarchies within Western metaphysics, the claim to 'presence' is treated as a suppression of the uncertainties in which signifying systems function. In this context, in his celebrated critique of Ferdinand de Saussure's rules of structural linguistics, Derrida proposed that the sign operates in a fundamental uncertainty or undecidability. Adopting the proposition that the sign functions in a relationship between signifier (the mark or sound) and signified (the concept or unit of meaning), Derrida follows Saussure's description of language as an entirely conventional construction that enables our thinking of the world, yet works to reveal the instability that underlies the oppositions upon which this account rests.

In his description of the rules of structural linguistics, Saussure describes the functioning of language as a self-contained, self-regulating system through which meaning becomes *present*. To 'read' the sign is to *locate* the signifier, to *recognize* its place within the semiotic system, such that, as signifier and signified are defined in their opposition, the signified, the 'unit of meaning', becomes available *in* the formation of the sign. However, within Saussure's own terms, this claim can be read as resting on a contradiction. Within the self-regulated system Saussure proposes, the functioning of the signifier, its ability to join with the signified, is dependent not upon what the signifier *is* but upon *what it is not*. Indeed, the very self-containment of the system requires that the signifier be recognized, and so defined by the reader, in its relation of difference with all other signifiers. This means that, insofar as he claims that in the joining of signifier and signified meaning becomes *present*, Saussure can be accused of supposing that there is a realm of the signified, of 'concepts', somehow existing beyond the functioning of the signifier. Only by gaining access to such a realm could the play of difference, by which the signifier functions, result in the presence of meaning. Yet any such realm would both precede and exist beyond the self-contained, self-regulating linguistic structure.

To question the opposition of signifier and signified which Saussure assumes, however, is to doubt the very decidability of meaning under the rules of structural linguistics. If the signified is not a function of presence but, like the signifier, of absence and difference, then it follows that meaning becomes subject to the same processes of differentiation which permit the functioning of the signifier. Meaning becomes, like the signifier, not a function of *what it is*, but of *what it is not*. Indeed, where, as Derrida argues, 'the signified always already functions as signifier' (Derrida 1976: 7), meaning can never be finally 'present', for the move toward the signified finds itself caught in the endless play of 'difference' and so 'deferral'; always subject to *différance*. With regard to 'presence', then, and consistent with this critique of Saussure, 'deconstruction' works to reveal the contradictions, the play of *différance*, which claims to 'presence', and, similarly, to the 'genuine', the 'real', the 'authentic' – to that which would *precede* or *transcend* the functioning of the sign – necessarily suppress.

Under this description, Pontbraid's opposition of 'aura' to a 'simple actuality' sits uncomfortably within a deconstructive project. Emphasizing technology's *intervention* into the terms of live performance, Pontbraid opposes the 'classical presence' of theatrical representation to 'a new and different presence' uncovered in the erasure of 'aura', a 'presence' defined in a 'simple presentation' and so a presence implicitly linked to the authority of 'the real' (Pontbraid 1982: 156). This privileging of one 'presence' over another reflects the ambivalence of any deconstructive project, which, as Auslander notes, after Derrida, always runs the risk of confirming or reinstating the very 'structures of authority' it seeks, at once, to inhabit and critique (Auslander 1992: 25–6). Yet, in the case of the 'deconstruction' of 'presence' in the 'expression of performance through technological means', this risk is further complicated by the capacity of the media itself to *reproduce*, rather than simply erase, the terms of this aura's production and perception.

Rather than simply standing in opposition to Benjamin's position, Derrida's understanding of presence and the functioning of the sign is reflected in the complexity of 'aura' itself. Indeed, under Benjamin's account, the object's 'aura' is defined in the perception of an implicit division *in* 'presence', in the 'unique phenomenon of distance, however close it may be'. After Derrida, such a 'phenomenon' is consistent with the play of the signifier to which the sign is subject. Here, where the reader of any sign-system can locate the sign only in *difference* and *deferral*, then, *its place* is always already occupied by the trace of *what it is not*. By extension, the object or performer's claim to a singular or unified 'presence', to a 'unique existence at the place it happens to be', must remain contentious, always subject to the 'trace', or 'supplement', in which *this location* is set in opposition to any other. 'Aura', in this sense, in a seeing of the 'object' as being 'there and here', is not simply a perception of the 'transcendence' of the 'original', but a perception of the separation in which the *signs* of presence function: an occurrence in which *the sign of that which is here* is *seen* to defer elsewhere. That 'aura' is linked to the divisions of the sign is reflected, too, in Benjamin's example of the aura of natural phenomena, from which he derives his definition of its effect. Benjamin notes:

> The concept of aura [. . .] may usefully be illustrated with reference to the aura of natural ones. We define the aura of the latter as the unique phenomenon of distance, however close it may be. If, while resting on a summer afternoon, you follow with your eyes a mountain range on the horizon or a branch which casts its shadow over you, you experience the aura of those mountains, of that branch.
>
> (Benjamin 1992: 216)

Here, 'aura' arises in a self-conscious viewing of the 'natural scene', a falling, in this contemplation, toward a recognition of the 'pictorial' aspect of 'Nature', and so, implicitly, its cultural identity *as landscape*. In this moment, where the perception of 'the real' is contaminated by a perception of its identity *in representation*, the *divisions* and *deferrals* in which the sign functions are *seen* to come into play: this scene is *different*; it *becomes distant*, however close it may be. In this context, and as Samuel Weber points out, the perception of 'aura' may, paradoxically, be produced *in* 'reproduction', for '[w]here [. . .] what is "brought closer" is itself already a reproduction – and as such separated from itself – the closer it comes, the more distant it is' (Weber 1996: 88). Consistently with this, Weber notes, Benjamin's essay refers not simply to 'aura's' 'disappearance', but to 'the contemporary decay of aura' (Benjamin 1992: 216), to aura's depreciation (Benjamin 1992: 215).

It follows from this, too, that the erasure of 'aura' in mediation must come into question. Indeed, in this context, Weber goes on to propose that the operation of television is integral to aura's transformation and even *its production*. In the first instance, then, television's mediation of place and time plays on perceptions of 'the real', confusing distinctions between the occurrence, repetition and representation of events, as:

The minimal distance necessary to distinguish reproduced from reproduction, model from copy, repeated from repetition, is reduced, tendentially at least, to the imperceptible [. . .] one cannot even discern *that* or *when* reproduction or repetition, in the manifest sense of recording or replaying, is taking place.

(Weber 1996: 121)

Yet, in suppressing the divisions in which the sign is *seen*, television produces another division in perception itself. Proposing that 'television is *different*, not just from film, as has often been observed and explored, but also from what we generally mean by the word *perception*' (Weber 1996: 109, original emphasis), Weber observes that 'the "act" of viewing television does not "take place" simply *in front* of the television set, ——as it might were it simply to involve the viewing of *images*', for '[a]s the name of the medium says very precisely, one looks at a certain kind of vision' (Weber 1996: 118, original emphasis). In presenting this 'vision', Weber argues, television provokes a *doubleness* in perception, for

[W]hat we see, above and beyond the content of the images, is someone or something seeing. But that someone or something remains at an irreducible distance from the television viewer: and this distance splits the 'sameness' of the instant of perception.

(Weber 1996: 122)

As a result, even as television suppresses its repetition of time and place, and so its functioning *in representation*, this splitting of vision means that 'what is thus brought close remains strangely *removed*, indeterminably *distant*' (Weber 1996: 124) in 'the *undecideable being of the television images we see*' (Weber 1996: 121, original emphasis). It follows, Weber concludes, that, '[i]n short, what the media bring closer is a certain separation, a certain distance' (Weber 1996: 161). Indeed, in this perception of a delay and difference *in watching*, television operates in a *reproduction* of the divisions in which the aura of natural phenomena is perceived. It follows that, in such mediation,

> [W]hat Benjamin calls the 'decline of aura' emerges here not as its
> simple elimination but as its alteration, which, however, turns out
> to repeat what aura has always been: *the singular leave-taking of the
> singular*, whose singularity is no longer that of an original moment
> but of its posthumous aftershock.
>
> (Weber 1996: 104)

Thus, in his re-reading of Benjamin, Weber proposes that, paradoxically,
'aura, despite all of its withering away, dilapidation and decline, never
fully disappears' but rather 'returns with a vengeance [...] in those forms
of representation that would, according to Benjamin's account, seem
most hostile to it: film, for instance, and now we can add, television as
well' (Weber 1996: 87). It follows that, finally,

> there is the very real possibility that aura will be reproduced in and
> by the very media responsible for its 'decline'. For what is clear
> from Benjamin's discussion, even though he does not say it in so
> many words, and what has become increasingly evident ever since,
> is that *aura thrives in its decline* and that the reproductive media are
> particularly conducive to this thriving.
>
> (Weber 1996: 101, original emphasis)

Weber's proposition is consistent with the assumptions underpinning
Derrida's deconstruction of Saussure's structural linguistics, while having wide-ranging implications for performance and its mediation. Under
Derrida's paradigm, the claim to presence is a *discursive claim*, made
in a suppression of linguistic, and so cultural, historical and political
contingency and contradiction. In the absence of the 'transcenden-
tal signified', then, the claim to 'presence', to the unique occupation
of *this place*, has no final foundation but is 'performative', in the
sense that it 'enacts that to which it refers' (Pearson and Shanks
2001: 69). Under this condition, that 'aura thrives in its decline' reflects its production in a double movement: in a 'presence' *fractured*:

in a perception of the divisions *in* the signs of presence, of repetition *in* mediation. It follows, consistently with Weber, that where 'aura' may be an effect *of* reproduction, the 'expression of performance through technical means' does not simply 'erase' aura, but, even in its interruption of 'classical' (live) 'presence', may *produce* it, *make it available*.

It is the performance of such *division* that underpins many of Acconci's moves across media and forms. Here, too, the structure of Acconci's work across a variety of media echoes Derrida's use of a 'trace-structure', to which Eleanor Fuchs directs attention in considering an 'aesthetics of Absence' in the theatre of Robert Wilson and Richard Foreman (Fuchs 1985). In the introduction to her translation of Derrida's *Of Grammatology*, Gayatri Spivak describes Derrida's 'structure of writing' as 'the sign under erasure', noting its '[t]race-structure, everything always inhabited by the trace of something not itself' that 'questions presence-structure' (Spivak 1976: lxix). In Acconci's practice, an analogous 'trace-structure' is evident in the tension between 'ground' and 'action' or 'instrument': in his disturbance of the medium or form *in use*; in the *oblique presence* that disrupts, contradicts or displaces attention. Hence, in his approach to the page, Acconci shadows that which is read with the *act* of reading; in approaching 'action', 'Performance' is denied *its proper place* before the viewer; in mediation and recording, Acconci presses toward the 'real' time and space of the viewer's encounter. In the development of his media-based installations, too, it is this division, and, particularly, video's ambivalent construction of place, its going on 'there and here', in which Acconci *acts out* a 'return' of presence.

This development is exemplified in *Command Performance* of 1974 (see Figure 3.3), which marked Acconci's entry into site-specific video installation while signalling his imminent withdrawal from live performance. An installation about performance, or, more precisely, 'about' the co-dependence of performer and viewer, *Command Performance* announced Acconci's conclusion that '[o]nce a place has been given to both agent and viewers, their places can be interchanged' (Acconci in Kirshner 1980: 20). Installed at 112 Greene Street, SoHo, New York, the arrangement

3.3 Vito Acconci. **"Command Performance," 1974.** *Courtesy Electronic Arts Intermix (EAI), New York.*

of *Command Performance* followed the architecture of this gallery space, one 'bisected by columns running down its length, from front to back' (Acconci in Kirshner 1980: 20), whereby:

> Farthest from the entrance, at the foot of one column, a video monitor faces a white stool placed at a second column; the stool is lit from above by a spotlight, and continuously shot by a video camera that shows the stool on a monitor in front of a third column, facing the entrance. The first monitor has a fixed tape: I'm lying down, seen from above, the way a doctor – or mortician – would see me: I'm addressing a viewer who might be sitting on the white stool, inviting the viewer to sit on the stool and appear on the screen, on the second monitor, putting on a show for other viewers as they come in.
>
> (Acconci in Kirshner 1980: 20)

Examining the performer's 'leaving', *Command Performance* begins in
the proposition that 'the art-space [. . .] can be supported on the memory
of the agent's presence' (Acconci in Kirshner 1980: 20). Accenting his
'withdrawal' by 'deadening' his image, refusing attention, closing his eyes,
as if to counter his *taking of this place*, Acconci's video performance gives
voice to an ambivalent 'reversal' of roles. Cajoling the viewer 'in a tour-
de-force of verbal play, talking, humming, dreaming, and singing' (Linker
1994: 61) of just under an hour's duration, he issues instructions to the
viewer that rehearse his own performance history and autobiography,
implicitly referring to his actions in *Reception Room* (1973), *Hand in Mouth*
(1970) and *Trappings* (1971), among others:

> (<u>Humming</u> <u>comes</u> <u>down</u> <u>harder</u>:) Du . . . Du . . . Du (<u>Humming</u> <u>like</u>
> <u>a</u> <u>taunt</u>, <u>like</u> <u>circus</u> <u>music</u> <u>gone</u> <u>crazy</u>:) Dududu – duduudu . . .
> Dududu-duduudu . . . Like a little dog . . . Jump up . . . Jump up on
> the stool . . . Sit up, come up to me. Beg . . . Dududu-duduudu . . .
> Dududu-duduudu . . . How do you think it feels . . . Show them
> your ass, stuff your hand in your mouth. Wiggle your prick around
> . . . It's your turn now . . . Now I don't have to be there anymore . . .
> You're my little puppet, it's your turn to play the fool for them . . .
> (<u>Humming</u> <u>fades</u> <u>off</u>:) Duu . . . Duuu . . . I'm losing you, I'm losing
> you . . .
>
> (Acconci in Kirshner 1980: 21)

Yet, in such 'autobiography', which concerns 'not so much revelation
of self but the use of [. . .] a kind of calling card to viewers' (Acconci
in Kunz 1978), Acconci acts out 'self' as 'narrative', as 'character': a 'self'
located in the tropes of 'fiction'. Here, specifically, Acconci plays on his
'performed persona', one reflecting

> the myth that had been made of me as a performer and that I had
> helped make myself: that myth demanded that I be involved not in

the world of books but in the world of bodies – that myth
demanded that my presence be sexual not neutered.

(Acconci 2001c: 356)

It is in this *leaving*, too, that, Acconci supposes, his work finally
approaches 'theatre': a theatre defined, paradoxically, in a giving up of his
'presence' in favour of the sign. Here, he notes, the gallery exhibits the
evidence of his 'self', such that:

Gallery returns to theatre. Image-structure:
spotlight – performance arena [...] The gallery is turned into
itself: the gallery is turned into, literally, a museum. This is where I
place my past in the spotlight, let it harden.

(Acconci 1979: 36)

Yet it is in this play of absence, too, that *Command Performance* elides
the opposition between performer and viewer. Constructing the visitor
as the object of this theatrical apparatus and so the *absent performer* of
his recollections, Acconci's 'leaving' mirrors the viewer's viewing of the
empty space or, in the case of participation, the stepping in and out of
'performance'. Here, too, *Command Performance* operates in a division
and play *between* spaces, where 'the tape is part of a whole situation'
(Acconci 2001: 362). In this respect, like others of Acconci's video
installations, *Command Performance* extends the operation of television
toward performance. In 1974, Acconci suggested that '[t]he more recent
pieces might be said to play on the notion of video 'dots': the monitor is
a point in a space that includes the viewer, a circle that's completed by
the viewer' (Acconci 2001: 362).

Such installation extends video's fragmentation and multiplication
of spaces and disturbance of the 'proper place', the unique or authentic
'location', in a 'splitting [of] the unity of place' (Weber 1996: 117). Writing
in 'Television, Furniture & Sculpture: The Room with the American
View' in 1984, Acconci emphasized video installation's disruption of the

unities of site through its operation in *differences*:

> Video installation is the conjunction of opposites [. . .] On the one
> hand, 'installation' places an art-work in a specific site, for a
> specific time (a specific duration and also, possibly, for a specific
> historical time). On the other hand, 'video' (with its consequences
> followed through: video broadcast on television) is placeless: at
> least, its place can't be determined [. . .]. Video installation, then,
> places placelessness.
>
> (Acconci 2001b: 376)

It is in the passages between 'place' and 'placelessness' that *Command
Performance* operates in a multiplication and exchange of spaces and
roles. In this exchange, too, *Command Performance* reflects the proposition that television is a *movement in place*, as Acconci articulates the
viewer's 'potential performance' in liminal spaces of exchange between
'performer' and 'viewer', 'mediated' and 'live', 'on' and 'off' screen. Indeed, the 'command performance' captured in this installation cannot be
entirely separated from either Acconci's fantasy or the viewer's watching.
Thus, where Acconci, on video, closes his eyes to *absent himself*, so, in
his monologue, he *displaces* the viewer toward performance. Yet, at the
same time, Acconci's demands, his pleading, will always *themselves* be
displaced, for the viewer can be no more than a figure of Acconci's
fantasy, in which he might '[d]ream myself into you. Dream myself
into the space'. Later, Acconci asserts: 'I don't know how to make you
concrete enough' (Acconci in Electronic Arts Intermix 2004). Consistently with this, *in action*, under the spotlight, the visitor's 'participation'
always 'differs from itself' (Weber 1996: 110). Inevitably *at variance*
with Acconci's instructions, and after Nauman's *Performance Corridor*, the
visitor's 'command performance' is always already 'a performance not
in the singular (the event, the act, the performance) but in the plural
(performative, repetitive and ritualistic) in which any one enactment
contains and anticipates traces of others' (Kraynak 2003: 30). In turn,
the visitor's 'act' is then subject to its *transmission* in the closed-circuit

system: to the media's *separation*, to 'placelessness'. It is, finally, in this occupation of multiple spaces that the visitor might 'take Acconci's place' as *Command Performance* works to locate the visitor-performer *there and here*: in Acconci's leaving, in the viewer's *becoming performer*. Here, Acconci works to cast the 'aura' of the 'live performer' over the visitors, inscribing 'his' performance into the divisions of 'their' actions, installing *his place* into 'their' location, so heightening their *presence* to themselves and others. 'Television', Acconci concludes in his essay 'Television, Furniture & Sculpture: The Room with the American View', 'confirms the diagnosis that the boundaries between inside and outside are blurred: the diagnosis that "self" is an out-dated concept' (Acconci 2001b: 372).

Acting in the Space Between: Studio Azzurro, Pipilotti Rist

Where Acconci's performance and early video installation focused on the performance of presence in the *divisions between* performer and visitor, subsequent video work has articulated action and interaction, and the mediated body's occupation of place, *in* the divisions of the media itself. Created in Milan in 1982 in collaboration between Fabio Cirifino, Paolo Rosa and Leonardo Sangiorgi, Studio Azzurro's work is grounded in dialogues between photography (Cirifino), visual arts and cinema (Rosa) and graphics and animation (Sangiorgi) while embracing prolific and wide-ranging commercial and artistic collaborations. Working, initially, in video installation, the group's consequent 'research on video art, our interest in theatre and cinema' (Rosa in Cirifino *et al*. 1999: 7) led, from 1985, to a series of major collaborations with the Italian post-avant-garde theatre director Giorgio Barberio Corsetti (Giannachi and Kaye 2002: 113–28) and, subsequently, toward increasingly complex, interactive 'videoenvironments' that incorporated the visitor into the execution of their work. Taking as their point of departure the passage of objects, actions and images *between* spaces, Studio Azzurro's earliest explorations with video focused on electronic mediation's apparent 'alteration' of the 'real' object or event. Thus, in an interview of 1994, Paolo Rosa recalled their early speculations over the effect of video's reproduction of 'landscape, the environment' and 'nature', a focus reflected in the first of their interactive environments, *Tavoli, perche queste mani mi toccano? (Tables – Why Are these Hands Touching Me?)* (1995):

> At the beginning we were primarily concerned with a specific concept: bringing a natural event into the foreground by focusing on an equivalent artificial event [. . .] a simple electronic drop that is made to fall repeatedly into a monitor screen can cause a very strong level of attention.
>
> (Rosa in Valentini 1995: 154)

For Rosa, such mediation effected an amplification of the event in its very reproduction: 'It is as if this phenomenon [. . .] were suddenly placed under a magnifying glass, a process that immediately brings it to the fore and gives it meaning' (Rosa in Valentini 1995: 154). In this context, the group's first installations addressed such transformations through a 'fragmentation of the space within the confines of the monitor and the surroundings in which it was placed' (Rosa in Valentini 1995: 141). For *Luci di inganni (Lights of Deceit)*, a series of object-based pieces including *Videoarmadio (Videowardrobe)* (1982) and *Videofumo (Videosmoke)* (1982), everyday objects and actions were articulated before and behind the screen in a series of 'small deceptions' (Rosa in Valentini 1995: 140) in which fragmented objects and their virtual counterparts formed a composite image. Here, Rosa notes:

> the screen had to be treated like the space of a small theatre in which the real object was mirrored, expanded, animated, the object being to create a constant dialogue between inside and beyond the

screen, between the physical stillness of the object and the mobility
of the represented image.

(Rosa in Valentini 1995: 140)

For Rosa, these objects expressed a mobility between the 'virtual' and the
'real' that, in retrospect, implied the notion of the interactive 'videoenvironments', in which the viewer's action, rather than the composite image,
effected a passage between spaces. Here, too, Rosa notes, in effecting the
object's 'disappearance' into mediation:

> I had become aware how paradoxically the more objects tend to
> lose their material essence, dissolve their physical nature into flux
> and data, the more they tend to disappear, the more their
> 'presence' gains ground.

(Rosa in Valentini 1995: 160)

In extending this, Studio Azzurro's mediation of 'landscape' and 'environment', but also objects and actions, worked against pictorial and cinematic
conventions that might announce their 'framing'. A major element in Studio Azzurro's work, Valentina Valentini observes, has been '[t]he removal
of the relationship between figure and background' (Valentini 1995: 139),
such that objects and figures *come closer*, as if they might take their place
in the space occupied by the viewer.

Here, too, the group's mediations have worked against the *immateriality*
of the electronic image in plays between metaphor and material effect.
Thus, following *Luci di inganni*, the site-specific installation *Il Nuotatore
va troppo spesso ad Heidelberg* (*The Swimmer Goes to Heidelberg too Often*)
(1984), which first brought the group to international attention, and the
videoenvironment *Il Giardino delle anime* (*The Garden of Souls*) (1997)
both mediated large-scale surfaces of flowing water whose instability,
Rosa suggests, 'is probably seen to closely resemble the electronic flow.
It is an element that has no shape, and tends to overwhelm other shapes,

changing them, redefining them, sweeping them away' (Rosa in Valentini 1995: 154). In interactivity, too, Rosa notes, the actions of spectators might participate in this play with materiality, for

> [w]hen the projection is made on wood, or on a carpet which shall be marked by an increasing number of footprints, the sensation of the matter itself, a feature peculiar to painting, is exalted.
>
> (Rosa in Cirifino *et al*. 1999: 45)

More specifically, in this bringing of the image closer, Studio Azzurro's videoenvironments invite interaction through interfaces that simulate functional aspects of that which they reproduce, so 'abolishing the need to decode the code' (Roveda in Cirifino *et al*. 1999: 53). Emphasizing, in his *Confidential Report*, the group's purpose 'to try and bring the work of art, the artistic artifice toward human gesture, to set artistic experience amidst the behavior of its viewers', Rosa emphasizes the importance of '[n]atural interfaces, as we have defined them, which do not make use of symbolic systems, [but] contribute to the fostering of actions and reactions that are pre-logical, instinctive, and which can be compared subsequently with more rational responses'. The 'natural interface' serves, even as the object 'disappears' into 'information', to restore its place to *activity*, to *use*. In this respect, Rosa considers that Studio Azzurro's practice effects a reversal of Marcel Duchamp's celebrated Ready-Mades, in which everyday objects were reframed within the gallery. Here, Rosa notes,

> we tried to do exactly the opposite of what Duchamp did. We are attempting to make works of art that relate directly to people's behaviour, and transform this behaviour into a part of the artistic experience, rather than extrapolating an object from its daily use and transferring it directly into an artistic context.
>
> (Rosa in Cirifino *et al*. 1999: 8)

Produced between 1914 and 1917, Duchamp's series of 'Ready-mades', including *Bottle Dryer* (1914), a snow shovel under the title *The Advance of the Broken Arm* (1914) and an upturned urinal as *Fountain* (1917), used paradox to expose the role of institutional and conceptual frameworks in the production of art. Presenting everyday objects selected, Duchamp later recalled, on the basis of 'a reaction of visual indifference with at the same time a total absence of good or bad taste' (Duchamp 1975: 141) in the manner of sculptural object, Duchamp's gesture at once rendered the utilitarian object beyond use while installing, in the place of art, objects of such familiarity that they might resist the gallery's distancing effect. Indeed, in this respect, the Ready-Made articulates and effects the divisions of 'aura': at once invoking the sense of an object's familiarity, its availability, its closeness, while subjecting it to frameworks that *produce* a sense of aesthetic 'distance'.

Studio Azzurro's 'inversion' of Duchamp similarly engages with the availability and 'presence' of the object. Defining the 'videoenvironment' as 'the place where things occur, a happening rather than a show; the stressing of the environment as the place where the interrelations between the electronic apparatus, the virtual reality and the physical space, the lived experience, take place' (Studio Azzurro in Valentini 1995: 145), Studio Azzurro's 'natural interfaces' *reproduce* the 'utility' of the object or figure subject to mediation. Yet here, in 'reversing' Duchamp, the group nevertheless stage 'the phenomenon of distance, however close it may be' (Benjamin 1992: 223). Thus, where the 'videoenvironment' mediates the object's *functioning*, bringing the virtual object or figure into the visitor's realm of action, what *comes closer* is the object's *difference*, its immateriality, its 'placelessness'. Here, in a final contrast to Duchamp's gesture, it is the visitor's *action*, in response to this *mediation of use*, that provokes a sense of the 'virtual object's' *being there and here*, and so an experience of 'continual shifts between what is actual and what is virtual' (Valentini 1995: 139). Indeed, it is in this *reproduction of utility*, in which 'the closer [the object] comes, the more distant it is' (Weber 1996: 88), that, as Rosa proposes, the 'presence' of the 'object' 'gains ground' (Rosa in Valentini 1995: 160).

It is in this context, too, that Studio Azzurro's interactive videoenvironments engage with the visitor's action *in* narrative. Here, in building on installation-based performances such as *Il Viaggio* (*The Journey*) (1992), which employed narrative fragments without seeking narrative resolution or closure, the group's interactive environments catch the visitor's attention in a dynamic between their own action and the narrative and fictional elements that these actions trigger. Thus, while Studio Azzurro seek to define 'an horizon of meaning' through the definition of a palette of narrative elements and possibilities, '[t]he user is not asked to participate only in a predefined narration but to "explore" and to "realize" in time, in space, in matter, the potential of a work/event'. 'Play', Rosa concludes in the *Confidential Report*, 'is an intrinsic component of all forms of interactivity [...]. Play is a threshold of access'. Here, too, not only are the 'real' and 'virtual' spaces in which the visitor acts subject to reversal and exchange, but the various 'times' of these elements' recording and mediation are re-played or conflated in the visitor's engagement. 'Interactivity', Rosa remarks in the *Confidential Report*, 'projects us inside representation'. In these interactions, he notes,

> you are not watching a story, but you are in it, there is no given
> evolution, but the spectator has to create his own. It is as if we
> were generating the necessary conditions and environment for a
> story that is taking place at that very moment, in the same time
> frame of the 'visionary' spectator.
>
> (Rosa in Valentini 1995: 155)

Where Studio Azzurro articulate virtual objects and narrative in this spatial play and exchange, Pipilotti Rist's video installations have engaged with video's definition in and of constructed, architectural and 'found' sites. Exemplified in *Open My Glade* (2000), Rist's occupation of the NBC Astrovision Panasonic video screen in New York's Times Square, such paradoxical plays from video's virtual spaces toward a performance of its 'real' sites are integral to much of her work. Influenced, Peggy Phelan suggests, by artists whose video work has been closely linked to performance, particularly Vito Acconci, the Austrian artist Valie Export and Joan Jonas, as well as Nam June Paik (Phelan 2001: 72), Rist has consistently challenged the spatial limit and frame of the video work. In approaching video, Rist emphasizes, 'I want to strip this dominating box of its conspicuous shape. I take it out of its context and plant it elsewhere' (Rist in Doswald 2001: 126). Extending Rist's focus on 'spaces within spaces', in which she notes, '[t]he moving picture' is 'itself is always a room within another room' (Rist in Obrist 2001: 26), many of Rist's single-channel tapes and gallery installations have reconfigured the visitor's spatial relationship with the monitor. For *3 Spitzen in den Westen, 3 Blicke in den Osten (3 Peaks to the West, 3 Views to the East)* (1992) and *Eine Spitze in den Westen – ein Blick in den Osten (A Peak into the West – A Look into the East)* (1992/9), Rist's installations required visitors to enter their head and shoulders into large, pyramidal architectural constructions projected from the gallery walls, so intervening into their encounter with the monitors and other visitors. For *Das Zimmer (The Room)* (1994/2000), 'an oversized couch and two large chairs made of hot pink Naughyde are arranged in the centre of a large room' (Phelan 2001: 67), Rist positions the visitor as child-size amid outsized furniture while a modest television is placed at floor level. Projection, too, has provided for a further elaboration of this extension of video space toward its site, as, Babias suggests, Rist has emphasized '[t]he viewer's confrontation with film as a bodily experience' (Babias 1996: 105). In a published conversation with the multi-media performance artist Laurie Anderson, on whom Rist's work has also drawn, Rist emphasizes:

> I like installations that really get you involved, that make you part of them, or that even work like a lullaby. When I do projections, I want people to go inside them so that colours, movement, pictures are reflected on their bodies.
>
> (Rist in Anderson and Rist 1996: 114)

In these contexts, *Open My Glade* extends Rist's interests in the 'spill' of projection, the blurring of 'video' into 'real' space. In Times Square, where, Rist suggests, 'physical space melts into virtual space', in being *screened off*, Rist *enters into* the virtual, architectural and 'real' site. Indeed, it is this potential collapse of the limits and separation of electronic media from the everyday social and architectural environment that underpins not only her modification of the monitor and its place, but many single-channel works. Such concerns are focused in a key single-channel tape, *(Entlastungen) Pipilotti's Fehler ([Absolutions] Pipilotti's Mistakes)* (1988), whose creation echoed Nam June Paik's interest in the unpredictable outcomes of the 'RCA-NSTC TV encoding system' (Paik in Ross 1993: 58). With particular relevance to this work, but speaking of her work as a whole, Rist has written:

> I work with video images that come out of improperly synchronized sequences, with shifts in the synchronization, when the image information is too fast or too slow. [. . .] I'm interested in the pictures that result when the RGB (red-blue-green) signal is out of synch [. . .]. I'm interested in feedback and generation losses, like colour noise and bleeds [. . .]. The faulty images reveal what is otherwise concealed.
>
> (Rist 2001: 108)

For *(Entlastungen)*, then, Rist compiled a series of 'the glitches and mis-cues of video transmissions' arising out of her work between 1986 and 1989, to produce a tape of 'all kinds of interference' (Phelan 2001: 47). The tape, Phelan argues, implicitly proposes that such images 'might offer clues to a kind of technological unconscious that can illuminate our own' (Phelan 2001: 41), so reflecting a breaking down of distinctions between Rist and 'her medium' whereby 'these supposedly faulty, chance images are like the pictures in my own subconscious' (Rist 2001: 108). In doing so, *(Entlastungen)* challenges the limits of 'video'. Here, the 'outside' of the medium, its 'exclusions', rush into the work, eliding distinctions between the 'proper' spaces of video composition and its distortions and failures. Here, like Studio Azzurro's projection 'into representation', Rist's work challenges video's separation from that which occurs 'around' it. By losing the body *in the video*, by reading the performance of self and site *into* the media, or in seeing the object 'gain ground' *in mediation*, these various practices bring video's spaces forward into the 'real spaces' of perception and action, into the 'social spaces' and the 'real time' of the viewer's activity.

Media Presence: Gary Hill's Projective Installations

Extending this, where Vito Acconci, Studio Azzurro and Pipilotti Rist have dramatized the divisions and reversals effected in mediations of body, object and site, the video artist Gary Hill has explored the performance of presence *in* meetings with the mediated image, an uncanny presence explicitly produced in representation. Ostensibly foregrounding *the image itself*, Hill's installations invariably begin in the projection of 'real-time' recordings that engage directly with the time and space of the visitor's looking. In *Viewer* (1996), for example:

> Slightly larger than life-size colour images of seventeen day labourers, facing out from a neutral background, are projected onto a wall, about 45 feet long, by five video projectors attached to the ceiling. [. . .] The men stand almost motionless, their movement limited to involuntary stirring – an incidental shuffling from foot to foot, slight movements of the hands, and almost imperceptible changes in facial expression. There is no interaction among them, each man standing quite alone and gazing out from the plane of projection toward the viewer.
>
> (Quasha and Stein 1997: 10)

Here, the 'performers' are explicitly met in their mediation: *fully visible* and *absent*. Running in a ten-minute continuous loop, and seemingly reflecting back to the visitor the attempt to apprehend through mediation, the *difference* of these images is asserted in their removal from the 'present' time and place, in *the fact* of recording. Yet, in this definitive removal of the recorded viewer, *Viewer* nevertheless works to upset the explicit 'distance' constructed in representations. Despite their evident projection, then, these images are presented in such a way as to suppress the apparatus of recording and reproduction. Emphasizing the viewer's 'encounter' with the viewed, these images thus evade any explicitly 'filmic' or fictional tropes and are projected seemingly 'unframed' onto the architecture of the room (Sans 1999: 72). In these recordings, originally composed separately and then composited together, Hill recalled, 'I wanted to avoid any notion of documentation' (Hill in Sans 1999: 72). Thus these projections recall and amplify Hill's direction of this real-time recording, in which, hired for an hour, each person

> was given the instruction to maintain eye contact with me – and the camera, which I was directly behind and in line with – for 20/30 minutes. The idea was not to stare *per se* but rather about two strangers making contact – viewing one another – being in a state of apprehending.
>
> (Hill in Sans 1999: 72)

In such projections, too, Hill notes, 'I want the body – literally and metaphorically – in your face' (Hill in Sans 1999: 73), in accordance with a key tension running through significant aspects of his work. In this respect, Hill notes, 'physicality has always been an important element [. . ..] and in many cases it questions conceptual structures used to make work and undermines the cognitive aspect by a sheer visceral presence' (Hill in Sans 1999: 71). In this context, too, Hill's work reflects a 'debt to Minimal art' and, Robert C. Morgan argues, a concomitant emphasis on the phenomenology of seeing (Morgan 2000: 8). Consistently with this, Hill accounts for his projective work in its activation of the 'real' space of viewing, noting that '[t]hese are works which activate a space in which the viewer is enfolded into the work and actively participates in self-conscious questions about viewing and being viewed' (Hill in Sans 1999: 71). In this context, such 'physicality' is found not simply *in the image*, which in any case emphasizes *flatness, immateriality*, but in this 'structure of experience' expressed in the projected image's effect on the time and space of viewing itself and, in this context, its subversion of its own removal in representation. In such video work, Hill remarks,

> the play with sculpture is very present, but even more so is the play on the word 'projection'. These are literally video projections and at the same time they are projecting out a certain look, perhaps a desire – any number of emotions. And we 'project' our view back to the projection and amongst ourselves in a space that continually inflects these words in many directions.
>
> (Hill in Sans 1999: 73)

In this space, then, Hill's projections create a paradoxical opening up to the viewer's 'performance', in which the image's *taking time*, but removal from *this time*, invites 'projection'. Here, the 'real' time of viewing becomes the measure of *Viewer*'s operation, even as the two-dimensionality of the image emphasizes its *being present elsewhere*. In their documentation of *Viewer*, George Quasha and Charles Stein recall:

> When we came into the room what we happened upon was *the view*. A room with a view, *inside*. The view is people looking *out* from where they are, in to where we are, here, in the middle of the space. It seems, perplexingly, that the view itself is viewing – viewing us [. . .]. In an environment that is saturated with viewing, at a certain point it's as though the space itself views – a topological displacement of agency.
>
> (Quasha and Stein 2001: 18)

It is a displacement of 'agency' amplified in the *particularities* of viewing that *Viewer* represents, as its presentation of the specificities and idiosyncrasies of 'looking' produce a simulation of *an exchange of view* between the recorded and the live. Quasha and Stein note:

> In *Viewer* the projection of the seventeen figures is very sharply focused (from an optimal distance, which is not close up to the

3.4 **GARY HILL.** *Standing Apart*, **1996 –DETAILS.** Two-channel video installation. **COURTESY DONALD YOUNG GALLERY, CHICAGO**.

wall). And as one engages this concrete focus, there is a personal charge relative to each of the men as one views it discretely; this is a human focus, a kind of individuation of attention. Then there is the *interactive focus*, by which we mean the phenomenon of focusing on the image of this *other* person in such a way that we ourselves seem to *get focused* [. . .]. This in turn produces a *field focus*, activating the whole of the viewing space, so that the shared sense enlarges and the other figures come alive in new ways.

(Quasha and Stein 2001: 22, original emphasis)

Such perceived interactivity, in which *Viewer*'s invitation to the visitors to 'project' their 'view' over this real-time recording, shifts subtly toward the double movement perceived in 'aura': the sense of 'distance', however close something may be. Thus, *Viewer* emphatically asserts the *difference* and *distance* between the spaces and times of viewer and viewed, yet in doing so creates a simulated interactivity that may seem to bring this image *closer*. Here, then, *Viewer*'s gesture of 'looking' plays on the visitor's

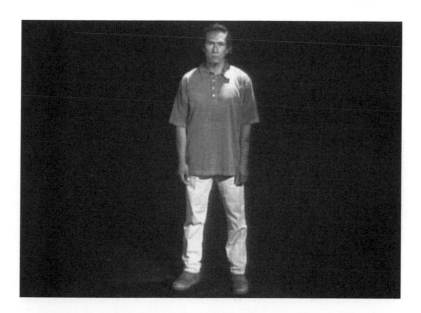

3.5 GARY HILL. *Standing Apart*, **1996 –DETAILS.** Two-channel video installation. **COURTESY DONALD YOUNG GALLERY, CHICAGO**.

perception of 'presence': '[t]o perceive the aura of an object', Benjamin notes, 'is to invest it with the ability to look at us in return' (Pearson and Shanks 2001: 95). Consistently with this, and with the dissonance of multi-media, Hill observes video's production of 'a reflexive space of difference' (Vischer 1995: 14), its 'capacity of having a presence and a distance at the same time' (Hill in Vischer 1995: 9). In these circumstances, Quasha and Stein suggest, the 'performance' of *Viewer* lies in the visitor's awareness and activation of the *space before* the projection, for '[t]he real 'event' is the performative space itself – a site, the very declaration of which allows the complex awareness of an engaged viewer. The event is an emerging awareness' (Quasha and Stein 2001: 24).

Where *Viewer* emphasizes this spatial complexity, *Standing Apart* (1996) (see Figures 3.4 and 3.5) approaches a further *division of the image*, in an extension of Acconci's sense that 'the television "shoots" images into the viewer: the viewer functions as screen' (Acconci 2001b: 374). Challenging the ability of the viewer to *stand apart* from 'its' projec-tion, *Standing Apart*, and its companion installation *Facing Faces* (1996)

3.6 **GARY HILL.** *Facing Faces*, **1996 –DETAILS.** Two-channel video installation. **COURTESY DONALD YOUNG GALLERY, CHICAGO**.

(see Figures 3.6 and 3.7), enmesh the viewer into their time-structure
while amplifying the doubling and division of the sign. Here, then, Hill
presents the viewers with another mirroring of their own looking, as,
in approaching *Standing Apart*, the visitors find themselves standing at
the apex of a triangle defined by asymmetrical but seemingly identical
projected images, while, for *Facing Faces*, the visitors encounter a doubled
portrait of the same figure on monitors installed, similarly, at head height.
Standing Apart, Hill notes,

> involves two separate (slightly larger than life) colour images of the
> same man projected onto two separate walls that meet at the
> corner [. . .] the effect is that one image seems to gaze out directly
> at the viewer, while at the same time, the second figure is looking
> at the first figure. About every two minutes the images switch
> positions: the second figure now gazes straight out at the viewer,
> while the first figure gazes at the second.

> (Gary Hill Studio 2002)

3.7 **GARY HILL.** *Facing Faces*, **1996 –DETAILS.** Two-channel video installation. **COURTESY DONALD YOUNG GALLERY, CHICAGO**.

Although mirroring the viewer's viewing, *Standing Apart* introduces
a disunity and multiplication into the experience of seeing and being
seen. First, the installation articulates the complexity of 'recording', as
the 'real-time' recording of the figure is played back in the 'real time'
of the viewer's looking. In this respect, *Standing Apart* plays on and
amplifies the paradox of 'real-time' recording. Thus, Hill points out, the
very meeting with such recordings renders the present time complex, as
the encounter 'happens in "the present" but the present has now gained
a complexity that quite literally includes the replayed past' (Quasha and
Stein 2000: 258). For Quasha and Stein, this complexity is amplified
in the apparent 'presentness' of the figures themselves, which calls into
question the capacity of the viewer to stand apart from the past it replays.
In this piece, they suggest, '[t]he time of the portrait is truly *other* to the
time of the viewing' and yet in the encounter 'this life-size projection of
a living, breathing entity imposes a time of its own which is unrelated to
the static time of portraiture [. . .]. Its time becomes our time as we view it

[. . .]. We are aroused to the intrinsic movement of being here – and being *there*' (Quasha and Stein 1997: 34–5). Here, too, the viewer's awareness of *acting out*, in the 'present tense', 'other' times is further amplified in the projected figures' relationship to each other, as the viewer's act and time of looking is re-enacted in their simultaneous and alternating attention. In these ways, *Standing Apart* engages with time-structures that are neither unified, singular nor simply *in* the present tense, as the experience or awareness of the 'acting out' of *other* times becomes part of the fabric of the work.

In *Viewer* and *Standing Apart*, the quality of 'being present' appears as a paradoxical effect of this multiplication: a presence performed *in* the absence of the figure; in the *acting out* of the 'past' times in the 'real time' of looking. As a result, these projective installations emphasize a phenomenon of closeness, however distant the figure is *seen* to be. It is a closeness that reflects upon and amplifies the media's transportation of vision: its claim to *presentness*, even as it foregrounds the divisions and differences in which it functions. Here, too, 'aura' becomes resurgent in the media, a 'mediaura' linked to the character and functioning of transmission, and mediation, itself. In this context, Weber concludes:

> What is condemned in the age of technical reproducibility is not
> aura as such but the aura of art as a work of representation, a work
> that would have its fixed place, that would take its place in and as a
> world-picture. What remains is the *mediaura* of an apparatus
> whose glance takes up everything and gives nothing back, except
> perhaps in the blinking of an eye.
>
> (Weber, 1996: 107, original emphasis)

Indeed, what is condemned 'in the age of technical reproducibility' is the uncontested 'location', the 'proper place' of the undivided object. In turn, *Viewer* and *Standing Apart* reflect this mobility, this articulation of locations and places. Thus, Quasha and Stein note, in its emphasis on difference and distance, *Viewer* appears to traverse 'real' and 'mediated' spaces:

No one's fooled when a video projector casts the image of a person upon the wall – and yet, it has its own reality, its own *intensity of view*. What shows up in this hypersensualized space is how these quite simple and ordinary people, whose living and breathing images are projected on the wall, are in fact quite powerful presences – unavoidably engaging and almost eerily present presences. Yet they are merely projections.

(Quasha and Stein 1997: 19, original emphasis)

Like the 'auratic object' which presents itself as 'more than what it is' (Pearson and Shanks 2001: 95), Hill's projections do not simply 'mediate' 'presence', for presence is not an 'originary point', an authentic or autonomous quality to be depleted in its reproduction and repetition. Indeed, where 'presence' is always already performed in the *space of difference*, in the divisions of the sign, so *Viewer*'s uncanny 'presence' is staged in the divisions of *aura*: as a presence *seen* in the division of the sign; in the repetition of the same *in difference*. Yet such a construction or performance of presence in mediation presents immediate consequences for the 'real' viewer. Indeed, where *Standing Apart* questions the visitor's capacity to separate themselves from their sense of this projected figure's 'being there', so this installation questions the 'presence' and integrity of the 'real' self whose view it mirrors.

CONFIDENTIAL REPORT ON AN INTERACTIVE EXPERIENCE

Tavoli, perché queste mani mi toccano?
(Tables – Why Are These Hands Touching Me?) (1995)

Interactive video environment, "Oltre il villaggio globale,"
Palazzo dell'Arte, Milan Triennial Exhibition.

Six tables, six virtually still figures – a woman lying down,
a fly buzzing on the tabletop, a drop of water obsessively
falling into a basin. This feeling of apparent calm is suddenly
disrupted when anyone touches the image – it reacts, it is
triggered, and a small part of its story unfolds.
The relationship between real and virtual is tested on
everyday materials, with no form of technological 'interface' –
the spaces are broken up, virtual and physical reality become
one. The meaning of this work is couched in the image's shift
from being a simple object of contemplation to becoming a
direct source of experience that impels the spectator to
interact with it.

In late 1994, after over 12 years of
experimentation in the field of artistic
expression and new technologies that had
reached fruition in works such as "The
garden of things" (*Il Giardino delle cose*)
and "The journey"(*Il Viaggio*), Studio
Azzurro embarked on a new line of artistic
research centered on the theme of
interactivity. The occasion for undertaking
this new endeavor was presented by the

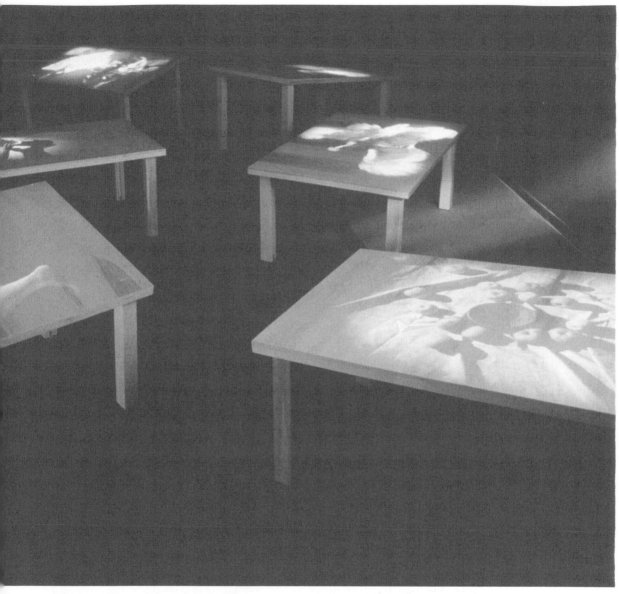

exhibition "Beyond the Global Village" (*Oltre il villaggio globale*), part of the Triennial Expo in Milan, where we presented "Tables - why are these hands touching me?" (*Tavoli - perché queste mani mi toccano?*).

In what follows, therefore, I propose some considerations based on this experience with the aim of addressing a number of intentionally disjointed concepts, some of which are inevitably linked to our artistic experimentation while others are expressed as a doubt or a question, and, in the process, to open them up to a larger discussion. This explains the choice to present this report as a sort of confidential communication, necessarily distant from the peremptory, definitive tone of a "manifesto."

1° INTRODUCTION

Interactivity has always been around; one could even say that it is the basis of human knowledge. But never before have we had at our disposal instruments and devices so sophisticated as to make things so completely changeable and interchangeable.

It could be said that in recent years we have gone from material that is fluid and unstoppable, the extreme condition of "looking at" something of which TV is the perfect symbol, to a material which is more malleable, more open to a condition of "letting itself be touched." The vast expanse of the communication and information horizon is developing in this direction, and not always with the noble aims of increasing people's participation, making systems more democratic, or

Coro (Choir) (1995)

Interactive video environment in two parts,
Mole Antonelliana.

A foot steps on a figure trampling it – it reacts, it moves, and
lets out a shout. Various feet cross a space, trampling many
figures that break up, raise their voices. Gradually a 'choir' is
brought to life through the movement of the bodies. In the
centre of the space there is a partially unrolled piece of felt,
a kind of large carpet – the projected images form a weave
that seems to replace the symbols and images found in a
traditional carpet decoration. The carpet as nomad territory,
as a meeting place, as a status symbol for secular or spiritual
power, all this is overlain with a new cosmography of inert
bodies that are ready to react as we pass, a metaphor for a
world order that is always being trampled on by the feet of
those in power.

simply responding to the needs of people,
who for too long have remained inert and
passive. Interactivity, then, opens up large
and serious questions which, once again,
need to be addressed from the exclusive
point of view of art. At the same time,
however, interactivity represents a great
opportunity to re-open a dialogue with the
general public, which in recent times has
seemed more and more estranged from

Totale della battaglia (Battle Overview) (1996)

Interactive video environment, "Luoghi di guerra in tempo di pace" Baluardo S. Paolino, Lucca.

This video environment, based on the 'battle of San Romano' by Paolo Uccello starts out as a set of pieces that has not yet been put together. It is the eye of the beholder that is free to decide the course the images will take. The two corridors, lined with a series of video-projections lead to a central area, where a truly spectacular setting has been installed. The scene is completed by the projection of a new overview of the battle. On entering the setting the spectator hears voices resounding, that inevitably lead him on – a succession of calls, screams, and clapping of hands starts up. The images called up by the sounds emerge from the water, the land, the leaves, with the spectator becoming the leading actor in the event.

contemporary art. An indifference that has imposed high costs on both parties: self-referential isolation for the artist, a decline of culture and sensitivity for the public.

Interactivity reopens a dialogue, recognizing that a process of creation or of information is not complete without the assumption of responsibility on the part of the user who is no longer just a spectator but a producer of an experience. The user is not asked to participate only in a predefined narration but to "explore" and to "realize" in time, in space, in matter, the potential of a work/event. This leads to a new sense of responsibility: that of artists who, having in mind a counterpart of this kind, are conscious that they are not merely designing a work of art but eliciting behaviors, gestures, reactions which will push them into confrontation with the delicate questions of ethics and even beyond to modern conceptions of anthropology. Interactive artists also know that they can lose control over the work itself, which necessarily changes form as a result of the interaction that they establish, but which must nevertheless maintain its meaning, the fruit of a deep process of ideation and design.

2° PROJECT HORIZONS
We wanted to address the problem of interactivity through a project, within an horizon of meaning, in order to avoid being pulled along by new necessities dictated by technological evolution.

We achieved our objective, trying to maintain continuity with our previous experience with video environments, by keeping two points clearly in mind: to create spaces for collective use and to use natural interfaces. Both of these elements were to concur in the formulation of a narrative hypothesis that had to be more than a simple exhibition of the device. Not a machine that narrates itself, but a machine that narrates.

3° SENSITIVE ENVIRONMENTS
The first meaning of our definition of "sensitive environments" is social space; contexts in which the interactive act is not confined to the individual dimension, as is unfortunately the case with most of these systems (one person engages in dialogue with the machine, others, if any, are limited to looking on). Contexts in which the dialogue with the machine is associated with an ongoing exchange, even a complicitous one, between the other people involved (a number of people participate in the interaction with the device while at the same time maintaining contact among themselves, an exchange and comparison of their reactions and sensibilities).

4° NATURAL INTERFACES
Trying to form relationships through simple interfaces, user-friendly systems beyond the realm of utilitarian interfaces like the mouse, the keyboard, data gloves or all the other devices that are tied to a technological reading of relationships. It's much better if our sensitive environments are without even so much as the shadow of an electric wire. This allows us to get a clearer view, not of technology, but of its effects, and allows for a more effective relationship between the immaterial world of images and sounds and the material world of the objects and spaces with which the work is completed. This creates the necessary conditions to reach a synaesthetic relationship not only among the different senses but also among their virtual replicas and extensions. (To touch the density of an image or the texture of wooden *Tables*, for example). "Natural interfaces," as we have defined them, which do not make use of symbolic systems, contribute to the fostering of actions and reactions that are pre-logical, instinctive, and which can be compared subsequently with more rational responses.

5° WOVEN NARRATIVES
The story, an ineluctable form of comprehension of the real world and, as such, a primary subject of artistic research, tends to assume a new and more complex physiognomy. Shedding the linear and didactic features of known forms, narrative is free to unfold in the parallel flow of the scenes and in the complex relationships among components.
No longer appearing in the guise of the single driving force represented by the literary or figurative or musical component, narrative becomes the warp and woof

generated by the interweaving of these and other forms. Vibrations, overlappings, oscillations, contrasts will be the backbone of this new narrative form. And it goes without saying that the viewer (whom we will have to learn to define in some other way) will have a fundamental role in identifying the wide range of possible variations.

6° FREEING THE IMAGE FROM ITS ARMOR

For a long time we used monitors arranged in various ways to try and free the visual image from confinement within the dimensions of a standard TV screen. The signal, passing synchronically from one monitor to another, broke out of the dimensions of the single screen, enlarging its field of play. Now, through the use of video projection, images are able to wander in space, free from their technological armor, displaying themselves against any number of material backdrops. Figures can now move about without frames, outside of the abstract, illuminated perimeters of cinema-scopes; but also outside of the conventional frame of the shot, positioning themselves on a variety of surfaces, carving out new niches for themselves from which to communicate.

To a certain extent, this condition may better represent that subtle and often invisible intertwining of real and virtual experience that exists in daily life as well as in the world of our imagination.

7° PICTORIAL MATERIALS

The projection of images onto wood or a carpet, which gradually fill up with prints, exalts the materiality which is so characteristic of the art of painting; the

Il Giardino delle anime (The Garden of Souls) (1997)

Interactive video environment (permanent installation).
New Metropolis, Science and Technology Center, Amsterdam.
From 2001, New York Hall of Science.

An expanse of electronic water. Something, very soon, is
bound to happen. While the feet continue to stick to the
watery surface, it moves, ripples, lights up, and a figure starts
to take shape among the little waves. This is a birth. The
images, like virtual twins of real bodies, come to life following
a narrative structure that harks back to the myth of Theseus
and Ariadne. The bodies re-emerge, perform their actions and
stop, awaiting another passage. Thus the dance of steps
begins, respectful, careful, and gradually becoming more and
more hurried and fretful. The music envelops the space and
the spectator in a wave of changing and intermingling sounds.

warmth of this medium and the pleasure
associated with a technique that has
played such a large role in the history of
art is in some way recovered. The images,
which move from the electronic and
"ascetic" to distribute their pixels onto
well-known surfaces, become more
familiar, they make us want to touch them,
to paint them. On many occasions we
have observed reactions which do not
distinguish the real from the immaterial
world; and not merely because of some
illusory trompe-l'oeil effect.

8° PLAYFUL ADVENTURES
Play is an intrinsic component of all forms
of interactivity, even the most archaic. This
enjoyment component may sound like a
synonym for superficial; naively falling into
the rules of a pre-programmed game. But
since we all know how to play, what it
really means is learning through
simulation to compose an experience by
way of an imaginary adventure. Just

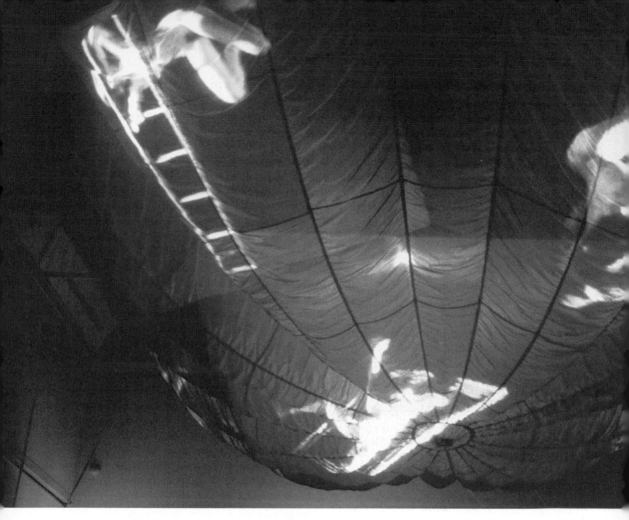

observe a child and you'll realize how it works. Play is a threshold of access. As such, it must lead you through layers of increasing complexity, where the rules you gradually come to know offer an extraordinary freedom of interpretation.

9° RELATION AND REACTION
Interactivity refers not just to a mechanism but to a relationship between its active parts. So it is not merely the complexity of the mechanism or its sophistication that are determinative, although we must recognize the catalyzing power of certain instruments and their capacity for generating interrelationships, but also their ability to produce a spark of intelligence, of that sensitivity that is created in the triangulation of system, person, and narrative. From this

point of view, it is not sufficient to define a relationship, even one between person and machine, by a series of predictable questions and answers. The relationship must be open to all possibilities.

10° SYMBOLIC SYSTEM
We often talk about technological instruments, language, devices in terms of new equipment to be added to the range of traditional tools. A computer is really not all that different from a paintbrush or a wrench. Such affirmations mask a deeper reality. The new instruments have a level of active intelligence which is incomparable to that contained even in the otherwise noble tradition of the paintbrush. It may be a pre-packaged intelligence, but it is no less active for that. If you don't "use" them,

Il Soffio sull'angelo (primo naufragio del pensiero)
(The Breeze of an Angel: thought's first wreckage) (1997)

Interactive video installation. Sala Fibonacci,
Pisa University, Pisa.

Three large parachutes, like clouds on which strange airy
figures float – angels, maybe, fallen from favor through
some misbehavior. These earthly figures are outlined, yet
hollow within – this is why they float in the air trying to grab
hold of objects, to hang on to them like shipwrecks clinging
to the floating debris. It seems as if all is couched in seeming
calm until the spectator's blowing doesn't reach the
parachute - it blows up and pitches the angel out of its
opaque fluidity, the angel's empty equilibrium could
explode or be blown far away. The parachute – a means of
survival – comes to life with many sounds: some soft,
modulated, sweet puffings, others fierce mechanical blasts.

these instruments are capable of "using
you," through their pre-arranged formulas
and ready-to-work programs. It could be
said that rather than instruments, they
amount to a system, a system of thought.
Just as an example, the role of interactive
technology in contemporary society could
be compared, despite its radically different
content, to the role played by perspective
in the Renaissance era. Has anyone ever
thought of perspective as a mere
instrument? It has been more appropriately
defined by some as a "symbolic system," a
system which contains within itself a way
of interpreting, conceiving, and
determining the reality of an era. The
instruments, the languages and the devices
of technology form a symbolic system that
determines a new point of view (or
point of life) from which to observe a
reality that they themselves, in a decisive
way, have helped to change.

11°   POINT OF LIFE

We are losing that sense of dominance
that was given to us by so-called point of
view, the glance that distances reality and
arranges it into a logical pattern, a
reassuring geometry. Interactivity projects
us inside representation, upsets the
geometry, excludes an authoritarian center,
triggers a dynamic of continuous
transformation; a point of life, as De
Kerchove has called it. It represents, in the
end, the scary need to move beyond the
illusion of seeing yourself in control to the
emotion of losing yourself in the chaos.
"Getting lost" is an essential feature of the
contemporary human condition, which can
foster a renewed capacity for "re-finding
yourself" or for "recognizing yourself" in
certain old and new values.

12° BRINGING THE WORK OF ART INTO HUMAN GESTURE

We have the impression that we are at the
end of the era initiated by Duchamp and

The Cenci (1997)

Musical composed by Giorgio Battistelli, Almeida Theatre, London.

The projected images of a video narrative that runs parallel to the words and actions of the actors, break up and move over the large cross-like area, which has become a stage. At times the images interact with the words and action, at other times they contradict them. The projected images act as a visual counterpoint that does not attempt to explain the text but rather to open it up to different interpretations and comparisons, that may help to get the audience involved to the point of inducing them to climb onto the cross at the end and interactively search for their own vision. All of this is set against a musical environment that imparts a narrative power, an expressive force that is able to take the words from the actor's mouths and spread them around the room, in the form of sounds, until they come into contact with the spectators' lips.

his ready-made works; his objects yanked out of the rituals of everyday life and provocatively sent away to the sacred atmosphere of an art gallery. The process now underway appears to be inverse; to try and bring the work of art, the artistic artifice toward human gesture, to set artistic experience amidst the behavior of its viewers, to move closer to their worlds. The term viewers, especially from this perspective, is certainly inappropriate; one should speak of co-authors.

13° DIFFERENCE AND CONVERGENCE

It would seem that the conditions have been created for conceiving the "Absolute Artwork," but we are more and more convinced that this utopian vision of the harmonious mixing of multiple artistic languages is really inappropriate, especially insofar as it restores the idea of the definitive and defining work of art; a polyphony of instruments intoning the same sublime aria.

This is not the time for that. We find much more convincing a position which posits the autonomy of the various media that concur in creation, media that come together to find points of convergence and areas of overlapping, but without neglecting their differences. In fact, it is precisely these non-homogeneous processes that create the pre-conditions for open and participatory narration. The very definition of "multi-media" itself may be interpreted in the same way; the parallel flow of different inputs, old and new, crossing, overlapping, clashing, and moving away from one another.

14° AN ECOLOGY OF DISAPPEARANCE

All works strictly tied to the contemporary technologies have a "contingent" character. Rarely, if ever, are they able to deposit themselves in a condition of physical permanence. Once the period of

their being on display has ended, they close back up into data, laser disks, or magnetic tape and end up being placed in some archive, in the hope of being pulled out again for some other occasion. They live, they exist, when they are being used, whether as a single edition or reproduced simultaneously into a large number of copies. The concept of the original work expires in favor of a new interpretation of "the work of art in an era of reproduction" called for by Benjamin. Not a work of art that is reproduced ad infinitum, multiplying its presence, but a work that is absent and reappears on request.

15° BETWEEN ACTION AND CONTEMPLATION

All of this stuff involved in this way of "acting," of "being there," inevitably conditions our whole way of thinking and the way we design our projects; we find ourselves involved more and more in itineraries that are interactive. But it may be well to specify that this dimension of action stands before, but not in opposition to, the dimension of contemplation. Even better, we could say that the two concepts are perfectly complementary and necessary to each other.

We are now moving out of a time which frustrated both these perceptive conditions: the entire information flow has been moving in our direction, towards us, and it has crashed into us. We have never had to force ourselves to move towards things. They have come into our homes, through simulation systems. We have lived a "state of seeing and knowing" estranged from our experience. All this has led to a state of passivity and inertia; conditions which are appropriate neither to a dimension of interactivity nor to one of contemplation. Now, interactivity, the art of acting and being there, may reopen the possibility of seeing at more of a distance, a glance

Dove va tutta'sta gente?
(Where Are All these People Going?) (2000)

Interactive video installation, Festival Vision Ruhr, Dortmund.

In the techno-global and interethnic village of the year 2000, the boundaries of renewed separatism abound. The dividing line between natural and artificial, between the real and the virtual world is shifting. In this work three automatic glass doors meet the spectator, opening wide, welcoming thresholds unopposed to any external presence. But on the other side of the glass screens the video-projected figures are moving frantically, smacking into the solid barriers erected by a different yet seductive culture that does not envisage the sharing of privileges. The interactive device takes its cue from the complexity of human relationships and the installation space is transformed into an "anthropological place," in which the opening and closing movements do not always occur as expected.

suspended in the depth of the senses. A double way of living things, of perceiving them, of inhabiting them.

16° RESPONSIBILITY
Over the years we have got more and more used to considering the "audience" as an abstract entity. People have become data, categories, percentages, ticket sales.

In the process of trying to trigger interactive narratives, observing user reactions and behaviors, almost as if we were involved in a little experiment of contemporary anthropology, we have rediscovered the condition of being fond of our "audience," of thinking of them as flesh and blood, and taking them into account, not as customers, but as people, with their own individual faces, their own souls, with the right to create an experience or to refuse to do so, to express themselves in their own way, to sculpt their own narratives.

This makes us feel the burden of a great responsibility: the realization that our projects involve, not only a work of art, but

also the behavior and actions of such highly differentiated personalities.

17° DESIRES

Interactivity has a potential for provoking short-circuits that could turn out to be dangerous. Once the expressive aspects exalted by the spread of interactive technologies (CD-ROM, Internet-type networks, video on demand, intelligent objects, etc.) are harnessed to the statistical sciences (which express themselves today in public opinion surveys, audience and market shares, etc.) it will be possible to measure in real time the

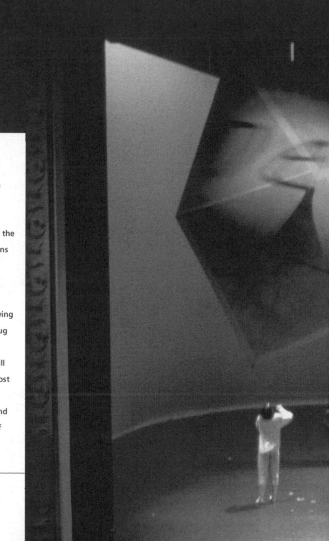

Wer möchte wohl Kaspar Hauser sein (2000)

Dance and video performance, choreography by Daniela Kunz Oper Theater Nüernberg.

An extremely subjective point of view that accompanies the fall from one point to the end point. The video projections project images that seem to belong to the world of children, with a touch of surrealism, an excess of reality, that make them feel alienated. Brightly colored elementary figures that acquire shape in the light following their long periods in darkness. In darkness Kaspar has dug his own world made up of small events, populated by insects and fluorescent animals. But this happy world will soon be filled by the most pompous conventions, the most treacherous rituals to such an extent that a distortion is produced. A data glove moves the images in real time and makes them interact with the dancers, seeking a form of dialogue that appears to respect all freedom but on the contrary becomes imposition.

reactions, the temperature, and the mood of an entire people. It may, finally, be possible to transform our social listeners or viewers into a kind of sensitive terminal, deceiving them into believing they are participating in a process of choice.

Desire is to be considered as an instrument of culture, not of mathematics, to be titillated whenever possible by the art of the unexpected.

18° EXPERIENTIAL WORKS

Interactive systems foster and conclusively define the shift, already in progress for some time in contemporary art, from the representation phase to the experiential phase. It is evident that these devices, this quest for relation, these narrative modes must function, first and foremost, as triggers of experiential processes. There is a real demand for movement in this direction; the reality that we are living is an already constituted reality, not least because of the overwhelming expansion of communicative instruments, of elements of representation, of induced images, of passively assimilated patterns of logic. This situation has created a need to find a way of reactivating this dead material. Works of

art that make use of technological devices can satisfy this need in part. They can act as laboratories for the generation of experiential prototypes, conducting experiments in the alchemy of reality and virtuality. They claim as their objective the emergence of the positive, poetic aspects of each individual personality.

19° RULES AND RANDOMNESS

In the face of the evident expansion of expressive possibilities one tends to forget the rules which govern them. When everything is possible, and often this has been the creed of a certain post-modernist conception, there is reason to think that there are no limits and no danger of falling into traps. In the technological dimension these signals of omnipotence and unlimited freedom are frequent. It is easy to forget that it is the very nature of the material itself that gives rise to very strict and calculated limitations.

The dimension of technological media can, on the other hand, lead to an excess of rationality, calculation, and inhibition. The complexity and the high cost of certain types of equipment can lead to exaggerated planning that squashes the

Tamburi a sud (Drums to the south) (2001)

Interactive video installation presented to the ICC on the occasion of the show dedicated to Studio Azzurro "Embracing Interactive Art" (Chorus and drums), ICC, Tokyo.

The installation is made up of four membranes or hides of approximately two meters in diameter, similar to large drums placed in one of the exhibition halls of the Museum. By beating each drum and interacting with the video-projected hands that appear on the surface, one may send the objects that materialize on the drum to a series of e-mail addresses. Anyone receiving the e-mail, a small hand that opens and offers a symbolic image, may log onto this site and send a small written message or a drawing of an object of their own choosing that somehow corresponds to the meaning of what they have received. This drum signalling that returns to its place of origin can help us integrate and shape the installation itself.

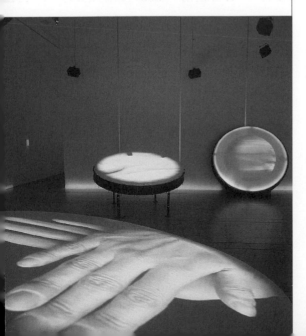

component of chance and randomness, of that confrontation with the unexpected that has always been a rich resource of artistic media. Interactivity can foster randomness, if it is thought of as an open dialogue in which there is not necessarily a one-to-one correspondence between questions and answers. It can elicit the unexpected, if there is complete respect for each of the participants in the process. These dialogues can be stimulated by the artist's work but they should not be planned; they must be allowed to flow between the parties' respective uncertainties, including those of the machines, that can become confused, forget, break down.

20° ET CETERA, ET CETERA

This point, whose provisional nature is evident from the title, was suggested to me by a complex work dedicated to Giacomo Leopardi and, more specifically, from some of his writings which I consulted in the preparation phase. I was struck by the naturalness, decidedly anti-academic, with which the poet makes use of ellipses or formulations like "etc. etc." to support his ideas, to accelerate his thoughts, to leave some space to the reader, to highlight the ductility and the instability of the material which is the object of some of his reflections. These blank spaces, these literary fadeouts, subtract nothing from the grandeur of his ideas, nothing from the refinement of his thought. On the contrary, they add a dark side in which we can find space to add our own modest interpretations. I would like to conclude this report by fading out in this, dare I say, interactive way, just to emphasize that this complex and still developing subject also has its dark side, still waiting to be discovered.

By Paolo Rosa
(Translated from the Italian by Gregory Conti)

Multiplying Media

Language and media seem natural partners and enemies. My interest is in their co-existence, their frictions and the humans caught in between.

(Jesurun 1993: 66)

Since the mid-1970s, and following the close link between video art, video installation and performance, the implication of the media's division of presence, action, place and representation has been integrated into overtly theatrical practices. Exploring relationships between live action, text, media, language and perception, this multi-media theatre has been associated in New York with the innovations of the Wooster Group, Laurie Anderson, John Jesurun, as well as Yvonne Rainer, Ping Chong, Meredith Monk and, more recently, The Builders Association. In Europe, the Italian post-avant-garde theatre exemplified by Mario Martone and Falso Movimento from 1979, Giorgio Barberio Corsetti's series of collaborations with Studio Azzurro from 1985 and, more recently, the performance company Motus has addressed the implications of media and mediation for understandings of history, narrative, text and site (Giannachi and Kaye 2002). In the UK, the performance company Forced Entertainment has established an extensive body of work in media-based theatre, installation and performance addressing the constructed nature of role, identity and place. Such developments have been broadly associated with a 'postmodern' performance characterized by quotation, appropriation, displacement (Auslander 1992; Kaye 1994) and a critique of the presence of the performer linked to deconstruction. Yet in its engagement with mediation, this multi-media theatre has also come to be concerned with the resurgence of that which media transforms: with the reassertion of 'presence', even as the conventional means of asserting the performer's 'place' and 'authority' are dispersed; with the convergence of media, performance and language, even as the theatre multiplies the means and channels of address; and with the return of narrative and role, even as the dissonance and *differences* of the media set 'character' and 'narrative' apart from themselves. It is a development reflected, in particular, in three generations of theatre practitioners: in the Wooster Group's definition of an explicitly multi-media practice grounded in their transformation of the 'Performance Theatre' (Bigsby 1985) of the late 1960s and early 1970s; in John Jesurun's exploration, from 1982, of converges and slips between electronic media, live performance and language; and in The Builders Association's reassertion of narrative through the divisions and multiplications of an explicitly media-based theatre.

Multiplication: The Wooster Group

Under the direction of Elizabeth LeCompte, the Wooster Group's theatre work has come to exemplify an overtly multi-medial practice articulated in distinct and simultaneous channels of address. 'Working', James Leverett proposes, 'at the point where the lens and the stage interact, contradict, complement, even interchange' (Leverett in Letzler Cole 1992: 91), an interweaving of 'live' and 'mediated' modes of work has become integral to their working methods, in which, Euridice Arratia notes in recording the company's preparations for *Brace Up!* (1991),

> the live performance, the mediated performance, and the sound
> score are developed simultaneously [. . .]. Monitors, video cameras,
> and Christopher Kondek, the video operator, are at all rehearsals.
> As [Jim] Clayburgh worded it, 'Since *Route 1&9* [1981],
> microphones and video monitors have been like performers, part
> of the company.'
>
> (Arratia 1992: 127)

The place of film and video in the Wooster Group's work has its roots in the company's earliest practices. Emerging out of Spalding Gray and Elizabeth LeCompte's development, with other members of the Performance Group, of the *Rhode Island Trilogy* (1975–8), the Wooster Group's first performances signalled a departure from the politics and aesthetics of a 'Performance Theatre' (Bigsby 1985) exemplified by the Living Theatre and the Performance Group itself. Led by Richard Schechner, and originating from his encounter with Grotowski's 'Poor Theatre' (Schechner in Kaye 1996: 174) in New York in 1967, the Performance Group's focus on the 'authenticity' of the performer's commitment, experience and 'presence' *in* performance also responded to the innovations and politics of the Living Theatre, the theatrical implications of happenings and John Cage's re-conception of music and theatre (Schechner 1969). Here, more specifically, Schechner sought to create an 'Environmental Theatre' (Schechner 1973) in which the performance of text would become subject to the personal, social and theatrical dynamics operating variously between performers and spectators. Yet, while the Wooster Group's exploration of framing, intertextuality, mediation and paradox has been taken to effect a deconstruction of Schechner's and others' attempts, in the context of 1960s' counter-cultural theatrical practice, to address the 'presence' of audience and performer (Auslander 1997), the Group's multi-media practices have also articulated a complex and equivocal response to this approach to the 'real' act of theatre or performance.

Evolved, initially, out of improvisation workshops led by Gray, the *Trilogy*'s departure from the 'psychological exploration' that, he recalled, 'had led to so much of The Performance Group productions' (Gray 1978: 87), was prompted in part by the theatrical responses to 'minimalism' which had emerged in 1967 and 1968 in work by Robert Wilson and Richard Foreman. *Sakonnet Point* (1975), which developed out of the Group's first informal workshops, thus followed Gray's exploration of dance improvisation with the postmodern choreographer Kenneth King and his participation in 'open evenings' of improvisation with Robert Wilson's loosely knit group, the Byrd Hoffmann School of Byrds (Gray 1978: 87). Taking shape in LeCompte's explicitly formal re-framing of Gray's 'personal-abstract improvisation movement', 'gestures', that, he recalled, 'grew directly out of our encounter with the theatre space' (Gray 1978: 87), the performance developed ostensibly in a meditation on aspects of Gray's childhood, yet emphasized the formal process of making the theatre piece. *Rumstick Road* (1977), the second part of the trilogy, emerged, in contrast, as a 'play' (Gray and LeCompte 1978) created in response to objects, recordings and dramatic elements connected to Gray's childhood, including taperecorded conversations with Gray family members and his mother's psychiatrist. Emphasizing the theatrical manipulation and re-framing of 'original' material, *Rumstick Road* re-presented ostensibly 'private' material relating to Bette Gray's mental deterioration and, finally, suicide in 1967. Consistent with *Sakonnet Point*, however, Gray argued that the piece offered 'no attempt to reconstruct the past' or 'in anyway create a gesture of memory' (Gray 1978: 87).

Gray's statement reflects a complex relationship between the Performance Group's emphasis 'on psychological honesty and full, emotive expression of feeling' (Gray 1978: 88) and the *Trilogy*'s production of contradictory and paradoxical relationships between 'private' and 'public', and between source, text, performance and reading. Thus, where the *Trilogy* implied a biographical and emotional 'honesty' connected to Gray's explicit exploration of 'a relationship with myself' (Gray 1978: 88), the performances foregrounded processes of 'mediation', transposition and representation. To this end, *Rumstick Road* explicitly re-framed Gray's apparently biographical material through the 'lecture-demonstration' and the 'examination', while its 'documentary' sources are stressed in the re-playing, re-enactment or lip-synching of recordings and in the projection of 'real' family photographs over performers. Here, too, these recordings are lent the mark of authenticity, in part, by the presentation of 'private' or 'illegally' obtained material in whose auditing which the audience may be implicated in a breach of confidence. Gray thus records his family members' discomfort in discussing events directly; he announces his playing of recordings his grandmother specifically requested him not to use; and, most notoriously, he signals his 'illegal' replaying of a secretly recorded telephone conversation with his mother's psychiatrist. Here, then, in contrast to the Performance Group's exploration of personal, social and theatrical transactions in order to *interrupt* the theatre's representations with the 'real' circumstances of their performance, *Rumstick Road* emphasizes the 'signs' of the real, the 'evidence' of 'authenticity'. Characteristically, too, this reversal provides the first of a series of linked paradoxes. In emphasizing the performer's *encounter* with the material at hand, *Rumstick Road* repeatedly directs attention toward 'the real recording', as if, in the lip-synching of audiotapes, for example, to demonstrate the incapacity of the theatre to capture or restore that to which its signs refer. Here, it seems, where 'real evidence' intrudes into the theatre's representations *in mediation*, 'live performance' functions as 'text' and 'sign'. Such reversals evidently counter the privileging of the 'live presence' of the performer in Schechner's work.

In this context, the third play of the trilogy, *Nayatt School* (1978), extended this logic while marking the Group's first direct incorporation of film into performance. Drawing on LeCompte's training in graphic design, *Nayatt School* further emphasized the edit, the cut and the radical interleaving of distinct elements. In a multiplication of highly referential fragments, David Savran records, *Nayatt School* brought together a 'wild assortment of texts' (Savran 1988: 102), including vaudeville comedy-horror sequences, excerpts from T. S. Eliot's *The Cocktail Party*, a scene, 'The Breast Examination', by Jim Strahs, as well as various musical and non-musical recordings, including a 1950s sound-recording of *The Cocktail Party* starring Alec Guinness. These disparate elements refracted Gray's personal history, while emphasizing multiple yet interdependent points of attention. Thus, David Savran suggests, the Group's incorporation of scenes from *The Cocktail Party* served to prompt reflections on a loss of innocence and a celebration of madness pertinent to both Bette Gray's suicide and Celia Copplestone's 'passion' (Savran 1988: 105). In this context, in Part V, 'The Fifth Examination of the Text: In Which Spalding Introduces the Children in Their Parts and the Man, the Woman and Spalding Play a Scene with Them (*The Cocktail Party*, Act III)' (Savran 1988: 104), a projection of Ken Kobland's record of the Group's rehearsal of the same scene with child and adult performers produced characteristically multiple implications. The film is projected over the whole space such that 'the live action is doubled by a film of a previous performance' (Savran 1988: 124–5), and Kobland notes that in 'going back into another time' the film 'was a constant next to the variables, the people who aren't there, which is also a part of *The Cocktail*

Party. Of the monologues. Of the past. Of the Wooster Group' (Kobland in Savran 1988: 107).

In including the film record of a past rehearsal, Kobland suggests, '[t]he idea was that the piece would be, with the film involvement, a piece of contradiction, of time passing in different ways' (Kobland in Savran 1988: 102). Echoing the times implicit in the overlaying or reconstruction of Gray's 'documentary' recordings in *Rumstick Road*, the film also emphasized a key characteristic of the Group's subsequent performances, in which the history of the Group, of their rehearsal and making of work, is selectively reproduced. The *Trilogy*, in this aspect, is a work 'about' the creation of theatre, in which, as Kobland implies, the history of *The Cocktail Party* is, simultaneously, the history of the Wooster Group. In contrast to the Performance Group's exposure of personal histories and group dynamics that construct a 'revelation' of the actor (Schechner 1970), however, the Wooster Group's reproduction of its *working practice* is caught within its play across *texts*. Thus, *Nyatt School*'s re-playing of the Group's rehearsal plays explicitly on 'the real' and its reproduction, offering an ambivalent retelling of their 'performance biography' that, even in emphasizing its recording of a 'real rehearsal', gains an explicitly metaphorical and so *textual* charge.

Such tactics continually construct the elements of these performances as caught within an *order of difference*. Thus, the film projection is read in the *different* times in which the performance now operates: in relation to the 'real' record; in its new contextual 'meaning'; in plays across 'actuality' and 'textuality' produced in its repetition and reproduction *here*. Here, too, the Wooster Group's re-use of material plays between 'repetition' and 'reproduction', as live and recorded performances are layered to articulate the group's restaging of their own and others' work. Such repetitions are not only linked to the open intertextuality of the Wooster Group's productions, in which texts, performances and films are appropriated and re-performed or reproduced, but refer, again, to the process of 'making theatre', and, in this, to distinctions between the 'live event' and its mediation.

Consistently with this, the Group's subsequent work has included radical reworkings of well-known texts into productions incorporating performance fragments from extremely diverse sources. Thus, *Route 1&9* (1981) set extracts from Thornton Wilder's *Our Town* against reconstructed blackface routines by the black vaudevillian Pigmeat Markham, while *L.S.D. (. . . just the high points . . .)* (1984) brought together Michael Kirby's play *The Hearing*, written in reference to Miller's *The Crucible*, with reconstructed rehearsal and film documentary. Yet, while the Group's work has, at various times, emphasized highly fragmentary approaches to texts and appropriations, the company has also pursued a rhythmic, spatial and visual *multiplication* in its articulation of performance *across* media. In this regard, the Group's compositions have worked against a sense of unity, wholeness or 'closure' not simply in the interweaving of radically distinct texts, but through practices and structures that produce and *accelerate* these differences. In certain respects, these structures are exemplified in the Wooster Group's most explicitly collagic work.

Through *Frank Dell's The Temptation of St. Antony* (1987) (see Figure 4.1), developed over a four-year period, the Group realized its most overtly complex collage of disparate theatrical, literary and philosophical texts. Achieving an extraordinary degree of reference, superimposition and dialogue between seven principal texts identified in the Wooster Group's published script (the Wooster Group 1996), in their rehearsal process, Suzanne Letzler Cole records, the company integrated at least fourteen distinct sources into the performance (Letzler Cole 1992: 94–6). Thus the piece explicitly incorporates reworkings of Gustave Flaubert's *La Tentation de Saint Antoine*, Ingmar Bergman's film *The Magician* (1958) and the unauthorized biography of Lenny Bruce, *Ladies and Gentlemen, Lenny Bruce!!* (1974) by Albert Goldman. At the same time, the performance draws on an edition of Flaubert's letters, videotapes produced in the manner of 'Channel J', a late-night New York cable channel talk show in which host and interviewees were nude, poetry by Geraldine Cummins and a history of the art of entertainment (the Wooster Group 1996: 265–6). Thematically, in relation to the texts it superimposes, the performance crosses polarities and oppositions, investing references to

4.1 FRANK DELL'S THE TEMPTATION OF SAINT ANTONY.
pictured: Ron Vawter.
photo: © Paula Court.

the metaphysical in allusions to obscenity and the obscene, confusing
the spiritual with references to vaudeville magic shows, the 'psychical'
and charlatanism. Shadowed, like many of the Wooster Group's performances, by the story of a performance company, here an itinerant
magic troupe, the production characteristically defers between narrative
lines and fragments and allusions to the making of theatre. Here, too,
and reflecting LeCompte's realization and instruction to the actors in
rehearsal that '[y]ou're in two plays at the same time' (Letzler Cole 1992:
118), *Frank Dell's The Temptation of Saint Antony* foregrounds a traversing
of media and texts, linked to the media's operation itself, and exemplified
in Ron Vawter's performance of its opening scene.

   In 'EPISODE 1: THE MONOLOGUE, in which Frank runs his
tape, and takes a call from Cubby' (the Wooster Group 1996: 267),
Vawter, ostensibly rehearsing his act in his dressing room, performs
Lenny Bruce's early alter ego 'Frank Dell'. Off-stage, 'Sue' occasionally
prompts, replies or throws remarks into Vawter's seemingly stream-of-
consciousness monologue, while above, and on monitors dispersed over

the audience, a silent tape of an interview with a nude young man and woman plays on. Here, Don Shewey recounts:

> Wearing dark glasses, sandals and a bathrobe, the central character of *Frank Dell's The Temptation of St. Antony* stands under a spotlight muttering into a microphone. Calling out instructions to an unseen engineer, he obsessively plays and replays scenes from a cable-TV nude talk show visible on a row of monitors above his head, dubbing in all the voices himself like a video ventriloquist. The dialogue these embarrassed looking nudists spout ranges from banal chitchat to metaphysical ruminations.
>
> (Shewey 1990)

Reflecting LeCompte's prompt in rehearsal for Vawter '"to link up" with an audiotape of Lenny Bruce's words whenever possible, "like a crazy person picking up signals everywhere"' (Letzler Cole 1992: 113), Vawter's monologue remains in an oblique relationship to the video. Performed with remarkable precision as he lip-syncs to the silent tape while apparently directing his attention elsewhere, Vawter explicitly mediates from live to video performance while giving voice to a series of 'absent' characters. Punning on 'the Medium', Vawter performs Bruce's rehearsal of 'Frank Dell', while wording the tape, and, in hesitations and pauses, issuing instructions to the Wooster Group technicians sitting behind the audience to rewind and replay the video, then to Sue, his off-stage assistant, while speculating on 'Cubby's' arrival. Here, various themes and references from the Group's source texts coalesce around Vawter's 'Act', as he implicitly touches on the psychical and the spiritual, the prurient and the metaphysical. Evidently for LeCompte, such themes and oppositions circulate around the figure of Bruce. Noting that 'Lenny Bruce always dreamed of getting into film', LeCompte recalls, the Group 'imagined that if he were alive today and made movies, he might have done Channel J-styled tapes', reflecting that '[i]n his final years he was very much like a visionary in the desert with the question left open as to whether he was insane or divine or whether the two have to go together'

(LeCompte in Letzler Cole 1992: 103). While Vawter's various 'voices traverse rather than inhabit characters' (Letzler Cole 1992: 250), the text is constructed in a similar movement across sources and oppositions to produce a layering of actions:

> *Maybe appearance is the only reality.*
> *Well, appearance is the only reality . . . and what an appearance.*
> *Uh, what you see is what you get.*
> *My prayers, my tears, my physical suffering is all turned on by your little*
>   *image here.*
> *Uh, Eddie? Eddie who?*
> *Eddie who? There must be some medicines. Medicines!*
> Sue, please what is it?
> An eddy of dead leaves, Frank.
> *OK. If I could feel love or pain or pangs of pity, I wouldn't be able to descend*
>   *to these feelings of portents and horniness that bless me and come to me in*
>   *my dreams [. . .] where are you from?*
> *Baltimore.*
>
> (the Wooster Group 1996: 271)

Here, Vawter/Dell/Bruce's monologue does not 'take place' within a single location. It may, for example, describe a series of rehearsals: Bruce's rehearsal of Dell; Dell's rehearsal of a monologue; Vawter's rehearsal of the lip-syncing of the tape; the 'prologue's' rehearsal of the themes of the performance. In this context, Vawter's 'Act' is defined, first of all, in the mobility and simultaneity of its signs, where one 'phrase' – one gesture, text, narrative or image – comes to function in *more than one scenario*. Thus, in 'rehearsing' Dell, Vawter 'plays' Bruce, while 'wording' the Channel J interview. As a consequence, at specific moments Vawter's turns of phrase come to occupy more than one position, be that Bruce as Dell, the interviewer responding to his interviewees, or Vawter alluding to St Antony: '*Well, appearance is the only reality . . . and what an appearance*'.

In this aspect, Vawter's 'Act' exemplifies a structural rhythm character-istic of Wooster Group performances. In bringing together the various elements of the Group's work, LeCompte emphasizes, the company aims 'to allow them to be in the space together, without this demand for meaning' (LeCompte in Kaye 1996: 256), noting:

> anything can co-exist together – without [. . .] losing its own uniqueness – without being absorbed and regurgitated. They are separate, and they can stay separate and at the same time inform each other – within the same work.
>
> (LeCompte in Kaye 1996: 257)

In turn, LeCompte has remarked that with regard to the actor '[e]ach performer has his/her own space, her own set of actions, her own "frame"' (LeCompte 1993). In this context, rather than asserting *the difference* between its points of reference, Vawter's performance comes to operate 'here' and 'there' simultaneously in a process of *distraction*. Here, it seems, Vawter's performance even 'differs from itself' (Weber 1996: 110) as attention is continually and simultaneously displaced from one narrative or contextual possibility to another. In this effect, too, the distinction between Vawter's 'phrase' and its repetition and reproduction becomes blurred. Indeed, rather than assert the stability of 'an order' in which 'live' events occur, then to be subject to delay and repetition *in mediation*, this performance is constituted in a continuous 'live' mediation of different channels of address.

Here, too, Vawter's performance asserts a multiplication of times as well as frames and *places*. Analogous to Elizabeth Ermarth's account of structures producing a 'postmodern time' in the novel (Ermarth 1992: 21), and which may be extended toward video and video installation, this inflection of one text and action across another marks a rhythm that unsettles *the time* of Vawter's 'Act'. Where in the novel, Ermarth notes, 'postmodern time' is established in narrative structures through which '[t]he story forces reader attention into play between alternate semantic systems' (Ermath 1992: 68), Vawter's performance poses the question of how to position, or read, what is done *in multiple contexts*. Thus, where Ermarth identifies 'rhythmic time' with alternating narrative possibilities in which 'each moment contains its specific and unique definition' (Ermath 1992: 53), Vawter's 'phrases' *traverse* media in simultaneous conjugations of *explicitly different* spaces and times: the 'live' Act; the 'fictional' rehearsal; the 'mediated' (recorded) interview. In this rhythm, too, Vawter's 'Act' reflects the crisis of the subject Ermarth identifies with the postmodern novel, where the question of 'who' and 'what' action is *present* comes to the fore. Writing 'On Form' with regard to *Brace Up!* (1991), which incorporated Chekhov's *Three Sisters*, LeCompte emphasizes:

> There is no 'Masha' on the stage. There is only the
> actor/performer. The audience makes 'Masha' from the actors'
> actions and the images which simultaneously occur in the stage
> world. The character is an accumulation of fragments of which the
> performer is the initiator. The character is a 'moment in stage
> time'.
>
> (LeCompte 1993)

In turn, this proposition returns to the question of how 'a moment in stage time' is constituted or structured: how the *times of performance* are effected.

In this context, the Wooster Group's later work departed from the extreme dispersal and fragmentation characterizing *St. Antony*, to explore the production of complete or virtually complete texts encompassing the time of performance while further developing this rhythmic complexity. Here, beginning with *Brace Up!*, which brought together a specially commissioned translation of Chekhov's *Three Sisters* by Paul Schmidt with the conventions of Noh theatre and popular Japanese television, the Group has gone on to engage with a wide range of canonical dramatic texts, including O'Neill's *The Emperor Jones* (1993) and *The Hairy Ape* (1996), as well as Racine's *Phèdre* in *To You, the Birdie! (Phèdre)* (2002). Implicitly engaging with a mediation or 'remediation' in which one text or set of conventions is filtered through another to produce a 'complex polyphonic structure' (Schmidt 1992: 156), these performances approach the combination of selected texts in ways consistent with

Vawter's traversing of character and context. Thus, in the making of *Brace Up!*, Arratia records, '[o]ne of the premises of the staging process was "to have always something that amplifies or goes against" what is being said or done onstage' (Arratia 1992: 130). Yet, in bringing apparently diverse practices together, Marianne Weems, the Group's assistant director and dramaturg from 1988 to 1994, notes,

> [t]he entrances and exits and some of the gestural language that's been worked into the piece come directly from the Japanese theatre. But they've been woven into the Chekhov; not just superimposed on it.
>
> (Weems in Mee 1992: 148)

Characteristically, these dialogues between structures, conventions and texts work to disperse attention from one point to another within the space. Thus, in her notes on *Brace Up!*, LeCompte's remarks 'On Fragmentation' indicate a series of exercises in displacement, in which live, mediated and recorded activities are bound one to the other while diverting attention away from a resolution of the relationship between their various spaces. Amongst these instructions, LeCompte notes:

> Performers on TV develop all relationships through a language of vocal and spatial displacements, i.e., the Baron speaks to a specific point on the upstage left wall to indicate that he is 'speaking to' the doctor.
>
> Performers on TV are also seen on stage from the back and in profile – and simultaneously on TV in close up. When the performers on the TV engage the lens directly, they are referring to the stage performers who spoke before them or after them [...].
>
> If dominant stage action is at stage left, then the TV performers' 'gaze' must be towards stage right – always pulling the centre away from itself as soon as it forms.
>
> (LeCompte 1993)

Reflecting on the performance's articulation in such distraction, Schmidt himself recalls the 'music' of *Brace Up!* as a series of 'calculated and rehearsed' layers, each of which asserts its difference in a 'complicated orchestral composition' (Schmidt 1992: 156) of reflexive elements. Including 'the text of Chekhov's *Three Sisters*; comments on the text by Kate Valk as the Narrator or myself as the Translator', Schmidt observes these distinct layers extending toward 'recorded music and sound effects performed on complicated machinery [. . .] live music and singing; fourth, the sound of the stage itself – furniture and props being moved about and handled; and fifth, the movement of bodies and the swish of costumes' and, finally, 'silence' (Schmidt 1992: 156). In this context, Schmidt, as translator and actor, discovered himself in a position of displacement from his own performance. Thus, throughout the piece, and in keeping with LeCompte's exercises, Schmidt sat facing a wall at the rear of the space as 'the audience sees my face in a constant close-up on a video monitor set downstage at the footlights, but I never see them' (Schmidt 1992: 152). Within this structure, he recalls:

> [w]e wanted to go with the mood, listen to the wind, identify
> ourselves with the emotional overtones of the background. And
> [LeCompte] was asking us instead to play against all that: to play
> one tempo on top of another, in other words, like a piece of music
> with one time signature in one hand and a different one in the
> other.
>
> (Schmidt 1992: 155)

In turn, in *Brace Up!*, and characteristically of the Group's performances, these rhythmic constructions are provided with another layer of complexity through set-piece dances and the play of live mediation and recorded video. Here, Arratia notes, in the rehearsal of *Brace Up!* '[t]he Wooster Group's dancing is made manifest throughout their work in the special attention to concrete time and space' (Arratia 1992: 135). Specifically, the Group worked to ensure that its choreographies remain rhythmically unpredictable, as if the performers might, in their dancing, move 'in and out' of their choreography's performance. Pursuing, at certain points, an overlaying of discrete choreographies (Letzler Cole 1992: 122), LeCompte's direction was explicitly aimed at a disruption or interruption of the rhythm of these dances in performance. Thus, Arratia notes, once established, their 'sharpness'

> is partially dismantled at the last rehearsals before the New York opening, with the performers hesitating slightly between movements, purposely missing transitions, stopping for a couple of beats, etc. The dances oscillate between 'being right on the beat' and 'not knowing what to do', between energetic exactness and an (apparent) relaxation, a contrast explored throughout the making of *Brace Up!*
>
> (Arratia 1992: 137)

Where the Wooster Group's dances work *across* rather than *in* a rhythmic unity, video itself introduces another and separate continuity into the performance. Here, the unfolding of images in the video's 'own' 'textual' worlds asserts an 'opening up' of *Brace Up!* to rhythmic orders apparently quite *other* to its principal textual sources. In this, too, the *drone* of video, the *operation* of the televisions and their physical manipulation by the performers on a series of runners integrated into the set, provide a further structural layer, which, at moments, may gain a specific metaphorical or narrative charge, as if the video itself might move 'in and out' of *Brace Up!*'s performance. In rehearsal, Arratia recounts:

> LeCompte is especially attentive to what happens unexpectedly, an image randomly revealed on the TV monitors, an unplanned gesture. For example, during one rehearsal the Hollywood film *The Harvey Girls* (1946) was on TV. LeCompte saw the fire scene in the movie as material for the beginning of Act III, the fire in Prozorov's town.
>
> (Arratia 1992: 130)

It is in this rhythm, too, that the Group's performances extend toward a disruption of the oppositions in which the conventional production of theatrical texts tends to operate: the distinction between 'performer' and 'character', 'live' and 'mediated', 'real' and 'representation'. Indeed, and echoing the tendency toward an 'opening-out-to-the-world' (Kaprow 1993: 114) evident in earlier multi-medial practices, the Wooster Group's layering of actions, spaces and times potentially extends toward an inclusion of 'temporality *in general*' (Blom 1998: 67) into its structural framework. Thus, in response to the Group's performance of *The Hairy Ape* in Paris in 2002, the critic Lynn Gardner recounted an earlier occasion in which

> [t]he performance began, but after about half an hour there was a technical glitch. The actors stopped acting. A ripple of anxiety ran around the auditorium, but everyone on stage seemed perfectly calm and relaxed, as if they had just broken off a game of cards. After a while the performance recommenced. The actors jumped straight back into the show, entirely unfazed.
>
> The next day I talked to LeCompte, Valk and Dafoe about what happened. They say they actually enjoy it when things go wrong [...] in a Wooster Group performance nothing is hidden; everything is open to view.
>
> (Gardner 2003)

Here, 'real time', the time of events, interrupts an 'inconstant' rhythmic structure: everything stops; then it continues. Extending the faltering of the Wooster Group's dances, and its performances' *crossing of times*, the 'stopping' of the performance becomes, here, for the performers, another of its rhythmic possibilities. Indeed, after Ermarth, and echoing video installation's measuring of multiple times (Oliva in Paik 1993: 16), this is an effect linked to the construction of performance in a multiplication of distinct 'phrases', where, in this case, '[performance] time is [...] a dimension of events' (Ermath 1992: 7).

It is in this attention to the times and spaces of performance, too, that the Group's work implicitly links an articulation of the media's divisions to a performance of 'presence'. In the first place, then, these structures explicitly act out the media's multiplication of times and spaces, posing *the question* of the performer's 'location': their occupation of this (live or mediated) space, in conjunction with another; their place 'in and out' of the performance's rhythms and times; their 'presence' to each other and the audience 'as performer' and 'in role'. Yet this very disruption of 'location' seems, for LeCompte, to be linked to perceptions of 'performer-presence'. LeCompte remarks:

> presence is something that I think is [. . .] always in conversation with the formal pattern. The formal pattern will tend to allow the performer to get lulled into feeling safe [. . .] the constant battle for me as a director is to find ways that an actor can be always present, always alive, always thinking this is the first and last moment that she's there – doing this thing.
>
> (LeCompte in Kaye 1996: 257–8)

The 'presence' LeCompte refers to arises, here, in rhythmic intrusion: in an *excess* produced in a being 'there and here' that resists a setting of the performer *in place*. Indeed, where the 'Act' moves 'in and out' of specific contexts, or, in these dances, falters 'in and out' of performance itself, 'presence' is articulated, in the Wooster Group's work, *in* the very divisions through which its theatre *integrates* media into performance.

In these various contexts, Mary Gearhart's photograph of Willem Dafoe's performance of Theseus in the Group's *To You, The Birdie!* *(Phèdre)* (see Figure 4.2) alludes to the articulation of precisely such a moment. Incorporating the Group's commissioned translation by Paul Schmidt of Racine's *Phèdre*, the Wooster Group's performance explores an intertwining and overlaying of 'real', 'mediated', 'recorded' and 'represented' times. Implicitly referring to Racine's adherence to neo-classical unities of time and place, *To You, The Birdie! (Phèdre)* incorporates the 'real time' of game playing, as the principal characters repeatedly return

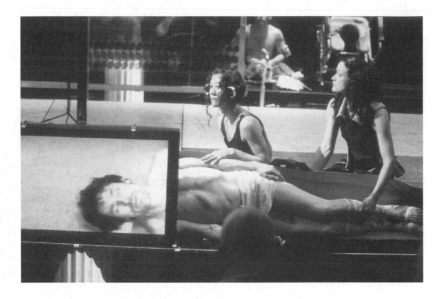

4.2 TO YOU, THE BIRDIE! (PHÈDRE).
   Directed by Elizabeth LeCompte.
   Pictured (l–r): Willem Dafoe, Koosil-ja Hwang, Ari Fliakos, Domonique
   Bousquet
   photo: Mary Gearhart.

to play a fast-paced game of badminton 'live' on the stage, as well as video recordings and live mediations of performers. As a counterpoint to the different continuities implied by the play's dramatic unities and the game's 'real time', the performance is continually fragmented and mediated, both in the soundtrack, which incorporates distortions and delays, and a system of mobile plasma screens that move slowly and smoothly in front of the actors to divide their bodies and performances. Within this framework, in the particular '"moment" of stage time' captured by Gearhart, Dafoe/Theseus' body is divided: split explicitly between screen and stage 'presence'. Indeed, this is a body whose division is multiplied, a body articulated not only through a division between 'live' and 'mediated', but also through the divisions of the mediated itself. Hence Dafoe/Theseus is 'seen' ('live' on stage) and, simultaneously, seen 'being seen' ('live' on screen, *via* the camera). In this process, Weber's proposition that the media's transportation of vision 'splits the "sameness" of the instant of perception' (Weber 1996: 22) is amplified by the Wooster

Group's particular mediation of the body, which has the 'staggered' character of a webcam broadcast, so playing on a confusion between the times of production, transmission and reception. Here, then, and analogously to LeCompte's observation of the necessity of resisting the 'security' of form, this mediation articulates Dafoe/Theseus' 'being there' in a conjugation of different orders of representation: in the 'theatrical' (represented) body of Theseus, now deferring to the 'live mediated' body, which refers to the 'real body' toward which the camera has, apparently, directed its attention. Such a moment explicitly extends the Wooster Group's address to the perception of 'presence' toward the media's un-fixing of the performer's *place*. In this moment, then, Dafoe/Theseus is presented in the body's transmission from 'there' to 'here': in a moment 'in and out' of fiction, 'in and out' of mediation. It is in precisely this move-ment, too, that the Wooster Group effects a performance of 'presence' in those media ostensibly responsible for its decline and depreciation. Here, then, Dafoe/Theseus' *place* is rendered uncertain in a conjunction and heightening of the movements and spaces of transmission, so articulating his 'presence' in deferrals between the 'real', 'live' and 'mediated' body, deferrals that evade the security of form and the erasures in which a representation of 'the character of Theseus' or 'the presence of Dafoe' would be performed.

Convergence: John Jesurun

Where the Wooster Group's work has emphasized a multiplication of the spaces and times of performance, the writer and director John Jesu-run's multi-media theatre has articulated these divisions while working toward a structural convergence between language, media and live per-formance. Here, in developing his work from *Chang in a Void Moon* (1982–95), a theatre performance presented, initially, in 36 weekly 30-minute episodes in serial form in 1982–3 and subsequently through a further fourteen episodes between 1984 and 1995, Jesurun has produced an extensive body of work quite different in tone and effect from the Wooster Group's performance-collages. Noting that, '[f]or me, the urge to use media comes from an area found deep in a pre-language state'

(Jesurun 1993: 69), Jesurun's theatre pieces produce a shifting ground on which to examine the individual's perceptual encounter with the world. Thus, in emphasizing that '[o]ne of the main concerns in my work is the use of spoken language and its structure, the many levels and layers through which a thought struggles to become words' (Jesurun 1993: 65), Jesurun takes recourse to the camera, the 'innocent eye', to describe the perceptive act as a move from the inside to the outside and *vice versa*, suggesting that

> [t]he innocent eye is essentially the pinhole through which one perceives. What the eye focuses on has as much to do with physical as well as mental processes occurring on both sides of it [. . .]. The human struggle to get from the inside to the outside and bring the outside to the inside is full of detours, pitfalls and discoveries in interpretation. There is a constant search for the correct translation.
>
> (Jesurun 1993: 65)

In this context, Jesurun's intertwining of live and mediated performance acts as a foil to an investigation of a deeper logic in perception. Thus, proposing affinities between the media's operation and the impulse towards speech, Jesurun looks toward the media's *excess* as a means of capturing the operation of language, remarking:

> In a sense the use of media is one step further away from the brain than the spoken word. But in other ways it is one step closer because we are capable of making it dissect the very language that set it into motion. It sees and remembers more than our physiology allows our sanity. We can even attempt to catch it and return it to its natural internal origins. It is a reflection of the sophisticated techniques our minds use to decipher, edit, reconstruct, contrive and adapt our personal and collective realities. These techniques are primal (automatic?). We are constantly looking for their origins.
>
> (Jesurun 1993: 65–6)

This emphasis is evident in Jesurun's earliest work. For *Chang in a Void Moon*, Jesurun drew on his three-year role as associate producer of the Dick Cavett Show, the rapid-fire talk show popular in the late 1960s and 1970s, while also marking his departure from independent filmmaking, on which he had focused since his training as a sculptor at Yale. Writing *Chang*'s 30-minute scripts at one sitting two or three days before their performance, Jesurun emphasizes that this 'was the first live piece but it was still working as film ... editing, cut, cut, never letting go of film' (Jesurun in Goldberg 1989: 74). Reporting on the first nine instalments presented at the Pyramid Club, New York City, Ronald K. Fried recalls Jesurun's application of overtly filmic conceits and contrivances to live performance, noting that *Chang*

> abounds in 'jump cuts' in which scenes begin and end in
> mid-sentence – or even mid-word – and other scenes begin
> instantly, with cinematic speed, in another area of the stage. Often
> scenes will, while in progress, suddenly jump ahead or backward in
> time [...]. Visual film-like effects are numerous [...]. Scenes are
> designed to recreate various camera angles available to
> a filmmaker.
>
> (Fried 1973: 75)

Employing various permutations of live, pre-recorded and mediated exchanges between performers (Fried 1983: 75–6), and replacing live actors with their recordings when they were unavailable, *Chang* unfolded in rapid transformations and accumulations of events, plot points and reversals, resisting any straightforward understanding of narrative sequence or coherence. As a result, in any one moment in *Chang*'s development, the accumulation of events and cross-references invited uncertainties over the status and location of particular scenes. At the beginning of each episode, Jesurun himself would report on key characters and events. Jesurun writes:

> *Antonio and Svetlana, their son Picablo, her mother Contessa Isabella*
> *married (in 1946) and divorced from Chang, the Contessa's maid*
> *Theresa, and the Infanta, played by a chair. The Contessa is a morphine*

addict. The Contessa adopted the Infanta after seeing her singing for
money in the streets of Rio de Janeiro. The Infanta's age is unknown. She
could be 7, she could be 40.

(Jesurun in Fried 1985: 58)

In this rapid, stream-of-consciousness sequence of events, Fried notes, Jesurun provided a 'fast-paced, fractured dialogue, often delivered in deadpan style', consisting of 'non-sequiturs, jokes, put-ons, insults, bits of rock lyrics and longer narratives that are sometimes lyrical and sometimes frightening' (Fried 1985: 58).

Here, too, Jesurun's blocking together of 'filmic' and 'theatrical' spaces rendered performances shifting and unstable to view. Thus, in *Episode #21* 'The Barbarities of Insulin' (see Figure 4.3), Contessa Isabella and Theresa are shown 'shot' from above, yet revealed to the audience frontally, supported by discreetly hidden platforms. In this crossing of spaces, Jesurun's composition of theatrical space echoes and extends his play of language, continually returning to puns, paradoxes, as well as simultaneous and sequential contradictions. In doing so, this performance calls into question the stability of the 'languages' of film and theatre through which it would be read. Indeed, in this flow and exchange between film and live performance, the more precise, the more 'successful' Jesurun's *simulation* of film, the more its language is disturbed. Recalling his impulse toward performance, Jesurun remarks:

As a filmmaker I began to wish for a way of breaking the relentless
inevitability of a spool of film/video unrolling. I began my first
theatre pieces as attempts to make films without filming them. To
take everything one could put through the lens of a camera and
present it live. The audience would be the camera and the film. An
innocent eye freed from the eyepiece of the camera. It was an
architecture of all the elements needed for a film. Script, actors,
film techniques (jump cuts, fragmentation of time, bird's eye views,
etc.) became the structure of the pieces.

(Jesurun 1993: 67–8)

4.3 John Jesurun, *Chang in a Void Moon. Episode #21.* 'The Barbarities of Insulin'.
Contessa Isabella (Ruth Gray) and Theresa (Helena White). Feb. 7, 1983,
Pyramid Club, New York.
Photo: Kirk Winslow.

Spatially, too, this simulation of the mediated *in* 'live performance'
foregrounds *division* and *separation*. Indeed, here, Jesurun's work *acts out*
the characteristics of the 'transmitted' image described by Weber: its
capacity to contain division and separation; to 'camouflage' difference;
to confound points of reference. In *Chang* these uncertainties are also
extended toward narrative time, as, Fried notes:

> Seemingly set in the present, *Chang* – especially in later
> episodes – crosscuts backwards and forwards in time within single
> episodes, resting in, among other places, Berlin in 1945, Saigon in
> 1946, West 52nd Street (the jazz club Birdland) in 1955, and
> London during the 1960s.
>
> (Fried 1983: 74)

In Jesurun's subsequent work, including *Number Minus One* (1984),
Red House (1984), *Shatterhand Massacree – Riderless Horse* (1985) and, from

1986, a series of increasingly complex 'fully integrated' pieces 'containing simultaneously synchronized interacting pieces of film and live performance' (Jesurun 1993: 68), including *Deep Sleep* (1986) and *White Water* (1986), his treatment of spatial and temporal context served to defer attention toward the process of language's unfolding. At the core of this focus, again, lay a conflation of theatrical and cinematic devices that subjects 'fictional' location, character and cause and effect to an intertextuality and ambiguity that amplify and play on linguistic uncertainty. In 1985, as his work moved increasingly toward a technical complexity in the intertwining of live and mediated performance, Jesurun commented:

> I don't necessarily want to determine space and time but rather
> focus attention on what is happening rather than when and where.
> I want the audience to think but not try to figure out the next part
> of the plot. There is no map to follow in viewing my work.
>
> (Jesurun in Fried 1985: 62)

It is a disturbance of reading effected not only in conflations and exchanges between pre-recorded, live-feed mediation and live performers, but, Jesurun notes, 'I also began using live cameras in several different positions to reveal and conceal the live action from all participants, audience included' (Jesurun 1993: 69). In this context, where '[a]ny sense of reality created in the theatre was constantly called into question':

> What held these elements together was the language. Verbal and
> visual interaction between screen and performers became as
> natural in my pieces as interaction between live performers. The
> video/film could not be separated from the live content. [...]. Live
> and prerecorded work could constantly connect each other. Over
> all there was an underlying and constant tension between them. An
> uneasy truce that always seemed on the verge of breaking down.
>
> (Jesurun 1993: 68)

In *White Water* (1986) (see Figure 4.4) Jesurun set twenty monitors around a rectangular, raked playing space, seating his audience on four sides. Performed by a boy, a man and a woman, the performance proceeds

4.4 John Jesurun, *White Water* (1986). Photo by Massimo Agus.

through rapid exchanges between six interlocutors: the three actors in the central space and, on screen *via* four upended monitors set at ground level, their recorded video performances of three other characters. Above the central playing space, the remaining sixteen monitors are set on 15-foot pedestals around the audience, playing ambient images periodically throughout the performance. Dramatizing a 12-year-old boy's attempt to convince his co-respondents of his vision of a floating apparition, the interrogation proceeds through shifts of meaning, perspective and position in such a way that the identity of the characters and their rec-ollection of events seem to be *produced* rather than reflected in their language's ambiguity. As *White Water* progresses, the actor's exchanges imply different places, times and purposes: a television studio, a court-room, then, by turn, a religious and secular inquisition. In the course of the interrogation, the pre-recorded performances, appearing at first on all four monitors at ground level, come to shift from monitor to monitor, changing places with the ambient images overhead. Jesurun's script marks the live dialogue in roman, the pre-recorded performances in italics. Thus, here, actor #1 (the boy) plays Mack (live) in dialogue with his own performance of the Producer (on video), while actor #2, playing Pegeen (on video) and Kirsten (live), advances the interrogation with a third 'live' character, DOC:

> PRODUCER: *And what is it exactly that you saw?*
> MACK: First I saw a light in the sky.
> PEGEEN: *Flashing?*
> MACK: Like a cigarette glowing in the dark except it was daylight.
> DOC: Was it an angel or something?
> MACK: Oh no it wasn't an angel it was something better.
> KIRSTEN: How do you know it wasn't the devil trying to trick you?
> MACK: Trick me into what?
> PRODUCER: *Trick you into thinking you saw something incredible.*
>
> (Jesurun 1987: 82)

As the exchange progresses, the script gains the character of a self-reflexive train of thought articulated by six figures that, in the live and mediated doubling of performers, implies a unity the 'play' gradually extends. Here, too, *White Water* reflects upon Jesurun's method of working that elides the signs of separate 'characters' or identities. Jesurun recounts that, in writing,

> I know who's going to say what, but I don't slow down to put in
> the speakers' names. When I go back to put the names in,
> sometimes I switch lines between speakers. The whole thing is one
> voice to me anyway, with several people speaking it who
> sometimes are characters and sometimes are not, who switch their
> identities back and forth.
>
> (Jesurun 1987: 76)

In *White Water*, this process is amplified by Jesurun's treatment of roles, in which 'I wanted the six characters to merge into the three actors to merge into one thing – I saw perspective lines meeting at the end' (Jesurun 1987: 76). As the performance comes toward its close, the distinction between roles, inner and outer dialogue and the vision itself becomes blurred. With the actors in darkness, the performance ends in mediation. Cortez, played on video by actor #3, asks the boy, Mack, now also on video with Kirsten:

> CORTEZ: *How many people are there in this room?*
> MACK: *Six.*
> KIRSTEN: *How many?*
> MACK: *Three.*
> KIRSTEN: *How many people are there in this room?*
> MACK: *Two.*
> KIRSTEN: *Who?*
> MACK: *You and me.*
> KIRSTEN: *How many people are there in this room?*
> MACK: *One.*
> KIRSTEN: *Who is it?*
> MACK: *Me.*
> KIRSTEN: *There, do you see it? There's a tiny little flame in the sky over*
>   *there, do you see it?*
> MACK: *Yes.*
> KIRSTEN: *Who is it?*
> MACK: *Me.*
>
> *All the video monitors go out.*

(Jesurun 1987: 142)

Here the flow of language itself overwhelms the attempt of its speakers to *make sense* of the events in which they appear to be caught. In this shifting of points of view, memory, purpose and knowledge between speakers, *White Water* also treats the distinction and exchange between 'the live' and 'the mediated' as parallel to its other linguistic plays and ambiguities. Thus, where its speakers or 'characters' are subject to unpredictable shifts in language, so their performances flow between live and recorded channels of address. Indeed, in Jesurun's dramatic worlds there is no clear distinction or priority between the live and the mediated, as the passage between them becomes, like language itself, an *engine of meaning* rather than a stable ground or opposition in which 'characters' can be located or 'narrative' placed. In such work, Jesurun has suggested, this equal weighting and unpredictable exchange implicitly reveals live performance as another mode of mediation. In this flow, Jesurun, notes:

> Every performance skirted on the edge of chaos [. . .]. It became a friction between naturally expanding live performing actors and strictly edited pieces of video/film. The language was so freely interspersed between the live and the recorded that the audience had to decide what and when to look [. . .]. The content of the piece at times became directly related to the actual struggle of the actors as they worked to maintain a common ground with their own mediated images. This also brought the use of actors into question. Are they mediated images? How much are they programmed in any theatre piece? Are they prisoners of the order of the words they have memorized? How much freedom do they have within these constraints? In a film do the rules allow them to be edited visually/verbally? and if this is allowed in film is it also allowed in theatre?
>
> (Jesurun: 1993: 68)

In many respects, it is in this flow between spaces that Jesurun's inscription of the mediated in the live, and *vice versa*, finds its clearest expression. Here, too, Jesurun's multiplication of the spaces for performance, developed and exemplified in pieces such as *Everything That Rises Must Converge* (1990), set the ground for his most overtly cinematic work. Yet, paradoxically, it is these explicitly cinematic works, in which everything is encountered in its mediation, that everything is performed live.

Presented to its audience by four 'live' performers, *Everything That Rises Must Converge* is constructed in twin aspects. Set before a white wall set across the width of the performance space, above which five monitors face their audience, the Queen and her interpreters, Freddie Mayfield, Joe and Mrs Peabody perform live, engaging each other and four other mediated performers in dialogue. Seemingly set at the Queen's court, the performance introduces themes of power, conquest and transformation, as dialogue is repeated in German and Spanish, while performers engage in apparently unselfconscious reflections on the difficulty of establishing meaning. As the play begins, the Queen (on stage) is offered a gift by Oscar (on video). Looking on from video is Phyllis, who acts as interpreter with Oscar to His Highness. A fourth mediated character, Lagrimas, is also in appearance. The Queen responds: 'Your language is powerful, disgusting and I have the right to choose the questions and revise the answers. Always I retain that right. It is my right by right of conquest. I've told you that before' (Jesurun 1997: 11).

In the ensuing exchanges, these characters' location becomes increasingly uncertain. By implication, the court may be a spaceship; the event to which they direct their attentions religious; the outcome may be war. Reflecting Jesurun's suggestion of his work that the script 'is disembodied from the actors [. . .] because, in a way, it's connected only to itself' (Jesurun in Fried 1985: 62), the import of specific phrases is transformed in their repetition and re-use:

> **YOUR HIGHNESS**: Prepare for reentry.
> THE QUEEN: What time is the convocation?
> MRS PEABODY: Just enough time to finish this glass of wine.
> JOE: It begins at three.
> **PHYLLIS**: Are you talking to me?
> **YOUR HIGHNESS**: Yes.
> THE QUEEN: Then get me my notes and I keep going.
> **OSCAR**: Get my notebook.
>
> (Jesurun 1997: 13)

As meanings and phrases are interrogated and re-tested, *Everything That Rises Must Converge* implies hidden information, the construction of secrets. In turn, this obfuscation itself appears to serve political purposes. The Queen remarks: 'It's precisely because it doesn't mean anything that they will imagine it does and become confused' (Jesurun 1997: 14).

This gesture, however, is also supported by the structural operation of the performance as a whole, for *Everything That Rises Must Converge* is realized across hidden spaces. Thus where the Queen performs 'live' to the audience before her in exchanges with His Highness on video, so, out of view, on the reverse side of the wall, His Highness, Oscar and Phyllis perform live to a second audience, as their performances are simultaneously mediated to the first. Symmetrically to this, the Queen and her interpreters' performance is captured and mediated live to the monitors above the wall facing the second audience. Engaging simultaneously with live and mediated modes, this design and performance articulate a series of reversals and conflations: here facing 'outside' to the audience is a casting of the mediated gaze behind, as the 'live' performance is played to the camera's gaze and confinement. In this operation, the 'play' articulates the language's themes of concealment, translation and dislocation, while reflecting, scenographically, Jesurun's construction of performance in twin spaces.

For the audience, too, this doubling of spaces has profound consequences. Thus, midway through this performance, in a reflection of the proposition that *Everything That Rises Must Converge*, the performers approach the wall, which, when pushed, 'rotates on its central vertical axis revealing the actors to the opposite side' (Jesurun 1997:9) (see Figure 4.5). As the wall turns, revealing audiences and performers to each other, Jesurun's tactic has a remarkable effect: the 'mediated' is revealed as 'live', the 'live' 'mediated'; 'everything' is exposed. Yet, as this wall rotates, and later in the performance, 'spins ten times and stops halfway, splitting the stage from front to rear' (Jesurun 1997: 99), the reading of oppositions in which the performance is constructed persists, as that which is revealed to be 'live' is read in the trace of its earlier mediation. Indeed, in this 'exposure', *Everything That Rises Must Converge* emphasizes its capacity to 'contain' division and separation: to *present* that which it appears to dissolve. In these respects, as elsewhere, Jesurun focuses not on the *opposition* between the live and the mediated but on the realization of one in the fold of the other; on the discovery of the mediated *in* the live, and *vice versa*. Thus, Jesurun asks:

4.5 John Jesurun, *Everything That Rises Must Converge* (1990).
   Photo: © Paula Court.

> Do these languages begin separately? [. . .] For me, the main
> concern is to get them back together. I find that despite obvious
> frictions [. . .] an almost musical relationship between voice, words
> and media allows these elements to be attracted, reunited,
> reorganized in their performance.
>
> (Jesurun 1993: 69)

It is precisely this possibility of the discovery of the live *in* the
mediated that provides the basis for Jesurun's most overtly cinematic
work. Drawing on *Black Maria* (1987) and *Blue Heat* (1991), *Snow* (2000)
sets its audience within a theatrical space in which all performance
is simultaneously hidden and available, live and mediated. Performed
outside an architectural space in which the audience is seated, *Snow*
simulates and enacts the live performance of television *via* twenty-two
cameras. Mediated and edited in real time from the surrounding sets to
four cinematic screens set inside the audience's space, *Snow* is performed
live by four actors and a fifth 'performer', a camera, 'Kit', whose 'point

of view' is simultaneously that of a camera, a computer programme, a simulated performer and the audience. Here, Jesurun suggests, the very absence in which this interactive, fifth 'character' functions invokes, for the audience, a paradoxical sense of presence in the 'live space' as they adopt 'its' point of view. Yet, reflecting the performance's broader themes of hidden spaces and information, this 'point of view' escapes *Snow*'s mediation of the 'live' performance. Indeed, Kit's 'view' is the 'interior view' of mediation itself, a view and 'presence' performed in a 'live mediation' that conflates 'inside' and 'outside', 'live' and 'mediated', technology and performer.

Return: The Builders Association

Founded in 1994, The Builders Association's large-scale multi-media theatre productions have foregrounded the mechanisms and processes of mediation while playing toward the unities and signs of character, place and narrative. Here, The Builders Association's work has marked a further reflection on the uncanny return of synthesis and unity in technologies of mediation. Thus, while the company's Artistic Director, Marianne Weems, was dramaturg and assistant director of the Wooster Group from 1988 to 1994, Weems' approach is marked by a focus on unified narrative structures, as she notes that '[n]arrative has been imploded by 'experimental theatre' to the point of meaninglessness [. . .]. My company's interest has been in reinstating narrative in a structural sense while at the same time incorporating technology' (Weems in Chalmers 1999: 60). In this context, The Builders Association's projects have increasingly foregrounded the 'interface between live and electronically mediated presence' (The Builders Association 2002) while playing on the *dissonant unity* of the media's 'camouflage'.

In this respect, and in a series of projects beginning with *Master Builder* (1994), the company has gone on to produce original scenarios and scripts, including *Imperial Motel (Faust)* (1996), written by John Jesurun; *Jump Cut (Faust)* (1997); and *Jet Lag* (1998–2000), created with the architects Diller + Schofidio and the writer Jessica Chalmers. Here, the company has frequently emphasized the juxtaposition, transposition and passage between live and mediated performance through overt divisions of the stage between theatrical (live) and cinematic (projected) spaces. For *Imperial Motel (Faust)*, a 'remaking of F. W. Mernau's 1926 silent film *Faust* using live actors' (Wehle 1999: 6), the company set a large video screen, some 6 feet high and 18 feet wide, above the main theatrical space and behind a gantry permitting live performers to stand before its projections. In this arrangement, however, the performance exposes the mechanisms by which images are composited or the screen illusion effected. As a result, characteristically, The Builders Association's audience sees at once a performance of the media's divisions and a return of a visual unity in mediation.

In extending this live performance of the media's synthesis, the company's work has engaged explicitly with the social and cultural implications of technology's construction of place, identity and experience. In this development, *Jet Lag* (1998–2000) marks a key departure. Created in collaboration with the architectural partnership Diller + Scofidio, *Jet Lag* offers two narratives of contemporary place. Rooted in 'real' events, the piece, Elizabeth Diller and Ric Scofidio recall, arose in response to a citation by the critic Paul Virilio:

> He spoke of a 'great American heroine' [. . .] who kidnapped her 14-year-old grandson and traveled with him from New York to Amsterdam, then Amsterdam to New York, back and forth 167 times over a period of six months in the attempt to elude pursuit by the boy's father. The father wanted his son to see a psychiatrist. After six months of continuous air travel, the grandmother finally died of 'jet lag.'
>
> (Diller and Scofidio in Chalmers 1999: 57)

Where this journey, they suggest, 'simulated domesticity for her grandson while in perpetual motion', *Jet Lag*'s other narrative mirrors this in reverse, through a protagonist who 'fabricated the bravado of movement while in constant stasis':

A British sailor (who Jessica Chalmers renamed Roger Dearborn)
joined a round-the-world yacht race. Dearborn was so driven by
the promise of media attention that he entered the race
ill-prepared. The sailor ultimately took two journeys. One took
place only in the media: Dearborn sent radio signals falsifying his
whereabouts as if he were actually circumnavigating; the other was
his actual journey, which consisted of sailing in circles for six
months in the South Atlantic, unable to admit his failure. He
ultimately died, possibly a suicide by drowning.

(Diller and Scofidio in Chalmers 1999: 57)

These stories articulate paradoxical movements in place. Thus, the
grandmother's constant travelling is subject to a 'deferred time' (Chalmers
1999: 60) and place produced in 'the boredom of the airport space, which
is neither here nor there' (Diller and Scofidio in Chalmers 1999: 58).
In parallel, Dearborn simulates a powerful narrative of his journey
though 'real space', a terrain that, for him, lacks all co-ordinates. In
these stories, the company focuses on the powerful metaphorical charge
of 'real' and 'virtual' places of passage and transit, characterized after
the anthropologist Marc Augé's account of contemporary 'non-place'.
Formed in the mobility of its users as a *passing over* of 'places' that
produces 'a sort of negative quality of place, an absence of the place
from itself' (Augé 1995: 85), 'non-place' describes a dislocation from the
'known' and 'settled' location. Forming 'the real measure of our time'
(Augé 1995: 79), Augé argues, 'non-place' thus derives from

a double movement: the traveler's movement, of course, but also a
parallel movement of the landscapes which he catches only in
partial glimpses, a series of 'snapshots' piled hurriedly into his
memory and, literally, recomposed in the account he gives of them
[...]. Travel [...] constructs a fictional relationship between the
gaze and landscape.

(Augé 1995: 86)

In its passages from the live to the mediated, *Jet Lag* performs a series of analogous double movements in its staging of technology and the live performer. The second story, Weems notes, focuses 'solely on the duo on the grandmother and the grandson in constant motion [. . .] as bodies continually passing through the space of the airport' (Weems in Chalmers 1999: 58). Here, the performers' live presence is set against projected renderings of these places in continual animation and structural repetition. In, contrast, in the first narrative, Jeff Webster, 'as the yachtsman Roger Dearborn',

> performs the entire 40-minute piece to camera, either recording logs or news footage, or talking (through a series of lags and delays on his MIC) to the other characters who he never sees. He is isolated and framed by the technologies that form his 'boat' on stage.
>
> (Weems in Chalmers 1999: 58)

Here, Webster performs a simulation of Dearborn's pretence, explicitly revealing the elements and mechanisms of his performance's mediation in order to act out a theatrical repetition of this 'journey'. Thus:

> Onstage we see him in front of a small screen whose content he controls: calm or turbulent sea, day or night, good weather or bad, windy or not. In front of him sits a video camera which he can control. The camera sees his image against his controlled backdrop; the two are synthesized and broadcast to the audience on the large screen behind him.
>
> (Diller and Scofidio in Chalmers 1999: 59)

Webster performs 'live', to camera. Simultaneously, his performance is (re-)mediated to the cinematic backdrop. Here, *Jet Lag*'s elements cohere in a simulation of a webcam broadcast that, Diller and Scofidio suggest, purposefully effected a state of continual motion or movement in place, even to the point of inducing a sense of motion sickness (Diller and

Scofidio in Chalmers 1999: 58). Here, too, and characteristically of The Builders Association's work, these events are re-enacted through the very technologies to which they refer, as, Chalmers suggests, '[t]he characters attempt to control their situation with technology, but they also become legible to the outside world, and to the audience, through technology' (Chalmers 1999: 59). Indeed, in *Jet Lag*, and similarly in the later *Alladeen*, the performance of place, identity and narrative are inextricably bound to the performance of media itself, both in the theatre and in the narratives these performances represent. Thus, in *Jet Lag*, 'non-place' is invoked in a play on the 'undecidability' of the transmitted image, on the media's capacity to *bring closer* places, objects and stories, whose production *in mediation*, and so absence from *this place*, is explicit. It is this uncanny confusion (Weber 1996: 121) that The Builder's Association's 'return' to narrative, to the description of character and to the rendering of dramatic place in architecturally modeled projections acts out and serves to heighten. Thus, rather than pursue a fragmentation of narrative and 'character' through the divisions and multiplications in which the media inevitably function, these performances operate *in reproduction* of the media's capacity to synthesize, to assert the 'unities' it would seem to defeat. Yet, in exploring and stating the mechanisms by which these effects come into play, this work always announces and performs the media's *becoming* separation, the *camouflage* under which its simulations take their effect.

SNOW (2000)
Written, Directed and Designed by John Jesurun
4 live actors, 22 cameras

This work is a continuation of my exploration into the nature, content and impetus of languages including the spoken, electronic, visual and verbal. Intricate interrelationships seem to continually compound with the daily arrival of new technology. From the struggle between form and content emanate elaborate issues such as reproduction, privacy, transfer, interpretation and ownership of content. It is a rich and confusing world of boundary-less communication brought about by the internet, satellite and microwave communication. Because of the human need for privacy these new ways of sending, receiving and intercepting information have expanded into new forms of encryption that stretch beyond government, laws or logic. These to me have a direct relation to our own internal human ways of interpreting, hiding and revealing layers of meaning. Parts of my work have explored the idea of "points of view" – physical, verbal, emotional, spatial, intangible – as integral pieces of the perception of a reality. The human struggle to bring the outside to the inside and bring the inside to the outside is an ongoing process of detours, deceptions and discoveries in interpretation. There is a constant search for the relevant point of view. Early on, this interest led me to the use of the camera. For me it became not only an extension of curious eyes but a participant and presence in itself. Organic to a camera's particular charisma was a dispassionate omnipresence, an ability to see things from any point of view and an apparent inability to lie. Added to this was a reluctance to get emotionally involved or reveal anything about itself while implicating whomever fell under its gaze. All the reverse can also be true depending on the camera's operator and subject. Part of the impetus for the Virtual Actor comes from a "character" in my piece BLACK MARIA (1987). In this piece five synched film projections surround the audience, including the ceiling. Every scene was shot from five points of view, leaving the audience in the center of the visual presentation. The central character in this piece was represented by a voice which interacted with other characters and also narrated. The projections implied "what he saw" from five different angles. His presence was indicated only by the sound of his voice and the continually shifting visual point of view which he shared with us. His body was wherever the audience was.

Through Brooklyn Academy of Music's Arts in Multimedia Program, I was able to work with two scientists at Lucent Technologies. It offered me an opportunity to continue to explore further the unique predicament of this "character." Kit August had been working on computer programs that could help teach language. Dan Lee had been working with a version of a camera which could be "taught" certain reactions to what it "saw." It could recognize faces according to its program. In the context of my work, what and how it "saw" became a window into personality. Its way of learning and its mechanical characteristics became part of its "personality." The process involved the teaching of "where to look" and "who is who" – some of the most basic components of human interaction. I was inter - ested in how we could implicate a unique presence in live space by introducing its point of view. Eventually we tied a prerecorded actor's voice to the camera to complete its presence. It could interact with other live actors by looking at them and verbally engaging them in pre-scripted conversations. For me this was a very rudimentary way of building a character from the bottom up. In this process live actors themselves had to learn how to interact with this new participant. There is an intangible element brought about by the struggle to communicate between a live and virtual actor that tells its own story. The virtual actor was developed for use in my piece SNOW (November 2000). The design of this piece physically integrates with its theme of concealment. Walls completely encircle and separate the audience from four live actors. All the action is transmitted by 22 live video cameras and is viewed on screens. The "Virtual Actor" played an integral speaking "character" that was never seen although the audience could hear what it said and see what it saw. Its speaking "point of view" moved around the set on a 90 ft. track. The object for me was not to control everything about the camera but to introduce another kind of element into the scenario that couldn't be completely controlled. In early trials the camera at times seemed to do what it wanted or to become "confused," undecided. In these situations there was always an immediate sympathy for it amongst the cast and crew. To us it felt like an inexplicable, distant echo of an attempt at "free will." For me there is a lot of potential in these moments of "confusion." This is one of the areas I wish to explore further as well as teaching the "entity" enough information to make simple decisions based on what it "knows." Certainly its creation influenced its character. It played a character/narrator who is overwhelmed by the dominance of his own point of view. He eventually renounces his part as narrator and steps out of the story. As I wrote his lines, the character developed as a combination of obsessive, distracted, present and absent at the same time. It's one wandering eye gave it the very human quality of being in a persistent state of wondering who it is and what it is doing there.

SET DESCRIPTION: INTERIOR: The audience sits within an enclosed center square area which measures 24 ft. by 24 ft. The room seats 75 people. The walls are 9 ft. high. Inside, the carpeted floor and walls are dark blue. Four 9 ft. by 12 ft. screens, one above each wall, slant downward at 45 degree angles toward the audience. The audience enters through a passageway from the lobby. For the performance this passage folds into two doors that are closed and made flush with the walls of the viewing area. Two small windows in these doors occasionally reveal action on the outside as actors walk by. The audience is completely separated from the live action.

EXTERIOR: Directly on the other side of the wall surrounding the audience area are four 6 ft. wide hallways which connect four rooms, each on one corner of the outside space. Each room is about 12 ft. by 12 ft. All of the live action takes place within this outside space. Four live actors on radio microphones inhabit the halls and rooms during the performance. The action is transmitted to the screens in the center viewing area by 22 cameras placed throughout the acting space. The 22 camera views as well as prerecorded material are in a constant state of live edit on the four screens. All live sound is transmitted to speakers inside the viewing area. A track is suspended from the outside wall of the viewing space. The computerized camera runs on this track and is able to circle the hallway almost completely. Its movements along the track can be controlled by an operator in the control room but it also has the ability to move by itself according to whom it is programmed to follow. The camera itself is programmed to recognize, focus, pan and tilt to view its subject. This camera entity represents the unseen fifth character in the piece. This character/camera (virtual actor) has a voice accompaniment. Room 1 is the control room. which serves as the actual technical control room for the piece. Lights, sound, video computers and technicians are all in this room. This room also serves as the control room in the "play." Room 2 is a dressing room, Room 3, a living room, Room 4, an office. Other action takes place in the hallways.

CONTENT: SNOW concerns what appears to be a major television and film studio churning out an endless series of programs for popular consumption. The television shows the company makes and broadcasts are in fact encrypted private messages sent for clients such as large companies and governments. All shows are constructed in code to conform with the client's message. Compartmentalized, isolated code processors set up the equations. Another department translates them in to random physical determinations. These are given to oblivious staff writers as required pieces of story content. They write the shows to formula without knowing that every word, color, plot device, actor and sound is encoded to a specific meaning within a universe of increments. When the show is broadcast the designated receiver with the correct code can translate the show into the message. The content for the general public is the typical television format. Unknowingly the five characters, an executive, a producer, a writer, an office intern (played by the virtual actor) and an actress struggle to conform to the subcontext the required format requires. Cricket, the studio's most popular actress, known to company executives as "her master's voice" finds that her voice and face are the axis of the entire encryption system. The "story" itself falls apart as the characters struggle to assume the role of narrator and take control. **SNOW performed November 2000, Seattle Washington, produced by the New City Theater, Seattle and Shatterhand. Support provided by Rockefeller MAP Funds, the BAM/Lucent Arts in Multimedia Program and the Flintridge Foundation *Technical director – BenGeffen,Video Technical director – Tim Coulter, Virtual Actor Program Designer – Dan Lee, Entity track Design – Bill Ballou, Media Manager – Kelly Wilbur, Technical Coordinator, Lucent Project – Mike Taylor. ACTORS – Valerie Charles, Peter Sorensen, Mary Ewald, Jojo Abaoag, Peter Crook. MUSIC by Black Beetle, Rebecca Moore

SCENE 24 – I THOUGHT I WAS SUPPOSED TO HIDE

CRICKET (ACTRESS), LEE (PRODUCER), AND KIT (EXECUTIVE) in Kit's office.

KIT: ......We're having a little trouble with your interpretation of some of the lines

CRICKET: My interpretation?

LEE: You're invisible, transparent – we can see right through you

C: Isn't that what you always wanted from me? Transparency?

K: Yes, but now it's too much. You haven't hidden yourself well enough

C: I hide myself perfectly inside every character you give me.

L: It's not enough. You haven't hidden yourself inside yourself well enough and
that is what is necessary here.

K: You're slipping. You're putting too much emphasis on how you say things.
It's throwing the rhythm off. Sometimes it looks like you actually believe what
you're saying. That you really know what you're talking about.

C: With these scripts? That'll be the day.

 L: And we don't mind so much but other people do. You feel things too violently and deeply and so....

C: So what? It's hard enough working without a director. And all those geeks
constantly taking notes.

L: You know we never use directors. We don't need them. They just confuse
things. The coordinators and writers take care of everything. You've been here
long enough to know that these things direct themselves.

K: As long as everyone involved doesn't get too involved.

C: I've always done whatever you asked.

L: Always–

K: But truthfully you've become a freak.

L: A Halloween mask.

K: Casper the friendly ghost.

C: Boo!

K: You've moved past that natural mediocrity – you've gotten too good for your
own good.

C: How would you know the difference?

K: I was an actress once too you know.

C: You thought you were – I never did.

L: Then think of it from the audience's point of view. You don't know what it's
like having to watch you year after year.

C: You don't know what it's like. To be driven like a camel up the hill and down
the hill day by day – a little pack mule dragging your shit along the cliff side trying not to slip off. And I am very good at it.

K: But not so much anymore. You're starting to slip and stumble off the path.
Get off before you get pushed off.

C: It's that weird intern isn't it? He's been spying on me. What did he tell you?

L: It's not the intern, it's the endless list of weekly brain battering miniseries you've memorized backwards and forwards and forwards and backwards. The wave after wave of desolate desolation you send out on your face night after night.

K : Now, go and rearrange your face and get another job or don't get one – you don't need it.

L: Get another life or just get a life.

K: You've been everything, now you can be anything. Or at least pretend to be.

L: We're all pack mules delivering the message. Shows and actors come and go but the message forever stays and must be sent. It's not the singer, it's the song.

C: You've turned me into some kind of electronic airbag, a red hot chili pepper, and I didn't even know it. Going through my motions like an idiot puppet head. What an awful way to live. Emotion mining in the school of black memories!

L: Don't be so dramatic.

K: Now where were we? You have one year left of your contract. Five more shows. It won't be renewed. You've gotten away with murder and now it's murder time so be grateful to get away without spilling a drop of blood in the blood bath.

C: What's happening here?

L: Nothing is happening here.

K: Something is happening here and you don't know what it is, do you, Mister Jones?

L: Stay away from that intern.

C: Why?

K: "I knew a girl who tried to walk across a lake. Of course, it was winter and all this was ice. It's a terrible thing to do, you know."

L: They say the lake is as big as the ocean.

K: "I wonder if she knew about it?" ("Walking On Thin Ice" by Yoko Ono)

L: Farewell, my concubine.

C: Hiroshima, mon amour.

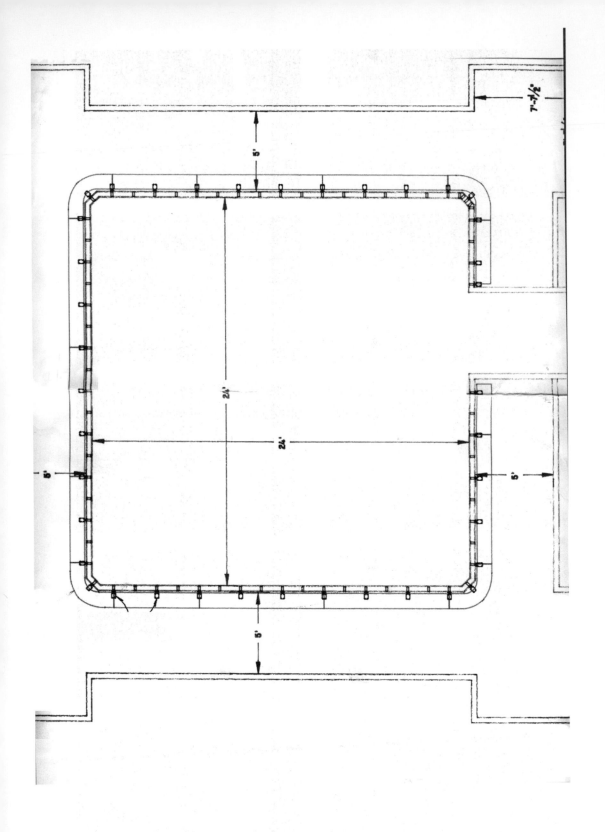

Conclusion:
Seen and Unseen

> there is no essential unity among those things that seem to resemble
> each other or that are assembled together under the name of video.
>
> (Derrida 2000: 21)

In its 'implication of a unique presence in the live space', John Jesurun's
Snow reflects upon the media's capacity to effect a convergence of
opposing terms. In this way, *Snow* is explicitly articulated in a series
of paradoxical conjunctions: in the performance of the 'live' in the
'mediated'; in a 'presence' produced in the virtual actor, 'Kit's', absence
from view; in the audience's occupation, *inside*, of the place of this 'unseen'
'performer', *outside*. In these respects, Jesurun's theatre foregrounds a key
aspect of the multi-media practices approached through this book, in
which the *performance* of media and mediation articulates a collision
of apparently distinct or mutually exclusive conditions, positions or
places. Thus, in his first departures in video art, and following John
Cage's formulation of a 'silence' in which the boundaries and limits of the
musical work were to be dissolved, Nam June Paik explicitly pursued such
a conjunction and exchange. Here, Paik's video has emphasized, variously,
a spontaneity and unpredictability effected in hardware's operation, the
juxtaposition and conflation of apparently distinct rhythms, times and
tenses, and the reproduction of 'real'/'live' events, measures and processes
in the 'live'/'real' time of mediation. For Acconci, too, video extended his
screening off and dispersal of the body in his articulation of performer-
presence; his attempt to *come closer* in mediation, to challenge and refigure
the dynamic and power relations that underpin the performance of site
and of private and public space. Subsequently, in the Wooster Group's
theatrical performances, the multiplication and mobility of signs, texts
and media, work, in their very displacement of the performer, to 'find ways
that an actor can be always present' (LeCompte in Kaye 1996: 257–8).

In the broader development of video art, video installation and multi-media theatre, this tendency toward a collision or conflation of terms and elements also persists. Thus, Bruce Nauman, Dan Graham and Joan Jonas deploy video and mediation to uncover the inscription of a plurality of times and tenses in the 'presentness' of spatial experience and subjectivity. In Gary Hill's work, the affective 'presence' of the projected *Viewer* challenges the separation between 'real' and 'virtual' spaces and subjects; in Studio Azzurro's videoenvironments, the dissolution of objects in mediation allows a paradoxical return *in use*, whereby 'the more they tend to disappear, the more their "presence" gains ground' (Rosa in Valentini 1995: 160). In *Open My Glade*, Pipilotti Rist acts out a blurring of boundaries between real and virtual 'sites', challenging video's separation from that which occurs 'around' it, from the places and sites of its production and reception. For John Jesurun and The Builders Association, too, through their very different modes of production and presentation, place, narrative and identity become inseparable from the media's operation. Here, where language and media converge, or where contemporary understandings of place, politics and identity are formed and encountered in electronic media, theatre's intertwining of 'live' and 'mediated' performances and 'presences' *inhabits* the processes they describe. More broadly, in these developments, too, these practices interrogate and amplify aspects of the media's operation. In particular, where the transmitted image's division of place and time is 'camouflaged' in the persistence and continuity of its vision, so this work explores the transformation of that which the media 'brings back': the 'undecidability' of the divided image in which vision is *brought closer*; the uncanny quality of a 'presence' and subjectivity seen to be defined 'there and here'.

In approaching this 'transposition of vision' (Weber 1996: 116), too, these practices frequently return to *the seen and the unseen*. *Snow* artic-ulates its themes of concealment in technology's *exposure* of multiple performances, scenes and narratives, in an emphasis upon the *availability* of points of view and perspectives in 'real time'. It is a rhythm reflected in Jesurun's documentation, which emphasizes the mechanisms of me-diation, surveillance and vision, while representing the camera's gaze as seemingly 'empty'. This relationship between the seen and the unseen also extends toward theatre and performance that has explicitly addressed the return of 'the mediated' *in* the 'live'. Thus, in Fiona Templeton's reproduction of Michael Ratomski's gestures in *Recognition*, in Jesurun's construction of theatrical space in *Chang in a Void Moon*, or in Vawter's 'Act' in the opening scene of *Frank Dell's The Temptation of St. Antony*, the presence or inscription of media and mediation in live performance is made explicit. Nor is this articulation of the media's operation limited to the theatrical representation of film and video or the 'live' performance of filmic constructs. From 1983, Vito Acconci's work has developed in a transposition of his concerns with the performance and mediation of the body and its sites, and of the dynamics between public and private space, toward public art and architecture. Extending his articulation of the site of performance as 'a meeting place, a place to start a relationship' (Acconci 1979: 34), Acconci's extensive architectural practice and work with the Acconci Studio has created proposed and built projects for sites across North America and Europe. In Acconci's collaboration with the Mekons, *Theater Project for a Rock Band*, this link between place, performance, media and architecture is made explicit in a mobile architectonic installation. Performed at the Brooklyn Academy of Music, New York, in 1995, and designed by Acconci Studio for installation into 'a space of any size and any shape', the *Theater Project* transposes Acconci's concerns for the dynamics between public and private space into a performance architecture, which, over 45 minutes, acts out 'the making of an architecture, and the making of a song, and the making of a band'. Articulating a dynamic between seen and unseen, proximity and distance, individual and group, Acconci's project effects and narrates the construction of a community of watchers and their subjection to performance. Here, this architectural place operates in a spatial mobility, complexity and division, in which Acconci and the Mekons map their claim, and perform a return, to theatrical unity and authority.

As Samuel Weber, Rosalind Krauss and others propose, there is no 'essential unity' underlying the practice of video, no 'recursive structure' (Krauss 1999: 7) to realize from within its operation. In its various crossings of live and mediated performances, the multi-media practices addressed in this volume have emphasized the instability or 'undecidability' characterizing the transmitted image and the performance of mediation. Yet, in exploring and amplifying the media's division, multiplication and dispersal of 'events, bodies, subjects' (Weber 1996: 117), these multi-medial moves between video, installation and performance have persistently returned to an interrogation of the media's capacity to *bring back* into recognition that which they divide or disperse. In this context, in its crossing of practices this work has consistently re-presented the *performance* of subjectivity, site, presence and 'Nature' in the media's *camouflage*, in the *return of the same in difference*. Indeed, in the explicit operation of these works across multiple spaces, times and channels of address, the performance of media and mediation has come to articulate uncanny descriptions and mirrorings of its audiences' occupation of the 'real' spaces and times of viewing.

Acconci Studio and the Mekons
THEATER PROJECT FOR A ROCK BAND, 1995
BAM, at the Dia Center for the Arts, NY
Fabric walls & ceilings, motors, lights, wood, narrative voice on audiotape, live band
(voice, guitar, bass, accordion, drums)
12' x 44' x 44'; 45-minute performance

The theater is a hexagon that can be installed in a space of any size and any shape. The performance is the making of an architecture, and the making of a song, and the making of a band.

The hexagon is divided into six trapezoids of audience seating, facing the center; each trapezoid is surrounded, at the sides and at the front, by three-foot high walls; suspended above each audience-sector is a trapezoidal ceiling, twelve feet high.

In the center of the hexagon is a smaller hexagon, a wood 'stage' with a triangular opening in the middle, inside which sit three technicians, one for sound and one for light and one for motorized movement.

At the rear of each trapezoid is a wood scaffolding that holds a triangular platform six feet high; on each platform is one member of the six-member band, a 'personal performer' for each sector of the audience.

The walls and ceiling 'perform': from the low wall at three sides of each audience sector, another wall might rise, doubling the height – above each sector, the ceiling might descend to a height of six feet. There are different combinations of movement: the stage might be walled off from the audience – each audience sector might be walled in, and shut out from the others – the performers might be together, above the ceiling, while the audience is left alone below.

While the architecture moves in space, the performers move toward each other in time. The performance consists of forty-five one-minute segments, a minute of the Mekons' *100% SONG,* divided into six sections. Each section begins in darkness, with a narrator's voice: the narrator loses his voice, and throws his voice – he wishes the band was meeting as if for the very first time – he realizes other people ('you') were there all the time – he gathers together with 'us' to make a world – he can't go home again, and gets lost in the crowd – he invites everyone to the dance. As the narrator stops speaking, the lights go on and the band performs. First, each band-member performs one minute of the song alone; then two band-members perform together, then three together, then four, then five; finally, all the band-members perform together, forming a band.

The rise and fall of the architecture isolates band-members, or joins them in different couplings and groupings. In each segment, a cold white spotlight from behind floods each performing band-member; the spotlight throws a shadow onto the ceiling or the wall; the band-members who aren't performing are bathed in colored light, they're out of the spotlight. At the end, spotlights flood all the band-members in glaring light; shadows loom like giants over the audience.

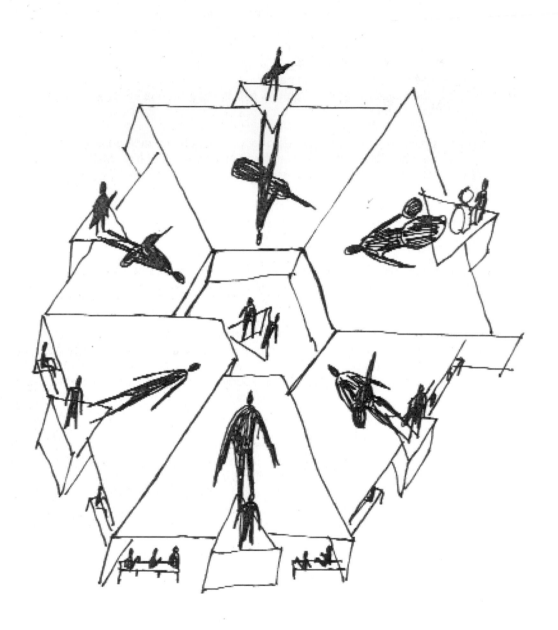

THIS IS A SIMULATION OF A SONG
are YOU ASHAMED OR WHAT?
HERE IS CRUELTY SO STRONG
CRUELTY WITHOUT BEAUTY
IN YOUR COUNTRY YOU HAVE NOTHING
A PARADISE OF VIOLENCE
A PARADISE OF NUFFINK
HOW COME YOU TASTE SO GOOD?

PEOPLE WORKING ALL DAY LONG
NOW THEY'RE GOING OUT
TO JOIN US ALL IN OUR SONG
FOR THE INDUSTRY OF NIGHT
LA LA LA .... etc

JESUS WALKING ROUND the GARDEN
WE'D LIKE TO THANK HIM for this SONG
We'd like to Thank him for these BEERS
We'd like to Thanke him for our CAREERS
DIG HIM UP AND ASK FORGIVENESS
Assembled on the Ground like a MAN
He's the monster from LOCH NESS
in a Halo and A DRESS
people working etc ......
THE WIND & WATER SINGING
where the naked are tied
From TIP to TOE, stroking
Delicate SKIN..... LA LA LA......

Vito Acconci/Mekons
THEATER PROJECT FOR A ROCK BAND: Scenario for motorized walls &
ceilings, lights, rock band, narrative voice

Three spotlights behind each band-member, one above and two to the
side. When a band-member is performing, the spotlight is white,
harsh: it casts the band-member's shadow onto a ceiling or wall
of his or her compartment. When a band-member isn't performing
for the time, his or her compartment is washed in colored light,
softer light.

SW = side wall. FW = front wall. C = ceiling. P = performer,
band-member.
P1: drums. P2: guitar, vocals. P3: vocals. P4: bass. P5:
accordion, vocals. P6: guitar, vocals.
Song: 100% SONG.

I. Dark.
    Narrative voice: 'Once I refused to talk, they forced me to
    sing for my supper. So I lost my voice, and I threw my voice,
    and I threw myself into their hands and mouths and bodies and
    down their throat and up their ass and through their veins.
    Take me, I said (though who could hear me with my tongue up an
    ass-hole). Take me, I said: Lift me out of my body and make my
    heart sing...'

    1. FW1/3/5 rise.
        Light casts P1 onto FW1.
        P1 performs one-minute song alone.

    2. FW1/3/5 stay up, as
        C2/4/6 fall.
        Light casts P4 onto C4.
        P4 performs one-minute song alone.

    3. FW1/3/5 stay up, and C2/4/6 stay down, as
        SWa/c/e rise.
        Light casts P2 onto SWa.
        P2 performs one-minute song alone.

    4. FW1/3/5 and SWa/c/e stay up,
        and C2/4/6 stay down, as
        SWb/d/f rise.
        Light casts P5 onto SWd.
        P5 performs one-minute song alone.

    5. FW1/3/5 and SWa/c/e & b/d/f stay up,
        and C2/4/6 stay down, as
        C1/3/5 fall.
        Light casts P3 onto C3.
        P3 performs one-minute song alone.

    6. FW1/3/5 and SWa/c/e & b/d/f stay up,
        and C1/3/5 & 2/4/6 stay down, as
        FW2/4/6 rise.
        Light casts P6 onto FW6.
        P6 performs one-minute song alone.

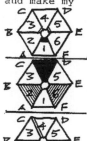

II. Dark.
Narrative voice: 'I wish they would wish they were meeting as if
for the very first time. I wish they would wish they didn't
recognize each other -- their minds go blank but their bodies
are hot and full of every other body but the one that's here.
The loss of history makes them constantly curious and continuously
horny...'

7. FW1/3/5 & 2/4/6, C1/3/5 & 2/4/6,
    and SWa/c/e retract, as
    SWb/d/f stay up.
    Light casts P1 onto SWf,
    and P2 onto SWb.
    P1 and P2 perform one-minute song together.

8. SWb/d/f retract,as
    C1/3/5 fall.
    Light casts P3 onto C3,
    and P5 onto C5.
    P3 and P5 perform one-minute song together.

9. C1/3/5 retract,as
    SWa/c/e rise.
    Light casts P4 onto SWa,
    and P5 onto SWc.
    P4 and P5 perform one-minute song together.

10. SWa/c/e retract,as
    FW2/4/6 rise.
    Light casts P2 onto FW2,
    and P6 onto FW6.
    P2 and P6 perform one-minute song together.

11. FW2/4/6 retract,as
    C1/3/5 and 2/4/6 fall.
    Light casts P1 onto C1,
    and P4 onto C4.
    P1 and P4 perform one-minute song together.

12. C1/3/5 and 2/4/6 retract,as
    SWb/d/f rise.
    Light casts P5 onto SWd,
    and P6 onto SWf.
    P5 and P6 perform one-minute song together.

13. SWb/d/f retract,as
    FW1/3/5 rise.
    Light casts P1 onto FW1,
    and P3 onto FW3.
    P1 and P3 perform one-minute song together.

14. FW1/3/5 retract,as
    SWa/c/e rise.
    Light casts P2 onto SWa,
    and P3 onto SWc.
    P2 and P3 perform one-minute song together.

15. SWa/c/e retract, as
     C2/4/6 fall.
     Light casts P4 onto C4, and
     P6 onto C6.
     P4 and P6 perform one-minute song together.

16. C2/4/6 retract, as
     SWa/c/e & b/d/f rise. .
     Lights cast P2 onto SWa&b,
     and P5 on SWd&e.
     P2 and P5 perform one-minute song together.

17. SWa/c/e & b/d/f retract, as
     FW2/4/6 rise.
     Light casts P2 onto FW2,
     and P4 onto FW4.
     P2 and P4 perform one-minute song together.

18. FW2/4/6 retract, as
     SWb/d/f rise. .
     Light casts P3 onto SWb,
     and P4 onto SWd.
     P3 and P4 perform one-minute song together.

19. SWb/d/f retract, as
     SWa/c/e rise.
     Light casts P1 onto SWa,
     and P6 onto SWe.
     P1 and P6 perform one-minute song together.

20. SWa/c/e retract, as
     C1/3/5 fall.
     Light casts P1 onto C1,
     and P5 onto C5.
     P1 and P5 perform one-minute song together.

21. C1/3/5 retract, as
     SWa/c/e & b/d/f rise.
     Lights cast P3 onto SW b&c,
     and P6 onto SWe&f.
     P3 and P6 perform one-minute song together.

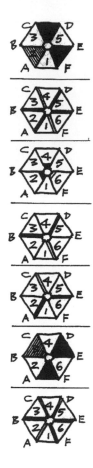

III. Dark.
Narrative voice: 'You mean you were here all the time – when all the
while I thought I was all alone here stranded in the jungle, when all
the while you thought you were all alone here lost in the clouds, when
all the while she thought she was all alone here lost at sea, when all
the while he thought he was all alone~~here lost in space...'

22. SWa/c/e & b/d/f retract, as
     C1/3/5 fall, and FW1/3/5 rise.
     Light casts P1 on C1. P3 on FW3,
     and P5 on C5.
     P1, P3 and P5 perform one-minute song together.

23. C1/3/5 and FW1/3/5 retract, as
    C2/4/6 fall, and FW2/4/6 rise.
    Light casts P2 on FW2, P4 on C4,
    and P6 on FW6.
    P2, P4 and P6 perform one-minute song
    together.

24. C2/4/6 and FW2/4/6 retract, as
    C1/3/5 fall, and SWa/c/e rise.
    Light casts P1 on C1, P2 on SWa,
    and P3 on SWc.
    P1, P2 and P3 perform one-minute song
    together.

25. C1/3/5 and SWa/c/e retract, as
    SWb/d/f and FW1/3/5 rise.
    Light casts P3 on SWb, P4 on SWd,
    and P5 on FW5.
    P3, P4 and P5 perform one-minute song
    together.

26. SWb/d/f and FW1/3/5 retract, as
    C1/3/5 .& 2/4/6 fall.
    Light casts P5 on C5, P6 on C6,
    and P1 on C1.
    P5, P6 and P1 perform one-minute song
    together.

27. C1/3/5 & 2/4/6 retract, as
    SWa/c/e and FW2/4/6 rise.
    Light casts P2 on FW2, P4 on SWc,
    and P6 on FW6.
    P2, P4 and P6 perform one-minute song
    together.

28. SWa/c/e and FW2/4/6 retract, as
    SWb/d/f rise, and C2/4/6 fall.
    Light casts P4 on C4, P5 on SWd,
    and P6 on SWf.
    P4, P5 and P6 perform one-minute song
    together.

29. SWb/d/f retract, as C2/4/6 stay down,
    as C1/3/5 fall.
    Light casts P6 on C6, P1 on C1,
    and P2 on C2.
    P6, P1 and P2 perform one-minute song
    together.

IV. Dark.
   Narrative voice: 'We are gathered here tonight as if in a
   city. Since the city has been wiped out, we bring our own.
   Better yet, we don't have to bring anything to this party, we
   make up our own city as we go. We build it up as we build
   ourselves up. Once a citizen has been expelled from the city,
   the citizen becomes the satellite city. Then two citizens
   together make a metropolis, and three citizens together make a
   country, and four citizens together make a world...'

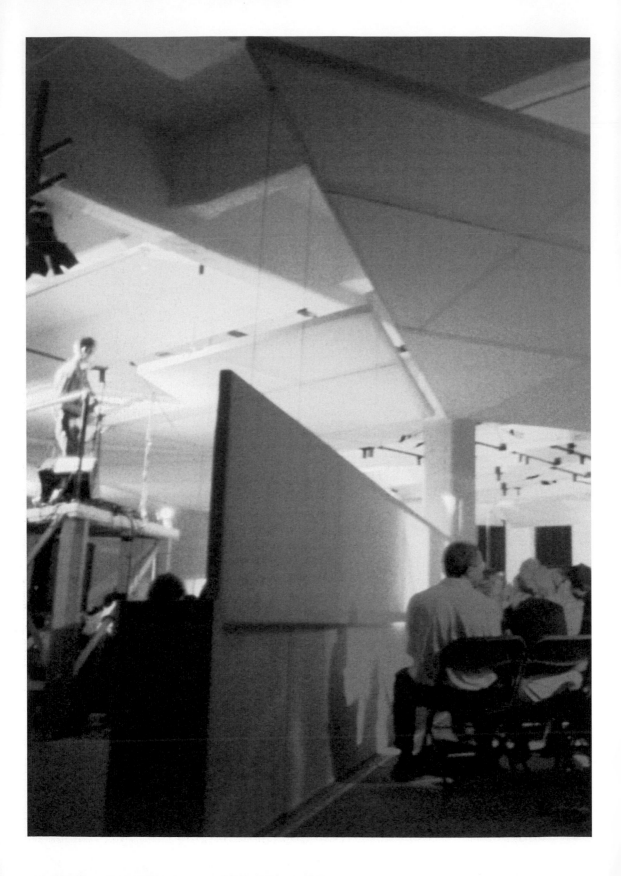

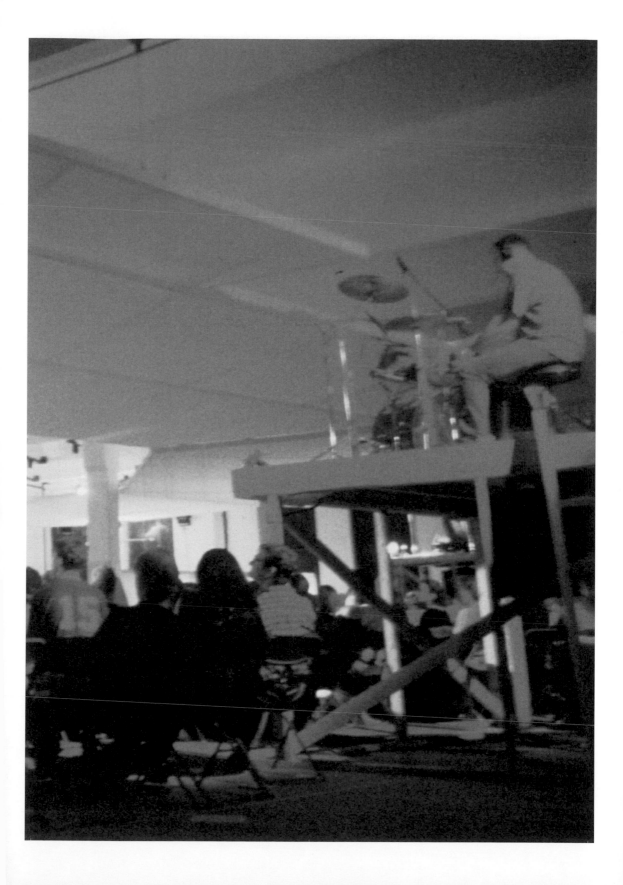

30. C1/3/5 & 2/4/6 stay down, as
    SWa/c/e rise.
    Light casts P1 onto C1, P2 onto SWa,
    P4 onto C4, and P5 onto SWe.
    P1, P2, P4 and P5 perform one-minute
    song together.

31. C1/3/5 & 2/4/6 retract, as SWa/c/e
    stay up, and SWb/d/f and FW1/3/5 rise.
    Light casts P2 onto SWb, P3 onto FW3,
    P5 onto FW5, and P6 onto SWe.
    P2, P3, P5 and P6 perform one-minute
    song together.

32. SWa/c/e & b/d/f and FW1/3/5, retract,
    as FW2/4/6 rise, and C1/3/5 & 2/4/6
    fall.
    Light casts P3 onto C3, P4 onto FW4,
    P6 onto FW6, and P1 onto C1.
    P3, P4, P6 and P1 perform one-minute
    song together.

33. FW2/4/6 and C2/4/6 retract, as C1/3/5
    stay down, and SWa/c/e & b/d/f rise.
    Light casts P1 onto SWa, P2 onto SWb,
    P3 onto C3, and P4 onto SWd.
    P1, P2, P3 and P4 perform one-minute
    song together.

34. C1/3/5 and SWa/c/e & b/d/f retract,
    as C2/4/6 fall, and FW1/3/5 & 2/4/6
    rise.
    Light casts P5 onto FW5, P6 onto C6,
    P1 onto FW1, and P2 onto C2.
    P5, P6, P1 and P2 perform one-minute
    song together.

35. C2/4/6 and F1/3/5 retract, as F2/4/6
    stay up, and SWa/c/e & b/d/f rise.
    Light casts P3 onto SWb, P4 onto FW4,
    P5 onto SWe, and P6 onto FW6.
    P3, P4, P5 and P6 perform one-minute
    song together.

36. F2/4/6 and SWa/c/e & b/d/f retract,
    as FW1/3/5 rise, and C1/3/5 & 2/4/6
    fall.
    Light casts P2 onto C2, P3 onto FW3,
    P4 onto C4, and P5 onto FW5.
    P2, P3, P4 and P5 perform one-minute
    song together.

37. C1/3/5 & 2/4/6 retract, as FW1/3/5
    stay up, and FW 2/4/6 and SWa/c/e
    rise.
    Light casts P6 onto SWe, P1 onto SWa,
    P2 onto FW2, and P3 onto FW3.
    P6, P1, P2 and P3 perform one-minute
    song together.

38. FW1/3/5 & 2/4/6; and SWa/c/e retract,
    as SWb/d/f rise, and C1/3/5 & 2/4/6
    fall.
    Light casts P4 onto C4, P5 onto SWd,
    P6 onto C6, and P1 onto SWf.
    P4, P5, P6 and P1 perform one-minute
    song together.

V. Dark.
   Narrative voice: 'Come and get me, I dare you. You've got the
   numbers, you've got the power: you can drown me out. I'm just
   a voice crying in the wilderness; but the bulldozers are
   coming over the horizon, and the builders are poised at the
   edges. Come and get me; I can't go home again. Come and get
   me; I'm not myself. Who am I then? Who's who anyway? Lost
   in the crowd, I found my way, and founded a city to boot,
   underfoot...'

39. SWb/d/f and C2/4/6 retract, as C1/3/5
    stays down, and SWa/c/e and FW1/3/5
    rise.
    Light casts P1 onto C1, P2 onto SWa, P3
    onto FW3, P4 onto SWc, and P5 onto C5.
    P1, P2, P3, P4 and P5 perform one-minute
    song together.

40. C1/3/5 and SWa/c/e and FW1/3/5 retract,
    as C2/4/6 fall, and SWb/d/f and FW2/4/6
    rise.
    Light casts P2 onto C2, P3 onto SWb, P4
    onto FW4, P5 onto SWd, and P6 onto C6.
    P2, P3, P4, P5 and P6 perform one-minute
    song together.

41. SWb/d/f and FW2/4/6 retract, as C2/4/6
    stay down, and SWa/c/e and FW1/3/5 rise.
    Light casts P3 onto SWc, P4 onto C4,
    P5 onto FW5, P6 onto SWe, P1 onto
    FW1.
    P3, P4, P5, P6 and P1 perform one-minute
    song together.

42. C2/4/6 and SWa/c/e and FW1/3/5 retract,
    as C1/3/5 fall, and SWb/d/f and FW2/4/6
    rise.
    Light casts P4 onto FW4, P5 onto C5, P6
    onto SWf, P1 onto C1, and P2 onto SWb.
    P4, P5, P6, P1 and P2 perform one-minute
    song together.

43. Swb/d/f and C1/3/5 retract, as FW2/4/6
    stay up, and SWa/c/e rise, and C2/4/6
    fall.
    Light casts P5 onto SWe, P6 onto C6,
    P1 onto SWa, P2 onto FW2, and P3 onto
    SWc.
    P5, P6, P1, P2 and P3 perform one-minute
    song together.

44. FW2/4/6 and SWa/c/e and C2/4/6 retract,
    as FW1/3/5 and SWb/d/f rise, and C1/3/5
    fall.
    Light casts P6 onto SWf, P1 onto FW1,
    P2 onto SWb, P3 onto C3, and P4 onto
    SWd.
    P6, P1, P2, P3 and P4 perform one-minute
    song together.

VI. Dark.
    Narrative voice: 'Never mind your own PC. What about your
    very own PP? No, no, that's not what I mean. I mean your
    very own personal performers. Have they left you in the
    lurch, and gone back to join the band? Can your personal
    performer be in two different places at once? But, if that's
    so, does that mean nobody has to move? Nobody move, nobody
    move. At the same time, everybody dance, <u>everybody</u> dance...'

45. FW1/3/5 and SWb/d/f retract, as C1/3/5
    stay down, and C2/4/6 fall.
    Light casts P1 onto C1, P2 onto C2, P3
    onto C3, P4 onto C4, P5 onto C5, and P6
    onto C6: the band is together, up in
    the air.
    P1, P2, P3, P4, P5 and P6 — the entire
    band -- perform one-minute song together.
    After about half a minute, SWa/c/e rise,
    then FW2/4/6, then SWb/d/f, then FW1/3/5:
    the audience is separated from one another.
    As the band is finishing their one-minute
    song, C1/3/5 & 2/4/6 retract.

Bibliography

Acconci, V. (1971) unpublished notes to the untitled project for Pier 17.

—— (1978) *Vito Acconci*, Luzern: Kunstmuseum Luzern (pages unnumbered).

—— (1979) 'Steps into Performance (and Out)', in A. A. Bronson and P. Gale (eds) *Performance by Artists*, Toronto: Art Metropole, 27–40.

—— (1982) *Recorded Documentation by Vito Acconci of the Exhibition and Commissioning for San Diego State University*, San Diego, Ca.: San Diego State University (audio cassette).

—— (2001 [1974]) 'Some Notes on My Use of Video', in G. Moure (ed.) *Vito Acconci: Writings, Works, Projects*, Barcelona: Ediciones Polígrafa, 361–3.

—— (2001a [1980]) 'Notes on Work 1970–1971', in G. Moure (ed.) *Vito Acconci: Writings, Works, Projects*, Barcelona: Ediciones Polígrafa, 358–9.

—— (2001b [1984]) 'Television, Furniture & Sculpture: The Room with the American View' in G. Moure (ed.), *Vito Acconci: Writings, Works, Projects*, Barcelona: Ediciones Polígrafa, 371–7.

—— (2001c [1989]) 'Performance After the Fact', in G. Moure (ed.), *Vito Acconci: Writings, Works, Projects*, Barcelona: Ediciones Polígrafa, 353–7.

Anderson, L. and Rist, P. (1996) 'Laurie Anderson and Pipilotti Rist Meet Up in the Lobby of a Hotel in Berlin on September 9, 1996', *Parkett* 48: 114–16.

Arratia, E. (1992) 'Island Hopping: Rehearsing the Wooster Group's *Brace Up!*', *The Drama Review* 36, 4: 121–42.

Augé, M. (1995) *Non-Places: Introduction to an Anthropology of Supermodernity*, London: Verso.

Auslander, P. (1992) *Presence and Resistance: Postmodernism and Cultural Politics in Contemporary American Performance*, Ann Arbor: University of Michigan Press.

—— (1997) *From Acting to Performance: Essays in Modernism and Postmodernism*, London: Routledge.

(1999) *Liveness*, London: Routledge.

Babias, M. (1996) 'The Rist Risk Factor: When Dreams Twitch Like Dying Fish', *Parkett* 48: 104–13.

Bear, L. (1982) 'Interview with Vito Acconci', in E. H. Johnson (ed.) *American Artists on Art*, London: Harper and Row, 232–5.

Benjamin, W. (1992 [1936]) 'The Work of Art in the Age of Mechanical Reproduction', in W. Benjamin *Illuminations*, trans. Harry Zohn, London: Fontana Press, 211–44.

Bigsby, C. W. E. (1985) *A Critical Introduction to Twentieth Century American Drama, Volume III*, Cambridge: Cambridge University Press.

Blom, I. (1998) 'Boredom and Oblivion', in K. Friedman (ed.) *The Fluxus Reader*, Chichester: Academy Editions, 63–90.

Brecht, G. (1983) letter to Nick Kaye, December.

—— (1991) *Notebooks Vol. III*, Cologne: Walther König Books.

The Builders Association (2002) *Alladeen*, programme notes.

Cage, J. (1962) *0'00" (4'33" No. 2)*, New York: Henmar Press.

—— (1965) *Variations V: Thirty Seven Remarks Re An Audio-Visual Performance*, New York: Henmar Press.

—— (1968 [1952]) 'To Describe the Process of Composition Used in *Music of Changes* and *Imaginary Landscape No. 4*', in J. Cage *Silence: Lectures & Writings*, London: Marion Boyars, 57–9.

—— (1968a [1958]) 'Composition as Process', in J. Cage *Silence: Lectures & Writings*, London: Marion Boyars, 18–55.

—— (1968b [1958]) 'Changes', in J. Cage *Silence: Lectures & Writings*, London: Marion Boyars, 18–34.

—— (1968c [1958]) 'Experimental Music', in J. Cage *Silence: Lectures & Writings*, London: Marion Boyars, 7–12.

—— (1968d [1959]) 'Lecture on Nothing', in J. Cage *Silence: Lectures & Writings*, London: Marion Boyars, 109–27.

—— (1968e) '45' For a Speaker', in J. Cage *Silence: Lectures & Writings*, London: Marion Boyars, 146–93.

—— (1976) *A Year from Monday: Lectures & Writings*, London: Marion Boyars.

—— (1993) 'On the Work of Nam June Paik', in T. Stooss and T. Kellein (eds) *Nam June Paik: Video Time – Video Space*, New York: Harry N. Abrams, Inc., 21–4.

Cage, J. and Charles, D. (1981) *For the Birds: John Cage in Conversation with Daniel Charles*, London: Marion Boyars.

Chalmers, J. (1999) 'A Conversation about *Jet Lag*', *Performance Research* 4, 2: 57–60.

Cirifino, F., Rosa, P., Stefano, R. and Sangiorgi, L. (eds) (1999) *Studio Azzurro: ambienti sensibili, esperienze tra interattività e narrazione*, Milan: Electa.

Cottingham, L. (2002) 'New Wine into Old Bottles: Some Comments on the Early Years of Art Video', in J. B. Ravenal (ed.) *Outer and Inner Space: Pipilotto Rist, Shirin Nesat, Jane & Louise Wilson, and the History of Video Art*, Richmond, Va.: Virginia Museum of Fine Arts, 4–13.

Crimp, D. (ed.) (1983) *Joan Jonas: Scripts and Descriptions*, Berkeley, Ca.: University Art Museum Berkeley.

Cubitt, S. (1993) *Videography: Video Media as Art and Culture*, Basingstoke: Macmillan.

Cunningham, M. and Lesschaeve, J. (1985) *The Dancer and the Dance*, London: Marion Boyars.

Davis, D. (1993 [1970]) 'Electronic Wallpaper', in T. Stooss and T. Kellein (eds) *Nam June Paik: Video Time – Video Space*, New York: Harry N. Abrams, Inc., 118–19.

Decker-Phillips, E. (1998) *Paik Video*, Barrytown, NY: Station Hill Press.

Derrida, J. (1976) *Of Grammatology*, trans. Gayatri Spivak, London: John Hopkins University Press.

—— (1978) *Writing and Difference*, trans. Alan Bass, London: Routledge, Kegan, Paul.

—— (2000 [1990]) '*Videor*', trans. Peggy Kamuf, in R. C. Morgan (ed.) *Gary Hill*, Baltimore, Md: Johns Hopkins University Press.

Dienst, R. (1994) *Still Life in Real Time: Theory after Television*, London: Duke University Press.

Doswald, C. (2001) '"I Am Half-Aware of the World": Interview with Cristoph Doswald 1994', in P. Phelan, H. U. Obrist and E. Bronfen (eds) *Pipilotti Rist*, London: Phaidon Press, 116–29.

Dreschler, W. (1993) 'Sonatine for Goldfish', in T. Stooss and T. Kellein (eds) *Nam June Paik: Video Time – Video Space*, New York: Harry N. Abrams, Inc., 41–8.

Duchamp, M. (1975) 'Apropos of Readymades', in M. Sanouillet and E. Peterson (eds) *The Essential Writings of Marcel Duchamp: Salt Seller, Marchand du Sel*, London: Thames and Hudson, 141–2.

Electronic Arts Intermix (2004) 'Vito Acconci: *Command Performance*'. Online. Available HTTP: http://www.eai.org/eai/tape.jsp?itemID=1957 (accessed 12 October 2004).

—— (2006) 'Joan Jonas: *Organic Honey's Vertical Roll*'. Online. Available HTTP: http://www.eai.org/eai/tape.jsp?itemID=531 (accessed 16 June 2006).

Elwes, C. (2005) *Video Art, a Guided Tour*, London: I. B. Taurus & Co. Ltd.

Ermarth, E. D. (1992) *Sequel to History: Postmodernism and the Crisis of Representational Time*, Princeton, NJ: Princeton University Press.

—— (1998) 'Time and Neutrality: Media of Modernity in a Postmodern World', *Cultural Values* 2, 2–3: 355–67.

Etchells, T. (1999) 'On Performance and Technology', in T. Etchells *Certain Fragments: Contemporary Performance and Forced Entertainment*, London: Routledge, 94–7.

Féral, J. (1982) 'Performance and Theatricality: The Subject Demystified', *Modern Drama* 25: 170–81.

Feuer, J. (1983) 'The Concept of Live Television: Ontology as Ideology', in E. A. Kaplan (ed.) *Regarding Television*, Los Angeles, Ca.: American Film Institute, 12–22.

Fried, M. (1968 [1967]) 'Art and Objecthood', in G. Battcock (ed.) *Minimal Art: A Critical Anthology*, New York: E. P. Dutton, 116–47.

Fried, R. K. (1983) 'John Jesurun's *Chang in a Void Moon*', *The Drama Review* 27, 2: 73–7.

—— (1985) 'The Cinematic Theatre of John Jesurun', *The Drama Review* 29, 1: 57–72.

Fuchs, E. (1985) 'Presence and the Revenge of Writing: Rethinking Theatre after Derrida', *Performing Arts Journal* 26–7: 163–73.

Gardner, L. (2003) 'Absolutely Potty', *Guardian*, 9 May 2002. Online. Available HTTP: http://www.guardian.co.uk/Print/0.3858,4409761,00.html (accessed 6 January 2003).

Gary Hill Studio (2002) letter and covering material to Nick Kaye, 13 November.

Giannachi, G. and Kaye, N. (2002) *Staging the Post-Avant-Garde: Italian Experimental Performance after 1970*, Bern: Peter Lang AG.

Goldberg, R. (1989) 'You Are a Camera', *Artforum* 27, 5: 74–9.

Graham, D. (1979) *Dan Graham: Video/Architecture/Television*, ed. B. H. D. Buchloch, New York: New York University Press.

—— (1995) *Dan Graham: Video/Architecture/Performance*, dir. M. Shamberg, EA Generali Foundation and Sabine Breitweiser (videotape).

—— (1999 [1989]) 'Performance: End of the '60s' in D. Graham *Two-Way Mirror Power: Selected Writings by Dan Graham on His Art*, ed. A. Alberro, Cambridge, Mass.: The MIT Press, 142–4.

—— (1999a [1991]) 'Dan Graham Interviewed by Ludger Gerdes', in D. Graham *Two-Way Mirror Power: Selected Writings by Dan Graham on His Art*, ed. A. Alberro, Cambridge, Mass.: The MIT Press, 62–83.

—— (2001) *Dan Graham: Works 1965–2000*, ed. M. Brouwer, Düsseldorf: Richter Verlag GmbH.

Gray, S. (1978) 'Playwright's Notes', *Performing Arts Journal* 3, 2: 87–91.

Gray, S. and LeCompte, E. (1978) '*Rumstick Road*', *Performing Arts Journal* 3, 2: 92–115.

Greenberg, C. (1961) *Art and Culture: Critical Essays*, Boston, Mass.: Beacon Press.

—— (1962) 'After Abstract Expressionism', *Art International* 6, 8: 26–30.

Hall, E. T. (1966) *The Hidden Dimension*, Garden City, NY: Doubleday.

Handhardt, J. G. (2000) *The Worlds of Nam June Paik*, New York: Harry N. Abrams, Inc.

Hansen, M. B. (2004) *New Philosophy for New Media*, Cambridge, Mass.: The MIT Press.

Herzogenrath, W. (ed.) (1999) *Nam June Paik: Fluxus/Video*, Bremen: Kunsthalle Bremen.

Iles, C. (2000) 'Video and Film Space', in E. Suderburg (ed.) *Space, Site, Intervention: Situating Installation Art*, Minnesota: University of Minnesota Press, 252–62.

—— (2000a) 'Reflective Spaces: Film and Video in the Work of Joan Jonas', in J.-K. Schmidt (ed.) *Joan Jonas: Performance Video Installation 1968–2000*, Ostfildern-Ruit: Hanje Cantz Verlag, 154–63.

—— (2001) *Into the Light: The Projected Image in American Art 1964–1977*, New York: Whitney Museum of American Art.

Isozaka, A. (1993 [1989]) 'A Conversation with Nam June Paik', in T. Stooss and T. Kellein (eds) *Nam June Paik: Video Time – Video Space*, New York: Harry N. Abrams, Inc., 125–6.

Jameson, F. (1991) *Postmodernism, or, The Cultural Logic of Late Capitalism*, London: Verso.

Jesurun, J. (1987) 'White Water', in M. E. Osborne (ed.) *On New Ground: Contemporary Hispanic-American Plays*, New York: Theatre Communications Group, 73–142.

—— (1993) 'Breaking the Relentless Spool of Film Unrolling', *Felix* 1, 3: 65–9.

—— (1997) *Everything that Rises Must Converge*, Los Angeles: Sun and Moon Press.

Jonas, J. (2000) 'Organic Honey's Visual Telepathy (1972)', in J.-K. Schmidt (ed.) *Joan Jonas: Performance Video Installation 1968–2000*, Ostfildern-Ruit: Hanje Cantz Verlag, 106–7.

—— (2000a) 'Organic Honey's Vertical Roll (1972)', in J.-K. Schmidt (ed.) *Joan Jonas: Performance Video Installation 1968–2000*, Ostfildern-Ruit: Hanje Cantz Verlag, 108–19.

—— (2000b) 'My New Theater III, In the Shadow a Shadow (1999)', in J.-K. Schmidt (ed.) *Joan Jonas: Performance Video Installation 1968–2000*, Ostfildern-Ruit: Hanje Cantz Verlag, 139–43.

Kaprow, A. (1993 [1968]) 'Nam June Paik', in T. Stooss and T. Kellein (eds) *Nam June Paik: Video Time – Video Space*, New York: Harry N. Abrams, Inc., 114.

Kaye, N. (1994) *Postmodernism and Performance*, Basingstoke: Palgrave Macmillan.

—— (1996) *Art into Theatre: Performance Interviews and Documents*, Amsterdam: Hardwood Academic Press.

—— (2000) *Site-Specific Art: Performance, Place and Documentation*, London: Routledge.

(2006) 'Displaced Events: Photographic Memory and Performance Art', in A. Kuhn and K. McAllister (eds) *Locating Memory*, Oxford and New York: Berghahn Press, 173–97.

Kellein, T. (1993) 'The World of Art of the World: Nam June Paik as Philosopher', in T. Stooss and T. Kellein (eds) *Nam June Paik: Video Time – Video Space*, New York: Harry N. Abrams, Inc., 27–37.

Kern, S. (1983) *The Culture of Time and Space 1880–1918*, Cambridge, Mass.: Harvard University Press.

Kirshner, J. R. (ed.) (1980) *Vito Acconci: A Retrospective 1969–1980*, Chicago: Museum of Contemporary Art.

Knight Crary, J. (2002) 'Perceptual Modulations: Reinventing the Spectator', in J. B. Ravenal (ed.) *Outer and Inner Space: Pipilotto Rist, Shirin Nesat, Jane & Louise Wilson, and the History of Video Art*, Richmond, Va.: Virginia Museum of Fine Arts, 22–7.

Kramer, J. D. (1988) *The Time of Music: New Meanings, New Temporalities, New Listening Strategies*, New York: Schirmer Books.

Krauss, R. (1976) 'Video: The Aesthetics of Narcissism', *October* 1: 50–64.
    (1999) *A Voyage on the North Sea: Art in the Age of the Post-Medium Condition*, London: Thames & Hudson.

Kraynak, J. (2003) 'Bruce Nauman's Words', in J. Kraynak (ed.) *Please Pay Attention Please: Bruce Nauman's Words*, London: The MIT Press, 1–46.

Kunz, M. (1978) 'Interview with Vito Acconci about the Development of His Work', in V. Acconci *Vito Acconci*, Luzern: Kunstmuseum Luzern (pages unnumbered).

Larsen, E. (2000) 'Ordinary Gestures of Resistance', in E. Suderburg (ed.) *Space, Site, Intervention: Situating Installation Art*, Minnesota: University of Minnesota Press, 171–88.

LeCompte, E. (1993) '*Brace Up!*', *Felix* 1, 3. Online. Available HTTP: http://www.e-felix.org/issue3/Lecompte.html (accessed 16 March 2006).

Letzler Cole, S. (1992) *Directors in Rehearsal: A Hidden World*, London: Routledge.

Linker, K. (1994) *Vito Acconci*, New York: Rizzoli.

Lyotard, J.-F. (1984) *The Postmodern Condition: A Report on Knowledge*, trans. Geoff Bennington and Brian Massumi, Manchester: University of Manchester Press.

Maciunas, G. (1988 [1965]) 'Neo Dada in Music, Theatre, Poetry, Art', in C. Phillpot and J. Hendricks (eds) *Fluxus: Selections from the Gilbert and Lila Silverman Collection*, New York: The Museum of Modern Art, 25–7.

McLuhan, M. (1964) *Understanding Media: The Extensions of Man*, London and New York: Ark Paperbacks.

Manovich, L. (2001) *The Language of New Media*, Cambridge, Mass.: The MIT Press.

Mee, S. (1992) 'Chekhov's *Three Sisters* and the Wooster Group's *Brace Up!*', *The Drama Review* 36, 4: 143–53.

Merkert, J. (1974) 'Filmes Dé-coll/age 1963–1971', in W. Vostell *Environmen-nements/Happenings 1958–1974*, Paris: Musée d'Art Moderne de la Ville de Paris, 226–31.

Morgan, R. C. (2000) 'Gary Hill: Beyond the Image', in R. C. Morgan (ed.) *Gary Hill*, Baltimore, Md.: John Hopkins University Press, 1–16.

Morris, R. (1993 [1978]) 'The Present Tense of Space', in R. Morris *Continuous Project Altered Daily: The Writings of Robert Morris*, London: The MIT Press, 175–210.

_____ (1997) interview with Nick Kaye, New York, 8 April.

Morse, M. (1998) *Virtualities: Television, Media Art, and Cyberculture*, Bloomington and Indianapolis: Indiana University Press.

Nemser, C. (1971) 'An Interview with Vito Acconci', *Arts Magazine* (March) 20–3.

Obrist, H. U. (2001) 'Hans Ulrich Obrist in Conversation with Pipilotti Rist', in P. Phelan, H. U. Obrist and E. Bronfen (eds) *Pipilotti Rist*, London: Phaidon Press, 6–30.

Onions, C. T. (ed.) (1973) *The Shorter Oxford English Dictionary*, Oxford: Clarendon Press.

Paik, N. J. (1964) 'Afterlude to the EXPOSITION of EXPERIMENTAL TELEVISION 1963, March, Galerie Parnass', *fLuxus cc five ThReE*, June, New York: Fluxus Editorial Council (pages unnumbered).

_____ (1979 [1963]) 'New Ontology of Music', in H. Ruhé (ed.) *Fluxus: The Most Radical and Experimental Art Movement of the Sixties*, Amsterdam: 'A' (pages unnumbered).

_____ (1979a [1963]) 'Postmusic', in H. Ruhé (ed.) *Fluxus, the Most Radical and Experimental Art Movement of the Sixties*, Amsterdam: 'A' (pages unnumbered).

_____ (1993) *Nam June Paik: eine Data Base*, Stuttgart: Edition Cantz.

_____ (2000 [1962]) 'About the Exposition of the Music', in N. J. Paik, S. Abe and W. Herzogenrath (eds) *Fluxus/Video*, Cologne Verlag der Buchhandlung Walther König, 53.

_____ (2000a [1965]) 'Electronic TV and Color TV Experiment by Nam June Paik', in N. J. Paik, S. Abe and W. Herzogenrath (eds) *Fluxus/Video*, Cologne: Verlag der Buchhandlung Walther König, 90–1.

Pearson, M. and Shanks, M. (2001) *Theatre/Archaeology*, London: Routledge.

Phelan, P. (1993) *Unmarked: The Politics of Performance*, London: Routledge.

_____ (2001) 'Opening Spaces within Spaces: The Expansive Art of Pipilotti Rist', in P. Phelan, H. U. Obrist and E. Bronfen (eds) *Pipilotti Rist*, London: Phaidon Press, 32–77.

Pincus-Witten, R. (1977) *Postminimalism*, New York: Out of London Press.

Pontbraid, C. (1982) 'The Eye Finds No Fixed Point on Which to Rest', *Modern Drama* 25: 154–62.

Quasha, G. and Stein, C. (1997) *Viewer: Gary Hill's Projective Installations – Number 3*, Barrytown, NY: Station Hill Press.

_____ (2000 [1998]) '*Liminal Performance*: Gary Hill in Dialogue', in R. C. Morgan (ed.) *Gary Hill*, Baltimore, Md: Johns Hopkins University Press, 243–70.

——(2001) 'Performance Itself', in G. Hill, *Around and About: A Performative View*, Paris: Editions du Regard, 1–5.

Rist, P. (2001 [1989]) 'Title', in P. Phelan, H. U. Obrist and E. Bronfen (eds) *Pipilotti Rist*, London: Phaidon Press, 106–8.

Ross, D. (1993) 'A Conversation with Nam June Paik', in T. Stooss and T. Kellein (eds) *Nam June Paik: Video Time – Video Space*, New York: Harry N. Abrams, Inc., 57–65.

Sans, J. (1999) 'Viewing *Viewer*: Gary Hill Interviewed by Jérôme Sans', in A. Kold (ed.) *Gary Hill*, Aarhus: Aarhus Kunstmuseum, 71–3.

Savran, D. (1988) *Breaking the Rules: The Wooster Group*, New York: Theater Communications Group.

Schechner, R. (1969) 'Six Axioms for Environmental Theatre', *The Drama Review* 12, 3: 41–64.

——(ed.) (1970) *Dionysus in 69: The Performance Group*, New York: Farrar, Straus & Giroux/Noonday Press.

——(1973) *Environmental Theater*, New York: Hawthorn Books, Inc.

Schmidt, P. (1992) 'The Sounds of *Brace Up!*', *The Drama Review* 36, 4: 154–7.

Sharp, W. (2003 [1970]) 'Nauman Interview 1970', in J. Kraynak (ed.) *Please Pay Attention Please: Bruce Nauman's Words*, London: The MIT Press, 111–32.

——(2003a [1971]) 'Interview with Bruce Nauman 1971', in J. Kraynak (ed.) *Please Pay Attention Please: Bruce Nauman's Words*, London: The MIT Press, 133–54.

Shewey, D. (1990) 'Wooster Group Not Tempted by Conventionality: The Experimental-Theater Troupe Has Jumbled-up Flaubert for Its 'Frank Dell's the Temptation of St. Antony', *Los Angeles Times*, 27 August. Online. Available HTTP: http://www.donshewey.com/theater_articles/wooster_group_for_LA_times.htm (accessed 16 March 2006).

Simon, J. (1994) *Bruce Nauman*, Minneapolis: Walker Art Center.

Smith, O. (1998) *Fluxus: The History of an Attitude*, San Diego, Ca.: San Diego State University Press.

Sohm, H. (1970) 'Vorchronologie und Parallelen', in *happening & fluxus*, Cologne: Kölnischer Kunstverein (pages unnumbered).

Spivak, G. (1976) 'Translator's Preface', in J. Derrida *Of Grammatology*, trans. Gayatri Spivak, London: Johns Hopkins University Press, ix–lxxxvii.

Tschumi, B. (1994 [1975]) 'The Architectural Paradox', in B. Tschumi *Architecture and Disjunction*, London: The MIT Press, 27–52.

Valentini, V. (ed.) (1995) Studio Azzurro *Percorsi tra video, cinema e teatro*, Milan: Electa.

van Bruggen, C. (1988) *Bruce Nauman*, New York: Rizzoli International Publications, Inc.

Viola, B. (1995 [1976]) 'The Sound of One Line Scanning', in B. Viola *Reasons for Knocking at an Empty House: Writings 1973–1994*, London: Thames and Hudson and Anthony d'Offay Gallery, 153–68.

—— (1995a [1981]) 'The Porcupine and the Car', in B. Viola, *Reasons for Knocking at an Empty House: Writings 1973–1994*, London: Thames and Hudson and Anthony d'Offay Gallery, 59–72.

Vischer, T. (1995) 'Five Video Installations of an Exhibition', in T. Vischer (ed.) *Gary Hill: Imagining the Brain Closer than the Eyes*, Basel: Museum für Gegenwartskunst Basel Cantz, 9–24.

Weber, S. (1996) *Mass Mediauras: Form, Technics, Media*, ed. A. Chholodenko, Stanford, Ca.: Stanford University Press.

Webster, F. (1995) *Theories of the Information Society*, London: Routledge.

Wehle, P. (1999) 'Overlapping Worlds: The Builders Association and *Jump Cut (Faust)*', *TheaterForum* 14, 4–9.

White, R. (1979) 'Interview with Vito Acconci', *View* 2, 5–6 (whole issue).

Wijers, L. (1979) *Vito Acconci Talks to Louwriern Wijers*, Velp, Holland: Jan Brand, Kantoor voor Cultuur Extracten.

Wolff, C. (1996 [1960]) 'On Form', in R. Kostalanetz (ed.) *Writings about John Cage*, Ann Arbor: University of Michigan Press, 58–65.

The Wooster Group (1996) *Frank Dell's The Temptation of St. Antony*, in B. Marranca (ed.) *Plays for the End of the Century*, Baltimore, Md: Johns Hopkins University Press, 261–314.

Zippay, L. (1991) *Artists' Video: An International Guide*, New York: Cross River Press.

Zurbrugg, N. (1991) 'Nam June Paik: An Interview', *Lund Art Press* 2, 2: 131–40.

Index

Related titles from Routledge

Liveness:
Performance in a Mediatized Culture
Phil Auslander

Liveness: Performance in a Mediatized Society addresses what may be the single most important question facing all kinds of performance today. What is the status of live performance in a culture dominated by mass media?

By looking at specific instances of live performance such as theatre, rock music, sport and courtroom testimony, *Liveness* offers penetrating insights into media culture. This provocative book tackles some of the last great shibboleths surrounding the high cultural status of the live event. Philip Auslander asks, what is live performance and what can it mean to us now?

Hb: 978-0-415-19689-5
Pb: 978-0-415-19690-1

Available at all good bookshops
For ordering and further information please visit:
www.routledge.com

Performing Science and the Virtual
Sue-Ellen Case

This impressive new book from Sue-Ellen Case looks at how science has been performed throughout history, tracing a line from nineteenth century alchemy to the twenty-first century virtual avatar.

In this bold and wide-ranging book that is written using a crossbreed of styles, we encounter a glance of Edison in his laboratory, enter the soundscape of John Cage and raid tombs with Lara Croft. Case looks at the intersection of science and performance, the academic treatment of classical plays and internet-like bytes on contemporary issues and experiments where the array of performances include:

- electronic music
- Sun Ra, the jazz musician
- the recursive play of tape from Samuel Beckett to Pauline Oliveros

Performing Science and the Virtual reviews how well these performances borrow from spiritualist notions of transcendence, as well as the social codes of race, gender and economic exchange. This book will appeal to academics and graduates studying theatre and performance studies, cultural studies and philosophy.

Hb: 978-0-415-41438-8
Pb: 978-0-415-41439-5

Related titles from Routledge

Site-Specific Art:
Performance, Place and Documentation
Nick Kaye

Site-Specific Art charts the development of an experimental art form in an experimental way. Nick Kaye traces the fascinating historical antecedents of today's installation and performance art, while also assembling a unique documentation of contemporary practice around the world.

The book is divided into individual analyses of the themes of space, materials, site, and frames. These are interspersed by specially commissioned documentary artwork from some of the world's foremost practitioners and artists working today. This interweaving of critique and creativity has never been achieved on this scale before.

Site-Specific Art investigates the relationship of architectural theory to an understanding of contemporary site related art and performance, and rigorously questions how such works can be documented.

The artistic processes involved are demonstrated through entirely new primary articles from:

- Meredith Monk
- Station House Opera
- Brith Gof
- Forced Entertainment.

This volume is an astonishing contribution to debates around experimental cross-arts practice.

Hb: 978-0-415-18558-5
Pb: 978-0-415-18559-2

Available at all good bookshops
For ordering and further information please visit:
www.routledge.com